ideas

into

action

becoming a professional writer

Arnold Keller
University of Victoria

Addison
Wesley
Longman

Toronto

Canadian Cataloguing in Publication Data

Keller, Arnold
    Ideas into action: becoming a professional writer

Includes index.
ISBN 0-201-66447-X

1. Authorship. I. Title.

PN145.K44 2001   808'.02   C00-930218-2

0-201-66447-X

Vice President, Editorial Director: Michael Young
Acquisitions Editor: David Stover
Marketing Manager: Sophia Fortier
Associate Editor: Susan Ratkaj
Production Editor: Sherry Torchinsky
Copy Editor: David Peebles
Production Coordinator: Wendy Moran
Page Layout: B.J. Weckerle
Art Director: Mary Opper
Interior Design: Anthony Leung
Cover Design: Anthony Leung
Cover Image: Corel Stock Photo Library/COREL CORPORATION

1 2 3 4 5   05 04 03 02 01

Printed and bound in Canada.

TABLE OF CONTENTS

Preface   The New Professional Writer   iv

Part I   What All Professional Writers Need To Know   1

Chapter 1   Professional Persuasion   2
Chapter 2   Structures and Signals   18
Chapter 3   Writing Plain English   36
Chapter 4   Graphics   52
Chapter 5   Document Design   82

Part II   What Professional Writers Produce   101

Chapter 6   Correspondence   102
Chapter 7   Writing Instructions   128
Chapter 8   Writing Proposals   158
Chapter 9   Reports   184
Chapter 10   Writing Descriptions   208
Chapter 11   Writing for General Readers   234

Part III What the New Professional Writers Produce   253

Chapter 12   Writing for the World Wide Web   254
Chapter 13   Writing Media Releases   286
Chapter 14   Speaking to Groups   298

Appendix I   A How-to Guide For Fixing the Most Common
             Writing Mistakes   318
Appendix II A How-to Guide For Citing the Work of Others   346

Index   357

The New Professional Writer

In the Age of the Sound Bite and the Jump-Cut, Does It Matter If You Write Well?

Of course it does. Professionals write a lot, and those who write well, do well. Being successful has much to do with getting out messages, and the written word—on the page or on the screen—remains the critical medium. Professional writing—that is, writing for business, science, and the professions—has always been about bringing a specific content to a specific audience. However, in a technology-driven world with information literally moving at the speed of light, content and audience change rapidly. That requires a new kind of writing professional who can use technology both effectively and efficiently. *Ideas Into Action* provides help for such writers.

Who Is This Book For?

Ideas Into Action is for students who want to learn to write for business, government, or the professions. Today's workplace requires you to spend significant time writing. Moreover, economic pressures mean that you must not only write the content but also produce the finished documents—and do so quickly. That requires knowing how to use technology. *Ideas Into Action* offers practical advice to help you meet these new demands.

If You'll Write at Work, You'll Be a Writing Pro, But ...

Not everyone who writes at work writes well—that's an ongoing complaint of employers. Repeatedly, company executives despair over the absence of writing that's clear and accurate, that truly talks to their clients, to their employees, and to the world at large. Because good writing is the exception and not the rule, people who write well have a genuine career advantage.

But learning to write professionally overwhelms many bright people. Too often, they are given pages of rules that they have difficulty putting into practice. They need some sound, clear, and pragmatic advice—based on procedures rather than rules-to help them do what they must do every day.

Will You Need to Write Well?

Yes, especially if you aspire to middle or upper management or are planning to enter the professions or the sciences. There, you will be called upon to produce the documents—reports, proposals, correspondence, and much more—that are at the core of a modern economy. In addition, you will increasingly need to write electronically for everything from simple e-mail to Web pages.

There's no shortage of books offering to help. However, most have two major weaknesses:

1. They are rule-based rather than procedure-based. That means that you are not given a sequence of steps to follow but must infer those steps from a rule. For example:

   - Writing texts tell you to "know your audience and shape your message for them." But how do you find out what your readers know and what they need to know? What steps do you follow to translate such knowledge into a report that persuades them to accept your recommendations?
   - Texts advise writers to "omit needless words" and "use Plain English." But how do you tell what words are needless and what words aren't? What must you do to write plainly?
   - Grammar texts typically warn that "two main clauses joined by a coordinating conjunction need a comma between them." But how do you put this rule into action? How do you determine if what's being joined are main clauses or something else?

2. They do not give you the skills you now need in an electronic economy. Technology is a moving target, of course, and any advice is doomed to obsolescence. You nonetheless need to know the technology that employers no longer merely hope for but demand.

Ideas Into Action isn't about rules: Knowing that you must do something isn't the same as knowing how. Ideas Into Action therefore replaces hard-to-apply rules about writing with step-by-step procedures, ideas, checklists, and practice.

What Are the Goals of This Book?

Ideas Into Action has three main goals:

- To provide you with fundamental ideas and practical, step-by-step instruction
- To demonstrate how technology can make writing more efficient
- To help you become credible and persuasive

To achieve these goals, *Ideas Into Action* continually tries to answer a central question: *What do I do next?* It approaches projects from the writer's perspective and helps you find solutions to immediate problems.

But *Ideas Into Action* doesn't simply offer procedures to be blindly followed; it also provides the ideas that must inform writing. The focus is on what you can carry to your computer today and keep in mind tomorrow. Each chapter has a four-part structure.

- Ideas provide an overview and general principles.
- Actions consist of step-by-step advice.
- Checklists remind you of key components.
- Exercises give you the chance to practice.

In addition, **WORKING SMARTER** sections appear throughout the book, showing you how to make writing more efficient with computers.

What the Book Covers

Part I deals with what all professional writers need to know:

1. How to persuade readers (and you're always persuading them)
2. How to organize your ideas and signal that organization to your audience
3. How to write Plain English, that is, clear, jargon-free prose
4. How to integrate graphics into your document, rather than using them merely to embellish
5. How to design documents are that attractive and easy-to-follow

Part II covers the standard documents that professional writers must produce—and produce efficiently:

6. Correspondence
7. Manuals and instructions
8. Proposals
9. Reports
10. Descriptions
11. Documents for general readers

Part III covers the tasks that professional writers are increasingly called upon to do:

12. Design Web pages
13. Write media releases
14. Speak in public

Finally, there are two "how-to" appendices:

Appendix I: Fixing the most common writing mistakes
Appendix II: Citing the work of others

The chapters include steps, checklists, and exercises keyed to each specific kind of document. In addition, there are many examples of real-world professional writing. There is also specific advice for testing and revising your documents, whether you work alone or with colleagues.

Online Components

The *Ideas Into Action* Web site is an integral part of this text because it enables readers to keep up-to-date without waiting for new editions. It also provides access to information and features that we could not include in the text without adding significantly to its cost. On the Web site, you'll find:

- Updates
- Additional discussions and techniques
- Additional examples
- Additional exercises
- Templates for various documents
- Links to professional writing resources
- Frequently-asked-questions
- An instructor's guide, including advice for teaching with technology
- Easy access to the author, so that you can ask questions or send comments

You can visit the Web site at <**www.pearsoned.ca/keller/**>.

Acknowledgements

I have incurred a number of debts in writing this book, and it is a pleasure to acknowledge them here.

I was fortunate in having the thoughtful advice of several reviewers: Ilona Ryder and Jannie Edwards, Grant MacEwan Community College; Janice Pearson, Toronto School of Business; Brent MacLaine, University of Prince Edward Island; and George Tripp, Fanshawe College.

I've benefited greatly by talking about professional writing with colleagues at the University of Victoria, particularly Kim Blank, Michael Cullen, Susan Doyle, and Elizabeth Grove-White. I'd like to especially thank Ruth Allison for her close reading of the chapter on instructions. At Camosun College, Anita Kess was equally generous with her comments. And over the years, I've learned much about writing from Ed Pechter of Concordia University.

At Pearson Education Canada, Susan Ratkaj and Sherry Torchinsky have been thorough and professional. David Peebles has been the copy editor every writer hopes for. Brian Henderson, a friend and editor for many years, played a key role in getting this book into print.

Closer to home, my family has been an unstinting source of encouragement and affection. My love to Polly, Jonathan, Emily, and Rebecca.

I am grateful to you all. The usual disclaimer has never been more true: The shortcomings of this book are mine alone.

Arnold Keller
Metchosin, British Columbia

PART 1

What All
Professional
Writers
Need to Know

1 Professional Persuasion

2 Structures and Signals

3 Writing Plain English

4 Graphics

5 Document Design

CHAPTER

1

Professional Persuasion

What This Chapter Covers

Ideas

The Social Act of Writing
Being Credible
Putting Readers First
      A Reader's First Question
      Keeping Readers Caring
      Targeting Your Audience
Finding the Right Evidence
      Presenting Evidence in Threes
      Showing the Bad Along With the Good
Using the Right Format
Taking Care of the Details
Testing With Real Users

Actions

Step 1: Analyze Your Readers
Step 2: Select Your Evidence
Step 3: Balance the Presentation
Step 4: Format Your Document to Meet Expectations
Step 5: Edit for Clarity
Step 6: Take Care of the Details
Step 7: Beta Test
Step 8: Revise and Retest

Chapter Summary

Checklist

Exercises

Learning Objectives	**At the end of this chapter, you will be able to explain:**

- The social nature of writing
- Three general principles of persuasion—accuracy, balance, and clarity
- The reader's main questions—*Why should I care?* and *Why should I care* now?
- Why you must analyze your audience before starting to write
- The different types of evidence—empirical, analogous, and anecdotal
- The persuasive power of *three*
- Why using the right format builds credibility
- How a physically attractive document persuades
- Why you must test your document with real readers

At the end of this chapter, you will be able to write persuasively by:

- Analyzing the audience
- Selecting appropriate evidence
- Balancing your presentation
- Formatting the document to meet your readers' expectations
- Editing for clarity and care
- Testing your document

ID**E**A**S**

You write to persuade; your career depends on it.

Persuasion isn't limited to obvious documents like sales letters or proposals. You are always persuading readers that you are credible and that they can trust you. For example, when you recommend a course of action, you want readers to be confident in your advice. When you instruct them in a task, you want readers to believe that pressing Button A won't lead to disaster. And even when you impart information in an apparently neutral voice, you are persuading readers to accept your picture of the world.

A credible writer is one whom readers believe. Your success as a writer will be measured by the degree that you persuade readers to accept you as trustworthy and act on your words.

To make readers believe you, you will be using rhetoric—that is, the tools of persuasion. Unfortunately, people often use the word *rhetoric* to imply something unpleasant, something dishonest or manipulative. We dismiss as mere rhetoric, for example, the promises of a politician or the claims of a soap commercial, assuming their authors want only our votes or our dollars. But rhetoric also has a long and distinguished tradition of helping writers express their own honestly held beliefs so that others will come to hold them too.

Professional writing is generally about getting other people to do something— buy a product or service, take a certain course of action, embrace a set of ideas. Successful professional writers, therefore, must use various rhetorical strategies to change the minds and influence the actions of their readers—for the benefit of those readers. This chapter describes some techniques that will help you be persuasive.

The Social Act of Writing

When you write, you build relationships much the same way as when you meet people face-to-face. In both cases, a set of social conventions establishes what is appropriate. For example, when you prepare for a business meeting, convention demands that you pick clothes that are literally "suitable" to the occasion. You leave your jeans or formal wear in the closet, opting for something more businesslike. Similarly, when you write, you choose your words so that you are neither vulgar nor stiff, avoiding both slang and pretension. When you ignore a social convention, you risk people thinking that you simply don't know how to behave. That makes them less likely to trust you.

Social and writing conventions change with time and place, of course, and those changes are not necessarily logical. In earlier times, for example, readers expected formality and ornate phrasing in correspondence. "My Dear Sir" and "I remain your humble servant" were common ways of starting and ending business letters. Although remnants of these expressions persist (as in "Dear Mr. Smith"), contemporary readers, who tend towards more informality, would think such elaborate language peculiar. One style isn't necessarily better than the other but rather more appropriate to its time and place.

A professional writer, therefore, has to be acutely aware of contemporary manners. This is not to suggest that you make Herculean efforts to stay on top of every passing fad. It does mean that you will have a better chance to build credibility—and get readers to buy what you're selling—if you know and fulfill their social expectations.

Being Credible

There are as many ways to be credible as there are readers and writers, but here are three general principles to start with:

Be informed. Writers have to know what they're talking about and get their facts and figures straight. How much does the Whizbang 2000 cost? How big is it? How long has it been around? What do other people say about it? Where can those opinions be checked? Because professional writing is about living and working in the everyday world, your information about that world must be thorough and accurate. When you get a fact wrong—even a small one—you undermine both your argument and your image as a knowledgeable professional. Unfair as it may be, unsympathetic readers will pounce on a single error of fact as proof that everything else you say is suspect. And even sympathetic readers may question your reliability.

Be balanced. Readers understand that you have a personal interest in what you write. Nonetheless, they expect you to present all sides of an argument fairly. Suppose you're encouraging them to buy your product: In addition to its virtues, they also need to know its limitations. What can't it do? How much will it cost to operate and maintain? How difficult is it to use? To learn? When you present both the bad and the good, your readers infer you are both informed and truthful. You present yourself as a disinterested, honest observer, not just someone with something to sell.

Be clear. The best ideas count for little if readers can't understand them. How you express your ideas, therefore, is critical to your credibility, and modern readers generally value Plain English over other styles. Plain English has become so important, in fact, that some jurisdictions insist on it for laws and contracts. In general, it promotes verbs over nouns, brevity over verbosity, and simple words over fancy ones. Plain English, however, is not a pure language that renders the universe objectively—no such language exists. ("All left-handed people are liars" is Plain English but false nonetheless.) Plain English is merely one style among many, but it best embodies current expectations for business writing. Chapter 3 discusses Plain English in more detail.

Let's now move from general principles to specific strategies.

Putting Readers First

With many kinds of writing (like diaries or journals), the writer is the only reader. As a professional writer, however, you have no such luxury: Your goal is to change the behavior of others. To do that, you must focus first and last on your readers, understanding what they need and what motivates them.

A Reader's First Question

A reader's first question is "Why should I care?" That's not because all readers are selfish but because the world makes so many demands on them. All of us filter the torrent of information that comes our way, deciding what to deal with immediately and what can wait or be discarded. We go through our mail, for example, quickly distinguishing the envelope with a real cheque from the one that says we may already have won a million dollars—in a contest that we've never entered. Because readers are necessarily wary, your first problem as a writer is getting them to open your envelope. That means telling them quickly why they should care about what's inside.

That, however, must be done honestly, not only for ethical reasons but also for pragmatic ones. If your readers open an envelope that says they've won a million dollars but find instead only a sales pitch, they'll be annoyed, not charmed. To fool a reader is to lose a reader. So make your pitch honest and immediate, as in these examples:

- When you are selling magazines, say so right away: "If you read *Popular Mortician*, we can save you money."
- When you are asking for help, say so right away: "I would like your help resolving a problem with my toaster."
- When you are asking for a donation, say so right away: "On behalf of the Downtown Fruit-Lovers Fund, I hope you can give money to those who love fruit."

Honest and direct opening statements like these don't guarantee, of course, that readers will care enough to stay with you. But even if they do stop reading, you won't have angered them and so lose a future opportunity.

Keeping Readers Caring

Having a reader care is merely a first step. You have to maintain that interest by continuously anticipating and responding to the reader's subsequent questions, starting with "Why should I care *now*?" Readers are more likely to keep caring if they see benefits for *them*. That requires you to view the world from their perspective, not yours. "I think the NoCaries 2000 is the best electric dental flosser in the world!" says only what you think—and why should readers care about that? How do they benefit?

What constitutes a benefit? As with other aspects of writing, there can be as many kinds of benefits as there are readers. Generally, however, people want to do better at what they're already doing, do it more cheaply, and (if possible) do it to make the world a better place. Here are some examples, expressed from the writer's perspective and then the reader's:

Doing Things Better

Writer's Focus: Our computer-dispatched trucks are now more efficient than ever.
Reader's Benefit: You'll receive your order in 24 hours.

Writer's Focus: We have added 10 new people to our technical support staff.
Reader's Benefit: You will be able to speak to a technician in less than three minutes.

Writer's Focus: Our software significantly improves the tracking of orders.
Reader's Benefit: You will track orders with three fewer steps than before.

Doing Things Cheaper

Writer's Focus: We've made the Whizbang 2000 give better fuel efficiency than ever.
Reader's Benefit: Your fuel consumption will drop by 10%.

Writer's Focus: We don't charge extra for long-distance calls during business hours.
Reader's Benefit: You will save 40% on long-distance charges during normal business hours.

Writer's Focus: Our new printer paper requires less ink.
Reader's Benefit: You will use 12% less ink with our paper.

Doing Good

Writer's Focus: Our paper is produced without chlorine.
Reader's Benefit: You will be using paper that is environmentally friendly.

Writer's Focus: All employees must be treated equitably.
Reader's Benefit: Adopting this policy will ensure equitable treatment for you and your employees.

Writer's Focus: It's everyone's duty to look after the homeless.
Reader's Benefit: We'll all feel better knowing that the homeless won't be forgotten at Christmas.

The second sentence in each pair stresses how the reader (or the world) will be better off. The first sentence in each pair, however, considers only the writer's perspective: *We* improved a product, *we* added staff, *we* think everyone should look after the homeless. Regardless of the validity of these views, they simply don't respond to the reader's fundamental and ongoing questions—"Why should I care now? How will this benefit *me*?"

Targeting Your Audience

Your document may focus on readers' benefits and still fail if you don't match the right benefits to the right readers. There's no point, after all, in telling someone who doesn't have cable what's on a cable-only channel at nine o'clock. It's faster, of course, to assume that everyone does have cable and compose a one-size-fits-all document. But it doesn't work well. Analyzing a specific audience takes more time but pays richer dividends.

Suppose you are selling copiers; you could send out a one-size-fits-all letter like this: "The Blurro 2000 produces clean copies quickly and cheaply." But you stand a better chance of making your sale when you target different kinds of readers differently, as in these examples:

To a comptroller: "In a time of escalating costs, your company can save money with the economical Blurro 2000."

To a production person: "Being able to produce crisp, clear, and easy-to-read copy shows your client that you're a professional."

To an office manager: "The Blurro 2000 will help your staff get work done on time by eliminating long lineups at the copier."

Focus, therefore, not only on the benefits, but also on the benefits for a particular reader that you identify as best you can. The Actions section later in this chapter suggests specific ways to analyze audiences.

Finding the Right Evidence

Readers of business, professional, and government writing expect evidence that's specific and concrete—facts and figures—and they are unlikely to be persuaded by anything else. They will not accept, for instance, a mere assertion that "Plan A is best" unless you first demonstrate that you came to that opinion by a reasonable process.

You can think of different kinds of evidence forming a continuum from hard to soft:

Empirical evidence (the hardest) is based on first-hand and objective observation of the world. It can include such things as specifications, prices, and the results of tests or surveys—indeed, any kind of concrete fact about which most people could agree. Let's assume you are to recommend the word processor that your department will purchase. Your readers will look for the evidence that responds to these questions:

- What word processing features do most people in the department now use? What features do they need? How do you know? Did you do a survey asking them? Did you observe them doing their jobs?
- What specific features do competing word processors have? How well are they implemented? What tests did you perform or review to verify that implementation? How were these tests carried out?
- What do the reviews from major computer magazines say about competing word processors? What has been the experience of organizations similar to yours?
- What do various word processors cost? Who quoted the prices? Is there a commitment from the vendor to deliver at that price?

In each instance, you have to answer with objective and concrete proof, and your sources must be reliable. Convincing evidence can come from your own demonstrably careful observation; it can also come from tests by reputable testers, product specifications supplied by software companies, dealer-published price lists or quotes, and so forth. In other words, your mere feeling that one word processor is better does not constitute evidence. Only a pattern of hard facts and figures will persuade.

Analogous evidence is data you find in contexts similar enough to your own so that you can generalize. That is, you can apply the experience of others to your situation. This can be persuasive, especially to back up empirical evidence. But it's also viable when empirical proof is not available. You must carefully establish, however, that reasonable comparisons can be made between the two situations. For example:

> The Accounting Department is roughly our size and does many of the same tasks, such as producing routine correspondence, reports, and brochures. They've used WordMagic for ten years and report (see the attached memo from Lesley Wynne) that each new release has increased their efficiency.

Although the two units differ, enough similarities exist (at least in this case) that you can apply the Accounting Department's experience to your own department.

You can find analogous evidence by speaking to colleagues and consultants or by reading the published literature. In all cases, you must demonstrate that your sources are reputable professionals with impeccable credentials and that you can legitimately map their context onto yours.

Anecdotal evidence is what people claim but cannot demonstrate empirically. Here are some examples:

- Ed Pechter has used both WordWrite and WordMagic but likes WordWrite better. He also says that's true of most of his colleagues.
- Kim Blank says that when he installed WordWrite, his computer crashed once a day.
- Elizabeth Grove-White says that she's always had good service from WordMagic's sales reps.

If 10 people all report similar findings, there's certainly an interesting pattern that deserves further study. But unless that study produces hard proof, anecdotal evidence remains just opinion, what people feel but can't prove. The plural of *anecdote*, science reminds us, is not *evidence*.

Presenting Evidence in Threes

You persuade not only with your evidence but also with its presentation. Chapter 2 discusses the *power of three* in more detail, but here's the basic concept: Grouping evidence in clusters of three is persuasive because three is the smallest number that shows a pattern. For example: Suppose you win the lottery this week; great, but it's only a happy accident. When you win again next week, that's interesting but probably just a coincidence. However, when you win it a third week, it's no longer accident or coincidence but *Providence*—that is, some force is shaping events into a meaningful pattern.

When you group ideas into threes, you appropriate the persuasive power of three. Readers infer that there is a pattern in your ideas, a kind of mini-Providence that confers legitimacy. They may not make the connection directly, but they will sense that you are controlling your material, arranging and shaping it into its true nature. That adds to your credibility.

Showing the Bad Along With the Good

We have said that one principle of credibility depends on writers being balanced. The world is always complex, and disadvantages and benefits usually co-exist. For example:

- Automating data entry costs some persons their jobs.
- Changing a corporate name and logo confuses customers.
- Installing a new water-treatment system is expensive.

You can, of course, simply ignore any disadvantages and hope readers won't be smart enough to recognize them. That approach is both unethical and risky. Readers may not immediately detect your deliberate omissions, but when they do, you'll have lost their trust. And that loss will extend beyond the particular issue you addressed.

Instead, meet each problem head on. For example:

- Although some people will lose jobs when we automate data entry, we will make every effort to find work for them elsewhere in the organization.
- Although some customers will be confused by our name and logo change, we will send them multiple notifications and offer them special discounts.
- Although the new water-treatment system is expensive, we will save money in environmental fines and earn much corporate goodwill.

It won't always be possible to find good news, of course, and you can't invent some. But once again, your goal is to persuade your readers and retain their trust. The more honestly you concede the bad news, the greater the chance they'll accept the good.

Using the Right Format

You also persuade by adhering to conventional formats, that is, explicit statements about how documents should look. Different kinds of professionals, for example, expect different ways of citing references or even labelling graphics. These conventions do not just magically appear; instead, a group of influential people decides and issues a public statement.

A format puts readers on familiar ground. For example, they immediately know where to find the summary or how to understand a reference. But adhering to a format also helps you as a writer by persuading readers that you are a knowledgeable member of their profession. It is analogous to choosing your clothes: Different situations demand different costumes. When your document fails to conform to an expected format, your reader may question your credentials and so hesitate to confer trust.

Given the number of professional associations that exist, it's not possible to give details about their preferred formats here. Consult the appropriate organization for this information; the *Ideas Into Action* Web site at **<www. pearsoned.ca/keller/>** provides links to several major ones.

Taking Care of the Details

How your documents look—that is, their physical appearance—sends a strong signal about the care you take with all other things. Readers generalize that a professional-looking manuscript presents professional ideas.

Although you naturally wish to be known and respected for your inner qualities, people will judge you on how you look, both in person and in writing. Readers infer, for example, that a document with spelling mistakes means that you don't care about the so-called little things. Pleading that you were rushed implies that you can't manage your time. Arguing that "it's only spelling" suggests that you simply don't know how to spell. In any event, why would readers expect the other aspects of your work to be any better?

A typo is a small thing, and everyone makes them from time to time. Readers forgive occasional lapses, but frequent ones undermine your credibility and your other efforts.

WORKING SMARTER

Spell Checkers

Spell checkers are invaluable for finding embarrassing mistakes but they are not foolproof. For example, if you use a perfectly good word in the wrong place (such as *its* for *it's*), the spell checker won't flag it. There remains no substitute for your own careful proofreading.

Also, a spell checker will often flag a correctly spelled word (such as a name). When that happens, you can tell the spell checker to ignore this word in the rest of the document. However, if the word is one which you use frequently (like your own name), you should add it to the spell checker's dictionary. The spell checker will then recognize the word in all documents.

Testing With Real Users

It's one thing to understand that writers must persuade readers; it's another to know if your document actually will. You can make only informed guesses about how readers will respond. But you can supplement that imperfect process by testing the document with real people.

Few companies now release products without going outside of their own labs to learn how end users respond. They invest heavily in focus groups and consumer trials. Software companies especially make beta testing—that is, trying out a pre-release version with real users—a critical part of development. Writing too requires similar beta—or, more accurately, usability—testing. Your goal is to verify those informed guesses about readers and their responses.

To beta test your document, you'll need people who have (or will assume) the characteristics of your intended audience. They must play the role of sympathetic but careful readers who will point out your document's weaknesses. A member of your actual audience is best, but colleagues or friends will do. And when no one is available, you yourself must become your readers, looking rigorously at your work from their perspective. Later chapters in this book discuss specific types of documents and give specific examples of what beta readers should look for.

Repeated testing and revising is a normal part of the writing process. Without it, all you have is guesswork.

A C T I O N S

The steps that follow are a general strategy for all your professional writing. Use them to supplement the steps in the later chapters on creating specific kinds of documents.

Note: Begin this process only when you have completed your preliminary research and have assembled the basic set of materials for the document you're writing.

Step 1: Analyze Your Readers

List the names of one or two key persons for whom you're writing, the ones who will decide whether or not to act on your advice. These will be your touchstone readers, that is, your reference points whom you will continually think of as you write. Write down as many facts as you can about them, including their likes and dislikes. Imagine them smiling or frowning as they read.

From the perspective of these touchstone readers, answer the following questions:

- "Why should I care?" Use that answer to draft the first sentence of your document.
- "Why should I care *now*?" Point to specific parts of your research that you can express as a benefit for a touchstone reader. What things does he or she wish to do better, cheaper, or as a larger good?

Apply the smile-or-frown test to your answers.

Step 2: Select Your Evidence

A. List the kinds of evidence your touchstone reader considers persuasive.
B. List the kinds of sources your touchstone reader considers reliable.
C. Locate these kinds of evidence and sources in your research.
D. Arrange your evidence in clusters of three.

Step 3: Balance the Presentation

A. List the items in your research that your touchstone reader would see as disadvantages. Respond to each of his or her potential objections by showing a counter benefit. Apply the smile-or-frown test to your responses.
B. Produce a cost-benefit statement that shows how the benefits for the touchstone reader will outweigh the costs. Apply the smile-or-frown test to this statement.

Step 4: Format Your Document to Meet Expectations

A. Select the professional style the touchstone reader expects (for example, from a particular professional association or house style sheet).
B. Design your document to conform to this convention (its citation style, margins, graphics captions, table of contents, etc.).

Step 5: Edit for Clarity

- Use nouns rather than verbs.
- Cut unnecessary words (warm-ups, throat clearing, redundancies, etc.).
- Use simple rather than fancy diction.
- Remove all sexist language.

Step 6: Take Care of the Details

- Check your spelling.
- Check for missing words.
- Check for grammatical errors.
- Make sure the copy is clean and readable.

Step 7: Beta Test

Ask a colleague or friend to play the role of the touchstone reader, explaining to him or her the expectations that person has. If no one is available, play that role yourself.

WORKING SMARTER

Grammar Checkers

As many writers have found out, grammar checkers are best used by people who don't need them. That's because even the best grammar checker generates wrong advice some of the time. For instance, it will say that that you've made an error when you really haven't; other times, it will miss a genuine mistake. In short, you must check the checker.

Grammar checkers have improved tremendously in the last few years. They now generate much less wrong advice (although that still doesn't help you determine when they're right). They now are very good at finding agreement errors, inappropriate diction, and missing words. In fact, the best grammar checkers not only spot a passive construction but can also suggest how to recast the sentence (although they still can't tell you when a passive is, in fact, appropriate).

Grammar checkers, therefore, are useful when you use them to alert you to possible mistakes. You then have to use your own judgment to decide if they're right or wrong. If you trust a grammar checker to be a magic correction machine, the results can be disastrous. As with spell checkers, there's still no substitute for human proofreaders.

Ask your tester to read your document and to consider these questions from the touchstone reader's perspective:

- Why should I care?
- Why should I continue to care?
- How will I benefit?
- Is this evidence appropriate?
- Is there sufficient empirical evidence?
- Does the evidence come from reliable sources?
- Do the benefits to me outweigh the costs?
- Is the language clear?
- Is the format acceptable?
- Is care evident throughout the manuscript?

Also ask your tester to apply the smile-or-frown test to your document.

Step 8: Revise and Retest

Based on your beta testing, revise the document. Repeat testing and revising as time permits.

CHAPTER SUMMARY

As a professional writer, you must persuade your readers to act—for example, to buy a product or follow a set of instructions. Because writing is social, you yourself must observe the social conventions, choosing appropriate evidence, language, and format. Otherwise, you're unlikely to persuade your readers that you're credible. And without that, they won't act on your words.

To persuade readers that you are credible, your information must be accurate, balanced, and clear. You must also answer a reader's first two questions: *Why should I care?* and *Why should I care* now? An audience needs to know how it— not you—will benefit by reading your document and following your advice.

You're most likely to succeed when you avoid a one-size-fits-all document but instead shape your message for a specific audience. You must select the right evidence, presenting it persuasively and fairly. You also need to ensure that your document is physically attractive. Finally, although you can make educated guesses about your document's persuasiveness, you must test it out with readers sufficiently similar to your eventual audience.

CHECKLIST

Who is the touchstone reader?

Why should touchstone reader care?

How will touchstone reader benefit?

Is the evidence appropriate?

Is there sufficient empirical evidence?

Does the evidence come from a reliable source?

Is the evidence presented in threes?

Do the benefits outweigh the costs?

Is the language plain?

Is the format acceptable?

Is there care throughout the manuscript?

Does the touchstone reader smile or frown?

Your additional comments:

E X E R C I S E S

Work in groups of two or three to do Exercise 1 and 2; do the others on your own.

Exercise 1

Assume you're writing a recommendation for a consumer electronic product (like a CD player or a camcorder) that you yourself own. The product description that came with it will list its features; express each one as a benefit for a typical purchaser. Then look at the product again for attributes your reader would see as weaknesses; stay within the bounds of truth but counter possible objections.

Exercise 2

Rethink the recommendation in Exercise 1 specifically for the instructor of this course. Consider the following issues:

 a.   Why should the instructor care? Why should the instructor continue to care?
 b.   What are the instructor's expectations and biases?
 c.   What kind of evidence would this person find acceptable?
 d.   Are any particular document formats required?

Apply the smile-or-frown test, that is, picture your instructor approving or disapproving each item.

Exercise 3

Repeat Exercise 1 with one of the following:

 a.   A course in professional, business, or technical writing
 b.   A car or truck
 c.   An ink-jet printer or digital scanner
 d.   A meat substitute (like a vegetarian hot dog or hamburger)

Your audience for this exercise is someone with whom you have worked or taken a course.

Exercise 4

Rewrite the recommendations in Exercise 3 for the following touchstone readers:

 a.   A friend in another college or university
 b.   Your mother or father (or other relation)
 c.   The instructor of another course you're currently taking

CHAPTER

2

Structures and Signals

What This Chapter Covers

[handwritten: |ɑː'tikjulit|]
[handwritten: 清晰明白地说]

Ideas

Keeping Readers Reading

Helping Readers Find Their Way

    Organizing Information

    Thinking Like a Reader

Making Promises to Your Audience

    ← Articulating Your Promise

Starting With a Problem *[handwritten: 应当，应该 ought to [verb]]*

    Showing That a Problem Exists

    Showing How Things Ought to Be

    Showing Possible Solutions

Taking Readers From Thinking to Doing

Signalling How You're Organizing Material

    Signalling With Headings

    Signalling With Words and Phrases

    Signalling With Punctuation

Exploiting the Power of Three *[handwritten: v.使用 vt.开拓，开发]*

Actions

Step 1: Imagine Your Readers

Step 2: Make Your Promise

Step 3: Make a List

Step 4: Reduce Your List to Three Headings

Step 5: Ask "So What?"

Step 6: Shift Each Item Under the Best Heading

Step 7: Imagine Your Audience Once Again

Step 8: Check That Your List Is Complete

Step 9: Write Headings

Step 10: Field Test What You Have

Chapter Summary

Checklist

Exercises

Learning Objectives

At the end of this chapter, you will be able to explain:

- Why you must both structure your material and signal readers how you've done it
- Why the most appropriate way of organizing information is the one that best serves your audience's needs
- Why you must make and keep promises to your readers
- How the various types of openings engage readers
- Why you should focus on problem-solving as a way to organize your document
- What are the various devices to signal your structure
- Why you can organize more efficiently with technology

At the end of this chapter, you will be able to:

- Implement a general strategy for organizing a document
- Describe your audience
- Formulate promises to your readers
- Select and test ideas for relevance
- Experiment with alternate ways of arranging material
- Test your document's structure against your description of your readers
- Write informative headings
- Field test your work

I D E A S

Keeping Readers Reading

Good writers are like good drivers: You always know where they're going.

Readers stop reading for many reasons. One of the most common is that they fail to see how your ideas connect, that it becomes their job rather than yours to sort through a mass of details and find the relationships. This chapter shows how to both organize your ideas and signal their relationships.

Helping Readers Find Their Way

It's the writer's job to get readers from A to B, to show how everything in a document fits together into a single structure. It's also the writer's job to make that structure easy to grasp. When writing flows, that is, when it moves gracefully from one idea to the next, readers see the overall shape and direction of a work. They may disagree with its ideas, but at least they can follow them.

To make your writing flow, you must do two things:

1. You must organize your material into a coherent whole, that is, create a structure with a logical progression from one idea to the next. Complex information can be arranged in a variety of ways, of course. You must choose the most appropriate and use it throughout your document.

2. You must signal to readers how ideas are organized, that is, make clear how each individual section of your document connects to the section before and to the one after.

Suppose you were writing a report about maintaining a bridge. You would include information about when it was built, its materials, its current condition, and various maintenance options. But you would also have to include signals, for example, statements that made clear *when* you were discussing the bridge's materials and *why* you were discussing them at that point. You must talk not only about the bridge but about the discussion itself.

Organizing Information

Let's assume you're writing a report about the poor customer service that your company provides. You have done some research and reached some tentative conclusions. You could start with several different issues:

- A list of common complaints
- The role of customer service within the organization

- The effect on profits of poor service
- The money the organization spends on customer service
- Good models of providing customer service

All of these approaches are legitimate, but each emphasizes something different. Moreover, whichever one you start with will influence how you present the others. How do you choose?

Thinking Like a Reader

The choice is less about you than about your readers. That is, the most appropriate way of organizing information is the one that best serves your audience's needs. For example:

- If your particular audience were primarily concerned with money, you might start with either the effect on profits or the amount the company spends on customer service.
- If your audience were middle managers responsible for delivering service, you might start with the most common complaints or how other organizations help their customers.
- If your audience were high-level managers concerned with the operational efficiency of the entire company, you might start with how the organization assigns responsibility for customer service.

WORKING SMARTER

Drag-and-Drop Editing

One of the great features of a computer is cutting information from one place and pasting it somewhere else. You can, of course, do that with keyboard commands or menus, but it's often more convenient to do a **drag-and-drop:**

1. Select some text (and/or graphics).
2. Keep the mouse button down.
3. Drag the cursor to the location where you want the text to appear.
4. Release the mouse button.

   Drag-and-drop is especially helpful when you are trying out various ways of organizing your material.

In other words, you first have to determine who your audience is, what they need to know, and what they know already. There is little point, for example, in telling money managers about specific techniques for providing customer service when they want to hear about costs.

In practice, of course, your audience may comprise several groups who want to know about several things. It's unlikely that a single way of organizing your material will satisfy them all; therefore, you have to identify your primary audience, your touchstone readers. These are real people with real names; you aren't forgetting about the rest of your audience but focusing on its key members. You want to visualize how your touchstone readers will respond to what you write. Simple-minded as it sounds, imagine them smiling or frowning as they read. What they consider important—that is, what will make them smile—determines how you'll organize your material.

Making Promises to Your Audience

Once you've identified your audience and their needs, think of your opening sentence as a promise about what will follow. For example: "Complaints about customer service seriously reduce our company's profits." This promises readers that they'll hear about customer complaints and the bottom line. If instead you discuss the merits of annual service contracts as opposed to per incident charges, you will have broken your promise. When readers expect to learn about customer service and profits, that's what they want and nothing else.

That opening promise should be an ongoing reference point for you and your audience. That is, as you present ideas, you should test them against your promise. If an idea doesn't contribute to keeping your promise, you must change either the idea or the promise. Your readers also will refer to that promise to understand how what you're talking about at a specific place contributes to the rest of what you're saying.

It's never easy imagining an audience's response. The best way to find out how well readers will follow your ideas is to field test your document with touchstone readers. Throughout this text, we provide questions for such test audiences to help determine where readers are confused.

Articulating Your Promise

A document's opening is often referred to as the lead. Professional writers take care not to obscure or bury the lead. Without a clear lead, readers are left wondering what the document is about. Even worse, of course, is having no lead at all, that is, no indication of where the document is heading.

There are three common ways to write a lead:

- Declaring a fact
- Asking a question
- Quoting a person

"Complaints about customer service seriously reduce our company's profits" declares a fact. It would make a good lead because it sums up the main issue of a possible report.

You can also lead with a question: "Why have complaints about customer service become so frequent that they affect our profitability?" This covers the same ground as a declaration but also engages the audience's curiosity; why *are* complaints so frequent? Readers find out by reading on.

You can also lead with a quotation:

> "Yesterday, I waited three hours for your customer-service technician to call back. By that time, I'd lost an entire day's work. This is the second time this has happened. I won't be buying from you again." So writes Joe Smith, a customer for ten years but apparently no longer.

Such a lead dramatizes the issue, as if the person being quoted were talking directly to your reader. It goes over the same material as the declaration and the question but is more involving—readers find themselves in the thick of the issue.

These three types of leads—the declaration, the question, and the quotation—form a continuum of engaging the reader. The declaration lays out the situation, the question arouses curiosity, and the quotation recreates a scene. This doesn't mean that you should start every report with a quotation; that would make your writing too mechanical and predictable. But it does mean that you have a choice.

However you frame your lead, you are signalling what's to come, providing an immediate impression of your document. The details may not be clear but the direction will be. If it isn't, you have something to revise.

WORKING SMARTER

Splitting the Screen

At times, you will find yourself editing a long document and having to scroll between distant parts of it. Rather than scrolling, split the screen into two windows, displaying a different section of the document in each window. Not only can you see more, but you can cut and paste (or drag and drop) between them.

Starting With a Problem

Professional writing is generally about problems, and the three types of leads all signal a problem that needs solving. If you use problem-solving as an organizing tool, it can be the basis of a straightforward, three-part structure:

- Showing that a problem exists
- Pointing out possible solutions with their pros and cons
- Recommending a solution to act on

  Let's look at each part more closely.

Showing That a Problem Exists

A problem implies two states: *how things are* and *how they ought to be*. Your reader expects to know how you intend to improve the present state. However, it's not enough merely to describe some problematic state: you must also say for whom it is a problem and how seriously it affects them.

For example, does poor service really affect profits? How badly? Are losses severe enough to warrant spending money? In other words, readers need you to distinguish between a tolerable situation and a truly bad one.

The best way to do this is to *show* readers rather than just *tell* them. Use concrete examples, case histories, anecdotes, and whatever other data you can find. Recreate the problem so that your audience can experience it—if not first-hand, then through your words.

Chapter 1 deals more fully with using evidence, but here is a brief example: Instead of saying, "Waiting times for service at our call centre are too long," begin with a narrative of real customers on hold, listening to endless recorded messages about how important their calls are but still never getting through to a real person. Such dramatizations need to be concrete with, for instance, the actual number of minutes a typical caller has to wait and the number of callers who just hang up. The more specific you can make your examples, the more convincing your case will be.

Showing How Things Ought to Be

Once you've signalled that a problem exists, you have to say how things ought to be. You can point to some set of existing objective standards, to the competition's performance, or to your own vision. For example:

- Customers should not wait more than three minutes to speak a technician.
- Customers should not wait more than one hour for a return call.
- Customers should not have to put up with rudeness.

Make your yardstick visible and consistent. Demonstrate that your standards are attainable because other people meet them—or could. You need to convince your audience that you're being both reasonable and rigorous.

Showing Possible Solutions

Having established that a problem exists, you can present possible solutions in two ways:

Go from the best solution to the worst. With this strategy, your first solution becomes the standard against which the others are compared. As you discuss the less attractive options, you remind the reader of what the best one will do and how each subsequent solution fails to equal it. You want to persuade the reader that the first option is really the only one.

Although you would need much more detail, here is an example of this strategy:

- A sophisticated Web site provides the best combination of effectiveness and low cost.
- Using live technicians exclusively provides as good service as a Web site but costs considerably more. Moreover, the high costs are ongoing whereas a Web site requires only periodic and relatively cheap maintenance.
- A pre-recorded telephone helpline or a fax system is inexpensive (and moderately effective) but unpopular with customers because of waiting times and long-distance charges. Our customers tell us that they already use the Web for many of their transactions.

Go from the worst solution to the best. Here you build upwards, ending with the strongest case. You stress the inadequacies of each preceding possibility until you reach the last one. You want the reader believing the final option is invulnerable and inevitable.

For example (and again, you would need more detail):

- A pre-recorded telephone helpline or a fax system is inexpensive (and moderately effective) but unpopular with our customers who prefer to speak to real people or use the Web.
- Using technicians exclusively provides good service but is expensive.
- A sophisticated Web site is effective, as other customer-service organizations have shown. It is expensive to set up but, even factoring in maintenance, it is still cheaper than using live technicians.

Whichever method you choose, give readers room to make their own judgments, to infer the best solution from what you're saying. Keep them actively engaged in making up their own minds—with your guidance, of course. Try for the middle ground: neither heavy-handed nor diffident about your ideas, neither hitting people over the head nor pretending you have no opinions.

What if you yourself don't know what solution is best? You can still use a form of either the best-to-worst or worst-to-best strategy. Eliminate the weakest possibilities from serious consideration. Then simply be honest about your uncertainty and present the remaining options and their consequences.

WORKING SMARTER

Saving Extra Material

As you revise a document, you may find a chunk of information that doesn't seem to fit but that you're reluctant to cut. Move that material to the very end of your document, labelling it "Extra Stuff." If you later decide to use it in a different location or remove it entirely, it will be easy to find.

Taking Readers From Thinking to Doing

It's not enough, however, merely to convince readers intellectually; you also have to show them what they should *do*. That is, you must leave them with not only a series of ideas but also recommendations on how they should act on those ideas.

Of course, your readers may disagree with your recommendations or, agreeing with them, be unable to carry them out. In such cases, you show both the actions and the consequences of not performing them.

Arrange your recommendations from most to least urgent. For example:

Recommendations: Create a Customer-Service Web Site
1. Allocate funds from the customer-service budget to reassign personnel from phone support to Web design.
2. If no current phone support person has the necessary skills, hire someone from outside the company.
3. Research what is done on other customer-service sites, both by our competitors and in other industries.
4. Start the preliminary design of the Web site by August 1.

Signalling How You're Organizing Material

To this point, we have been looking at structuring information. However, to make that structure apparent, you have to signal it to your readers. Signalling means indicating what you're going to do next, just as good drivers do. You don't want your readers to think you are the writing equivalent of a driver who turns without signalling.

Good writers always tell you where they're going. Let's look at three strategies for doing that.

Signalling With Headings

Informative headings are a key method of preparing readers for what they are about to read. Headings provide a preview and a context for what's to come. To be effective, however, headings should go beyond merely saying "Introduction" to more helpful statements like "Why We Have to Upgrade Our Customer Support." Similarly, instead of merely being "Recommendations," a heading should look towards what will actually be recommended (such as "Create a Customer-Service Web Site").

Here are some specific suggestions for writing headings:

- Write them only after you've written the section they introduce so that they genuinely reflect what that section is about. Otherwise, you risk making the ideas fit the heading, rather than the heading fit the ideas.
- Be relatively brief—less than ten words. Treat a heading as a summary, asking yourself what is the single most important idea that's coming.
- Revise headings. Treat them as full-fledged parts of your organizational strategy. As you revise each section of your document, revise the heading that characterizes it.

Signalling With Words and Phrases

Like headings, there are many words and phrases that signal the relationships among ideas. For example:

Signalling What Is to Come
- This report deals with . . .
- To conclude . . .
- Here are some examples . . .

Signalling What's Been Said:
- As we've seen . . .
- The examples we've just looked at . . .
- The preceding examples suggest . . .

Other words signal more complex relationships:

- **Sequence:** first, second, third, now, next, then, finally
- **Addition:** and, also, too, in addition
- **Demonstration:** for example, for instance, such as

- **Clarification:** that is, in other words
- **Logic:** therefore, consequently, because
- **Contrast:** but, however, on the other hand, nevertheless
- **Assertion:** indeed, of course, certainly
- **Spatial:** left, right, top, bottom, middle
- **Hierarchy:** most, least, equal

When you test a document, read it aloud to see if you have enough of these signals to tie together your ideas.

Signalling With Punctuation

Because punctuation is everywhere, it's easy to overlook its value as a signal. It is worth noting the signals given by the following:

Colon: What follows will amplify what has just been said.

> Example:
> There is one rule for providing service: The customer comes first.

Semicolon: What follows is as important to the meaning of the sentence as what has gone before.

> Example:
> Customer service is expensive; however, its lack is even more expensive.

Parentheses: What is inside is useful but not essential to the meaning of the sentence.

> Example:
> The Whizbang company has consistently provided better service (as measured by customer satisfaction surveys) than any of our competitors.

Dash: What follows is either a sudden interruption in the current idea or a parenthetical idea. (Parenthetical ideas are followed by a second dash.)

> Examples:
> Treat all customers with respect—even if they themselves are rude.
> Treat all customers—even those who are rude—with respect.

Bulleted List: All items in this list are equally important.

> Example:
> The ABC of customer service is:
> - Accuracy
> - Brevity
> - Courtesy

Numbered List: Items in this type of list are either a hierarchy or a sequence.

Examples:

1. Gold Service Plan
2. Silver Service Plan
3. Bronze Service Plan

1. Describe the problem in terms of keywords.
2. Search Help database for keywords.
3. Select the most likely result.
4. Explain the results to the customer.

Note that list items must be grammatically parallel. So, if the first item in the list is a noun (such as "accuracy"), all the other items must also be nouns (like "brevity" and "courtesy"). If the first item were a subordinate clause (such as "when you are accurate"), all the others must be too (such as "when you are brief" and "when you are courteous").

Exploit the Power of Three

Chapter 1 discussed organizing information into groups of three as a way to persuade readers that there is a pattern to your ideas. But grouping by threes is also important because most people can keep only a few things in their short-term memories. Most people simply can't remember a long list of items.

For example, suppose you want to discuss these separate items about customer service:

- Time waiting for first answer
- Time waiting for callback
- Technical knowledge
- Courtesy (or its lack)
- Cost of support to customer
- Cost of support to company
- Evidence of company losing customers
- Evidence of company losing profit
- Evidence of company losing reputation
- Examples of good customer service (within and without company)
- How the customer-service department is currently organized and managed
- How customer service fits into company's organization
- Training of customer support staff
- Salary for customer support staff

Although the issues on the list are all important, they lack focus. Dividing them into three groups gives readers just three main points to remember:

Customer Perspective
- Time waiting for first answer
- Time waiting for callback
- Technical knowledge
- Courtesy (or its lack)
- Cost of support to customer

Profitability
- Cost of support to company
- Evidence of company losing customers
- Evidence of company losing profit
- Evidence of company losing reputation

Management
- Examples of good customer service (within and without company)
- How the customer-service department is currently organized and managed
- How customer service fits into company's organization
- Training of customer support staff
- Salary for customer support staff

When you group ideas into threes—dividing and subdividing as necessary—you not only make it easier for readers to grasp ideas, but you appropriate the persuasive power of three. Readers sense that you are controlling, arranging, and shaping your material and that you have discovered its real nature.

WORKING SMARTER

Use an Electronic Outliner

To make organizing easier, do large-scale organizing with your word processor's outliner. (See your manual for the details.) An outliner makes grouping ideas onscreen much easier than on paper.

Equally important is that an electronic outliner lets you play "What if?", that is, experiment with various ways of organizing what you want to say. For example, you can ask what if "Technical knowledge" were under "Management" rather than under "Customer Perspective" and what if "Examples of good customer service" were under "Customer Perspective" rather than under "Management"? In the early stages of writing particularly, you want to keep your ideas fluid and your possibilities open. Because an electronic outliner makes "what-if" experiments relatively painless, you can change things as often as you want.

ACTIONS

There's no recipe for perfectly organizing your ideas, but there are helpful strategies. The general procedure is this:

- Clarify your topic in terms of a problem someone needs solved.
- Write down as many items as you can that relate to that problem.
- Group and regroup them under the most appropriate headings.

This is very much a planning process that comes between your research and your writing. That is, after you have gathered information about your subject, you're likely to have a mass of related but distinct items. You need to step back and order it for your particular audience. If you simply jump in and start writing, you risk not being able to see the forest (the big picture) for the trees (the individual pieces of information). And if you can't see the big picture, neither will your audience.

Planning the order in which to present complex information can't be done in a single session. Give yourself time to walk away from your work, so that when you come back, you can see it from a new perspective, approximating the distance of readers who don't understand the information as well as you do. A day between sessions works best; if that's not possible, a few hours will do.

Circle back to earlier steps as necessary and refine your organization as it develops.

Step 1: Imagine Your Readers

Ask "Who will read this?" Visualize your audience, imagining your touchstone readers. Who are they? Write down names and refer back to them frequently to make sure you don't forget for whom you're writing. Give one-sentence answers to the following questions:

- Why do the people on your list want to read about this?
- What do they need to know about?
- What do they know already?

Step 2: Make Your Promise

Write down the single most important thing that you will promise your readers. What problem needs solving? What question needs answering?

Step 3: Make a List

With an outliner or on paper, jot down your ideas as they occur to you. Go as fast as you can, not censoring yourself nor dwelling too long on a single item.

Step 4: Reduce Your List to Three Headings

Refine your list by asking what three main ideas emerge from what you've put down. Create three headings and three headings only.

If you came up with more than three headings, try to combine two of them. However, if you think you really need four separate elements, work with four headings. You can always revise later.

Step 5: Ask "So What?"

Take a step back and imagine your touchstone readers asking "So what?" to each point. How would you answer? Why is each point worth talking about? How does it contribute to the promise you've made to your audience?

Step 6: Shift Each Item Under the Best Heading

With your electronic outliner, play "What if?" Shift items under different headings and experiment with alternate structures. You can always change things back.

WORKING SMARTER

Working Smarter: Sorting

From time to time, you may find yourself with a list of items that needs to be alphabetized. For example, you may have created a list of works cited by cutting and pasting from various documents. Or you may have a list of names that you entered as quickly as you were able to think of them. Word processors can sort them by letter or by number (if applicable) in either ascending or descending order.

Just one caveat: Save your work before you sort so that you have something to fall back on if things go awry. Better yet, copy the raw data to a new document and sort it there. If the results are what you want, copy and paste back to the first document, replacing the unsorted version.

Step 7: Imagine Your Audience Once Again

Put your work away for a while. Leave it long enough that you can take a fresh look at what you produced. Don't omit this step—it's most often the critical step in learning to think like a reader.

When you return to your document, loop back to Step 1 and Step 2. Ask yourself:

* Does your list of headings satisfy the audience you've named? Repeat the "So what?" test for each idea: Does your touchstone reader need to know this? Would your work be weaker if it were cut? Does the idea distract your readers from your main points?
* Does your list keep your promise, that is, solve the problem or answer the question from Step 2? What needs adding? What needs removing?

Step 8: Check That Your List Is Complete

Check your topics again, making sure you can find specific places in your document where you answer these questions:

* Where is the problem clearly defined? For whom is it a problem?
* How severe is the problem?
* What solutions do you recommend? What are the pros and cons for each one?

Check the order of solutions, either best-to-worst or worst-to-best. Ensure that there is a progression in one direction or the other.

Step 9: Write Headings

Having decided on what information you'll include and its order, write informative headings that provide a brief overview of each section. Don't use vague terms like "Introduction" or "Conclusion." Give readers a summary and preview of what they're about to read.

Step 10: Field Test What You Have

Test your document. Ask a colleague to play the role of your touchstone reader. (If a colleague isn't available, you will have to play the role yourself.) Then talk through your ideas—don't just read from notes. Have a conversation. Make sure that a reasonably informed person knows what you mean.

You can always ignore any suggested revision. Your goal at this point is not to provide a finished product, but to see where you need to clarify, omit, or add.

CHAPTER SUMMARY

In order for your readers to follow the flow of your document, you need to structure it so that one idea leads logically to the next. You also need to signal how you've organized your ideas. When it becomes the readers' job to untangle a mass of material, they stop reading.

There are various strategies to lead an audience through a document. These strategies include making and keeping promises, choosing effective leads, focusing on problems, writing informative headings, and grouping material into *threes*. Technology can help you organize your document more efficiently.

You do general planning after you've completed your preliminary research but before you go too far with your writing. With a general plan in mind, you describe your audience, formulate promises, select key ideas from your research, experiment with different structures, and produce informative headings. Finally, as with all professional documents, you field test what you have produced.

CHECKLIST

List who your touchstone readers are, what they need to know, and what they know already.

State your promise in a sentence.

State the core problem clearly with solid evidence of what the problem is and for whom it is a problem.

Decide on your basic method of structuring ideas (that is, what you will discuss first, second, etc.).

Group information into threes where possible.

Discuss possible solutions to the problem, giving concrete reasons why you are recommending one solution and rejecting the others.

List the actions necessary for implementing the recommended solution.

Write informative headings.

Your additional comments:

EXERCISES

Work in groups of three or four to do Exercises 1 to 4; do Exercise 5 on your own.

Exercise 1

Generate a list of problems, a list of possible solutions, and a list of recommendations for reports on each of the following topics:

a. Improving personal safety in your neighborhood after dark (Write for municipal politicians, your member of the provincial legislature, and your federal MP.)

b. Reorganizing student government (Write for the executive of your current student government.)

c. Encouraging people to ride bikes in your town (Write for a local cyclist advocacy group.)

Exercise 2

a. Prepare outlines for the reports in Exercise 1, keeping to three main headings, each with its own three subheadings.

b. Apply the "So what?" test, saying why each heading and subheading is worth discussing at the point it appears in your outline.

c. Play "What if?", shifting headings and subheadings to see if you can find a more effective sequence. (This is best done with an electronic organizer.)

Exercise 3

For each report in Exercise 1, write a promise. That is, articulate the single most important thing that you want your readers to know. What problem needs solving? What question needs answering?

Exercise 4

Once you are satisfied with the promises you wrote in Exercise 3, revise your headings and subheadings as necessary so that you keep your promises more effectively. Add, cut, reposition, or reword headings and subheadings.

Exercise 5

Working individually, write the first sentence of each report in Exercise 1 in three different ways. Use the following kinds of openings:

a. Declaring a fact

b. Asking a question

c. Quoting a person

CHAPTER 3

Writing Plain English

What This Chapter Covers

Ideas

Why Write Plainly?
How Sentences Get Tortuous
Does Plain English Sacrifice Content?
Strategies for Writing Plain English
      Don't Bury the Verb
      Don't Bury the Subject
      Don't Write Long Sentences
      Cut to the Chase
      Use Plain Words
      Test for Usability

Actions

Step 1: Look Your Reader in the Eye
Step 2: Unbury the Verb and the Subject
Step 3: Make the Verb Active
Step 4: Locate the Words That Show Relationships
Step 5: Use Plain Words
Step 6: Cut to the Chase
Step 7: Test for Usability

Chapter Summary

Checklist

Exercises

Learning Objectives

By the end of this chapter, you will be able to explain:

- Why you should write Plain English
- How bad sentences get written
- How to use the strategies for writing Plain English
- Why you must field test for Plain English

By the end of this chapter, you will be able to write plainly by:

- Imagining your audience
- Unburying verbs and sentence subjects
- Using the active voice
- Reducing the number of relationships your readers have to track
- Replacing uncommon words with common ones
- Cutting words that do no work
- Field testing for Plain English

IDEAS

Why Write Plainly?

Plain English speaks clearly, directly, and honestly to readers so that they know what a writer means. It is both a movement (among consumer groups and legislators, for example) and a practice that demands words and syntax that aren't barriers to comprehension. Plain English does not oversimplify ideas but makes them clear; understanding a complex idea is difficult enough, after all, without having to struggle with the very language that conveys it. Neither does plain mean dull; just the opposite, in fact, because Plain English at its best is concrete and lively.

/'bæriəl/
n. 栅栏, 阻碍

We are all too aware when language isn't plain. We hear it in the wordiness of the bureaucrat, the timidity of the committee, the jargon of the expert. We recoil from such language because we know it both obscures what should be clear and lets the dishonest wriggle free. It misleads the mind and offends the ear.

Writers, however, can learn to see when their language impedes understanding, and more to the point, how to improve it. This chapter covers those techniques.

How Sentences Get Tortuous

/'tɔːtjuəs/ a. 扭曲的, 转弯抹角的

Why is this a dreadful sentence?

> It can be seen by a cursory examination of Freedonian geography that the country is much encumbered by being landlocked and by being circumscribed by swamps and that its attempts to hold back the mud (as the Dutch hold back the sea) have resulted in the unfortunate combination of great expense without commensurate efficacious results.

Why is this better?

> Freedonia is both landlocked and swampy, but its attempts to fix these problems have been costly and unsuccessful.

The quick answer is that the second version is shorter, and books about writing inevitably advise writers to shorten sentences. That's good advice, as long as you can figure out what to cut and what to leave. However, not every long sentence need be dreadful.

Why do people write long, tortuous sentences? One reason is that they discover their ideas only after they've written them down. That's a good strategy for a first draft. However, when we're not sure of what we want to say, we make lots of false starts and go down logical dead ends. All too often, unfortunately, the draft in which we discover our meaning is the draft we give our readers.

②

A second cause of long and tortuous sentences is <u>writers misreading their relationship with their readers</u>. That is, writers sometimes speak from on high—putting on their fanciest clothes, as it were—and confuse seriousness with pomposity. To appear authoritative, they insist that their special and complex knowledge can be expressed only through special and complex language. They forget that a reader may know little about a document's topic and still be as smart as its writer.

Such an approach is socially inept. To avoid making this mistake, imagine real, live human beings facing you and sharing a conversation. Throughout this text, we speak of touchstone readers, that is, actual members of your audience. We encourage you to picture those touchstone readers reading, smiling or frowning as they do. One way to keep them smiling is write nothing that you wouldn't say to them in conversation. That doesn't mean you lapse into slang or vulgarity; you simply look your reader in the eye and write accordingly.

Does Plain English Sacrifice Content?

A frequent worry writers have when they write plainly is that they will leave out important information. In fact, writing plainly helps them see their content more clearly. Consider the following paragraph in which a consulting firm outlines its method for assessing its client's computer network. Although a made-up company name has been substituted, this example is from an actual proposal:

> Amalgamated Consolidated Inc. proposes to assign a senior Technical Specialist to conduct up to three individual situation assessments of the network infrastructure during the course of this project. The assessments would review the quality of services provided, review the procedures and practices employed, and review the hardware/software configurations for <u>efficiency and effectiveness</u> as well as for quality of product. The reviews would conclude with a presentation of findings to management, along with recommendations for change where applicable. This process allows the on site resources to focus on providing the best possible day-to-day service while implementing ACI's total quality management initiative for continuous improvement. [103 words]

At its core, the paragraph says that a technical specialist will assess the client's network and recommend changes. The writer believed that because this was a legally binding promise to perform, prudence required spelling out what the consultant would do. Yet despite the legitimate need for prudence, much of the paragraph is unnecessary. For example:

- Readers already know they're reading a proposal from Amalgamated Consolidated Inc; they don't have to be reminded.

- Readers don't have to be told that the technical specialist will assess the network hardware "during the course of this project." When else would the specialist do this work?
- "Quality" already implies "efficiency" and "effectiveness."
- Readers aren't interested how the consultant arranges matters to ensure quality; they just expect it. They don't need to hear, therefore, that "This process allows the on site resources to focus on providing the best possible day-to-day service while implementing ACI's total quality management initiative for continuous improvement."

Here is a Plain English version of the paragraph:

> To ensure the quality of our work, a senior Technical Specialist will assess the PC network infrastructure up to three times, reviewing quality, procedures, and hardware/software configurations. He [or she] will then present his [or her] findings to management and recommend changes. [43 words]

Despite using less than half the words of the original, the Plain English version loses no important information. In fact, it reveals that important information is missing:

- What professional qualifications does the "senior Technical Specialist" have? Why should we trust him?
- Under what circumstances will the consultants perform "up to three" assessments? When will they do only two? Only one? Will the fee change?
- What procedures will the company follow?

So despite the length of the original, it leaves much unclear. It also sends a disturbing message that the consultants can't think clearly. Why would a client want to deal with them at all?

Strategies for Writing Plain English

Many writing books advise writers to observe the <u>ABC of writing—accuracy, brevity, and clarity.</u> That's easier said than done, and the famous advice to "omit unnecessary words" is sound but insufficiently precise. What follows, then, are some specific strategies for writing plainly.

Don't Bury the Verb

Verbs describe actions, that is, they tell readers what someone or something does. Nouns, on the other hand, tell readers that someone or something exists. When a verb becomes a noun—as when *decide* becomes *decision* or *provide* becomes *provision*—the action gets buried and the reader has to dig it out.

Here's an example:

The Freedonian military is always in the thoughts of King Ethelred the Delusional.

Whatever action there is (Ethelred thinking) gets buried in the noun *thoughts*. Readers have to mentally translate the noun back into a verb to know that somebody was thinking. That's not difficult, but it is tiresome, especially when readers have to do it continually. Tired readers are unhappy readers, and unhappy readers stop reading.

Consider these sentences and their revisions:

> I made the right guess about the winner of the big game.
> I guessed who won the big game.

> Her worry was concerning the outcome of her exam results.
> She worried about her exams.

> The consultant will conduct an assessment of the network.
> The consultant will assess the network.

The second versions are shorter (without sacrificing meaning) and more direct: People guess, worry, and assess—all actions the originals buried in nouns.

To find buried verbs look for a sentence's key actors and their actions. In *Revising Business Prose* (4th ed. Boston: Allyn & Bacon, 1999), Richard A. Lanham tells us to ask "who's kicking whom?" Similarly, in *Style: Ten Lessons in Clarity and Grace* (6th ed. New York: Longman, 1999), Joseph M. Williams tells us to think of the sentence as a mini-drama with a cast of performing characters. Either method unburies verbs so you see what's really going on in your sentence.

Some verbs get buried more often than others. Nouns ending in *ial, ion, ance, ence*, or *ment* are likely buried verbs. For example, look within *denial* and you'll see *deny*, within *inference* to see *infer*, and within *judgment* to see *judge*. Dig out your verbs so your reader won't have to.

The verb *to be* doesn't get buried as much as it buries other verbs, especially when it follows either *there* or *it*. Here are some examples:

> It *is* obvious that the fourth-quarter results are distortions.
> X distorted the fourth-quarter results.

> It *will be* essential for you to give an answer.
> You must answer.

> There *were* three weak reasons in Benson's explanation for her actions.
> Benson gave three weak reasons for her actions.

> There *is* no excuse possible for him to make for himself.
> He can't excuse himself.

Nothing is lost by cutting the *to be* constructions and much is gained. The real subjects—*X, you, Benson*, and *he*—move to the foreground. So do their real actions.

This isn't to say that *there* and *it* have no place, even when followed by *to be*. For example, *it* lets you avoid repetition and *there* can be a useful pointer:

> The gun went off; it was Quentin's.
> There they are!

But when you revise, both words should raise red flags.

Don't Bury the Subject

You can also bury a sentence's subject, making it difficult for the reader to see who did what. The most common offender the passive voice, that is, when the subject does not act but instead is acted upon.

For example:

> The decision was made to fire you.

The grammatical subject here is *decision*, but the real subject gets buried—the *who* that made the decision. Writers sometimes use the passive voice deliberately to hide what they don't want you to know. Compare "The decision was made to fire you" to "I decided to fire you" to see how the passive tries to deflect your anger.

To create a passive, you start with a form of the verb *to be* and then add another verb. For example:

> The ball *was* hit.
> The tofu *will be* prepared.

You can optionally add *by* and name the doer:

> The ball *was* hit by Emily.
> The tofu *will be* prepared by Rebecca.

But if you're going to name the doers anyway, use the active voice:

> Emily hit the ball.
> Rebecca will prepare the tofu.

The active voice sentences put the real actors—*Emily* and *Rebecca*—at the start of the sentence where readers of English normally expect them.

You can, however, use the passive voice quite legitimately either when the actor is obvious or when you don't know who performs an action:

> Muggers must be punished. [The courts must punish them.]
> The rare book was stolen. [We don't know who stole it.]

You can also use the passive voice when the doer isn't as important the action itself:

The Oscars will be announced on March 24.
Charley should be congratulated for his winning goal.
The Bastille was stormed in July.

Although you needn't hunt down and remove every passive you write, your prose will be more direct if you do get rid of most of them.

Don't Write Long Sentences

Another enemy of Plain English is the long sentence. Readers have troubles not when sentences exceed some arbitrary number of words but when they include too many relationships. Consider this made-up monstrosity:

> The Lower Freedonian man in the red jacket with the white stripes had gotten off the plane with the black markings under its wings which had arrived from the Lower Freedonia's capital city (Morosia) where the blonde woman in the red dress with the polka dots had just gone to when she heard that the Lower Freedonian secret police were following her, and she began to get tired from the weight of the cabbage rolls that she carried in her purse.

There are ten prepositions here, three relative pronouns, two subordinating conjunctions, and one coordinating conjunction. All connect one thing to another thing. For instance, *in* connects *man* and *red jacket*; *with* connects *red jacket* and *white stripes*; *under* connects *black markings* and *wings*, and on and on. You must hold all these relationships in your mind while keeping track of the central action (a man getting off a plane). Most readers simply give up, and rightly so.

How many relationships are too many? In a seminal paper, psychologist George Miller has shown that humans generally can keep about seven items in short-term memory—about half the number in the example above. (For details, see his article, "The Magical Number Seven, Plus or Minus Two: Some Limits on Our Capacity for Processing Information," in *The Psychological Review*, 1956, *63*, 81–97.) So a simple count of prepositions, conjunctions, and relative pronouns will tell you when your sentence is too long.

However, if the ideas in a sentence are themselves complex, seven items are likely too many. "Complex," of course, is always relative, and the best way to know if ideas are too complex is to test them with a real reader. We'll discuss such testing in the Actions section.

Cutting to the Chase

Sentences are also too long when they contain words that don't do any useful work. For example:

> In my personal opinion, Lower Freedonia's flag which is green and purple in colour has been the object of abuse, mistreatment, and defilement by every victorious

army that fought against Lower Freedonia in the country's military battles and history since the earliest days and times of past years.

The sentence says something simple: Lower Freedonia's opponents always abuse its flag. But many words don't do any real work:

***In my personal opinion*:** Can an opinion be anything other than personal? And given that the entire sentence is the writer's opinion, why mention "opinion" at all?

***Green and purple in colour*:** Why add "in colour"? Can a flag be green and purple in height?

***Military battles*:** Given the context, can the battles be anything other than military?

***Abuse, mistreatment, and defilement*:** Are there useful differences among these three words?

***Earliest days and times of past years*:** Can the past be anything but days, times, and years?

In *On Writing Well* (6th ed. New York: HarperResource, 1998), William Zinsser describes this kind of wordiness as "clutter." There are literally thousands of other examples, but here are some common ones, followed by their Plain English counterparts in parentheses:

- At this point in time (now)
- In the immediate future (soon)
- At one time in the past (in the past)
- Whether or not (whether)
- It is necessary to see that X is Y (X is Y)
- Completely perfect (perfect)
- Close proximity (near)
- Different variation (variation)
- First priority (priority)

The general principle with such words is simple: *Get rid of them.* You don't have to cut everything to the bone, but you do have to know what's important and what isn't.

Use Plain Words

Plain writing uses plain words. For example, you *read*, not *peruse*; you *think*, not *cogitate*; and you *walk*, not *perambulate*. Although each word in these pairs means the same as its mate, the two have different pedigrees.

Those pedigrees differ because French-speaking William the Conqueror conquered England in 1066. As a result, the language of the Germanic tribes he beat went from high status to low. The language of the ruling class became French. Over time, French merged with the local dialect, but words with French roots still carried the cachet of the winners. English-language writers still reach for the "higher" French word when they want to impress readers, even though that word is usually longer, more obscure, and less conversational.

Here's a crude example: A doctor hands you a plastic cup and points you towards the bathroom where a sign says "Urinate In The Receptacle Provided" What would you think if the sign said "Piss In This"? Centuries have passed since William conquered, but winners still *urinate* and losers still *piss*.

This is *not*—repeat *not*—a licence to be vulgar; that's a social offence. But you offend another social convention when you opt for the fancy word, when you talk down to readers rather than to them. Your place is between vulgarity and pomposity.

Everyday conversation uses everyday words, and in writing those words convey the immediacy of people talking. Conversation is neither slang nor unearned familiarity but one person speaking directly to another. This means that you use big words only when they convey your meaning exactly.

Testing for Usability

Like other complex things, writing must be tested. Your first tester will be yourself, of course, but that's not easy since we are usually too close to our writing to see its weaknesses. We also have too much time and ego invested to want to see. We need some distance, therefore, and here are some ways to gain it:

Read aloud. When you re-read your work silently, you often skip over errors. When you read aloud, however, your ear often will pick up what your eye will miss. Like real readers, you'll stumble over missing words, ideas that just trail off, or thoughts that don't connect. That stumbling is useful because it points you to where you need to revise.

Put time on your side. A blessing of short-term memory is that when you return to something that you've written, you look at it from a new perspective. A day between writing and re-reading will let you see your work anew and still let you remember what you meant. When an entire day isn't practical, try to put your writing aside for at least a few hours.

Work smarter. There's no magic software that transforms bad writing into good. However, the best grammar checkers flag inappropriate diction, missing words, some grammar and punctuation errors, and even passives. Think of them not as teachers who know all (they don't) but as assistants who remind you of what you know but forget.

However, real testing needs real readers. Earlier, we talked about touchstone readers, that is, real live human beings trying to understand what you've written.

Generally it's difficult to get actual members of your audience to look at your work. Instead, you must find friends or colleagues to play that role. Assure them that your hide is thick and you won't take their comments personally. Ask your testers:

- What was clear?
- What needed clarifying?

The answers to these questions will show you strong points in your prase that you can use as models elsewhere and weak points that you need to revise. The more specific your testers' comments, the better.

There's a large literature on usability that goes well beyond these issues. But doing even a relatively quick test will uncover problems you surely will have missed. You don't have to change everything your testers question, but you do have to pay attention.

A C T I O N S

Use the following steps after you've written a couple of drafts and have the basic content and organization in hand.

Step 1: Look Your Reader in the Eye

Imagine your touchstone reader, that is, an actual member of your intended audience. Write nothing that you wouldn't say in a face-to-face conversation.

Step 2: Unbury the Verb and the Subject

Change nouns to verbs so that the grammatical subject is also the sentence's most important actor:

1. Think of everyone and everything in a sentence as the cast of a play.
2. Identify the "star" of the sentence and the supporting players—ask "Who does what?"
3. Find the verb that names the star's action.
4. Find the verb that names the actions of other cast members.
5. Make the star the grammatical subject of the sentence.
6. Make the main verb the action the star performs.

Step 3: Make the Verb Active

A. Use your word processor to find the word *by*. Then:
   1. Look at the words that precede *by*. Do they consist of a form of *to be* followed by a verb?
   2. If so, look after *by* to find the real subject.
   3. Rewrite the sentence:
      a. Put the real subject before the verb.
      b. Cut the *to be* verb.
      c. Make the verb active.

B. Use your word processor to find a form of *to be*. Then:
   1. Check if a verb follows the form of *to be*.
   2. If so, locate the real subject by asking who performs the action.
   3. Rewrite the sentence:
      a. Put the subject before the verb.
      b. Cut the *to be* verb.
      c. Make the verb active.

Step 4: Locate the Words That Show Relationships

A. Use your word processor to find:
   Subordinate conjunctions: because, when, if, since, etc.
   Relative pronouns: that, which, who, etc.
   Prepositions: of, to, from, in, on, concerning, like, etc.

B. Rewrite sentences into shorter units, limiting the number of relationships to no more than two or three per clause.

Step 5: Use Everyday Words

Look for "fancy" words, especially those that come from French. Replace them with their Plain English equivalents.

Step 6: Cut to the Chase

Remove words and phrases that do no work.

Step 7: Test for Usability

To test your document by yourself:

- Let a day pass before testing entire drafts.
- Read the document aloud.
- Use software to flag inappropriate diction, missing words, grammar and punctuation errors, and passives.

To test your document with colleagues playing the role of touchstone readers:

- Ask "What was clear?"
- Ask "What needed clarifying?"

Revise as necessary, then test your revisions.

CHAPTER SUMMARY

Writing Plain English results in language that isn't itself a barrier to understanding. Plain English is clear and direct, without sacrificing important information. Neither is Plain English dull—it is, in fact, concrete and lively.

People write poorly when they haven't thought through what they need to say or when they try to impress others with convoluted sentences and fancy diction. Plain writing requires you to avoid both these traps and instead use some straightforward techniques: emphasize a sentence's verb and subject, reduce the number of relationships the reader must track, remove language that does no useful work, and use everyday words.

You can test your document for Plain English by reading it aloud and leaving yourself enough time to approach it with the eyes of a new reader. The best field test, however, is having someone else act as your touchstone reader.

CHECKLIST

Identify the touchstone readers; speak to them directly.

Identify the real subject and real action in each sentence.

Make the verbs active wherever appropriate.

Revise sentences with too many relationships.

Use plain words.

Cut to the chase.

Test for usability with yourself and typical readers.

EXERCISES

Exercise 1

Identify both the grammatical subject and the most important actor in the following sentences; then rewrite the sentence, changing the most important actor into the grammatical subject.

a. The decision to sue for damages that was taken on October 14, 1999 by Eliot Thompson involved the children who had purchased tickets to the afternoon performance of Pinocchio that had been cancelled.

b. There should be no hesitation whatsoever on your part to speak clearly about the government's failure to act on behalf of the disadvantaged.

c. Our beliefs were such that Parker and Fitzgibbons shared them, even when Harrison threatened them with legal action.

d. The necessity of repainting the upstairs of the house because of the shoddy work by the contractor has been verified by Jane Evers, the head of our local Better Business Bureau.

e. A full assessment of the University's computing infrastructure must occur before further expenditures are undertaken.

Exercise 2

Unbury the verb and rewrite the following sentences:

a. The collision of the two cars occurred at Sherbrooke and Connaught.

b. His assumption was that the Oilers would win at home.

c. The following day, however, the Premier's indications were that he would resign.

d. The doctor and I had a discussion about possible treatments.

e. It will be necessary for you to bring the money with you.

Exercise 3

Rewrite the following sentences, cutting or replacing words that do no useful work:

a. My own belief is that anyone who is six years of age or above would know better.

b. It is useful to note that the men and women who sit in Parliament have little choice and few options when the political parties of which they're members insist they to vote in certain ways.

c. My past memories of times gone by include wondering whether or not Grandma would make changes or modifications to her Christmas menu.

d. I have no plans at this point in time to travel to or visit any countries outside my own.

e. Thompson really has no use for virtually any of her ideas or concepts.

Exercise 4

In the following, change the passive voice to the active voice only when it improves the sentence.

a. An excellent three-course dinner was served that included an entrée, a main course, and a desert.

b. The consequences of not attending class were realized by Edward when he received his final grades.

c. The ball was thrown to the tight end by Tracy while he was scrambling to his right.

d. The cottage was vandalized, and we were heartbroken.

e. The judgment of the lower court was upheld by the higher court.

Exercise 5

Rewrite the following sentences to make them more conversational, without being slangy or vulgar.

a. The judgment I had made about not dispatching an invitation to you to my social gathering was based on indications that your fondness for me was non-existent.

b. The accumulation of particles of dust beneath your place to sleep has grown to obscure the appearance of our feline companion, Ralph.

c. Your inability to habituate to patterns of intensive cogitation over subject matter assigned you by faculty members in the courses for which you have registered will surely convey you to a lack of success at university.

d. Any recompense you garner while pursuing part-time employment must be transmitted to those with whom you have non-discharged debt obligations.

e. It will be insisted by those so charged with the responsibilities of upholding statutes passed by democratically elected governing assemblies concerning the movement of traffic specifically that vehicles of conveyance of persons and goods cease their forward motion when encountering traffic control signals whose hue is ruby in colour.

Exercise 6

Put the following sentences into Plain English.

a. Since there is a continuation of the operation of the disk drive, there is little reason for its replacement.

b. Unless there is co-operation on your part, we will have to effect a termination of your employment.

c. Canadians have often debated whether the state should put people to death for serious crimes.

d. The Personnel Manager has interviewed all the candidates, checked their references, and then asked for our advice. Interviewing all the candidates, checking their references, and then asking for our advice takes time but yields good results.

e. When the children from the village where Jock lived when he first got his job were visiting him in Toronto, he took them after they had arrived to the CN Tower to where they could see the view that he had told them about when he was there because he knew that it would be a treat for them to visit it.

CHAPTER

4 Graphics

What This Chapter Covers

Ideas

Why Writers Should Learn About Graphics
Instructing and Delighting
The Main Types of Graphics
       Photos: Showing It Exactly
       Diagrams: Showing the Essentials
       Tables: Presenting Information Concisely
       Line Graphs: Showing Trends
       Column Graphs: Showing Comparisons
       Pie Charts: The Parts and the Whole
       Flow Charts: Showing a Process
       Organization Charts: Showing Hierarchy
       Other Kinds of Graphics
Persuading With Graphics
Complex and Simple Information
Making the Abstract Concrete
       An Example From Logic
       An Example From Psychology
       An Example From Algebra
Helping the Reader See the Graphic
Overdoing a Good Thing

Actions

Step 1: Decide When to Use a Graphic
Step 2: Choose the Kind of Graphic
Step 3: Prepare the Graphic
Step 4: Integrate the Graphic Into Your Text
Step 5: Write the Callout
Step 6: Guide Your Reader Through the Graphic
Step 7: Test the Graphic

Chapter Summary

Checklists

Exercises

Learning Objectives

At the end of this chapter, you will be able to explain:

- Why professional writers must know about graphics
- What the main types of graphics are
- What the appropriate uses for each type are
- How graphics persuade
- When to use graphics and when not to
- How graphics help readers understand abstractions
- How to help readers look at a graphic

At the end of this chapter, you will be able to insert graphics into your documents by:

- Deciding when you need a graphic
- Selecting the appropriate type
- Preparing the graphic
- Integrating the graphic with text
- Writing the callout
- Guiding readers through the graphic
- Field testing

I D E A S

Why Writers Should Learn About Graphics

The time when professional writers dealt only with words has passed.

Professional writers now must know how to use graphics, not as mere embellishments but as ways of solving communication problems. Further, as employers continue to demand efficiency, being able to work with images becomes an essential skill. Writers are increasingly required to reduce costs by producing both text and graphics.

Ideally, a writer would call upon a trained artist for the graphics, but most writers don't have that luxury. They themselves must create the images or at least know how to integrate ready-made ones into their work. Fortunately, computer technology has made the necessary tools affordable and easy to use. Although the resulting graphics may not win design competitions, these images can still be effective.

This chapter, therefore, talks both about using graphics as part of a document's argument and about the computer tools for creating those graphics.

A Note about Examples: Professional writers use many kinds of graphics. Although this chapter gives numerous examples, it can't be exhaustive. The *Ideas Into Action* Web site at **<www.pearsoned.ca/keller/>** provides more examples, including those where colour plays an important role.

Instructing and Delighting

An old maxim about education is that it should instruct and delight, and the same can be said about graphics. The first job of a graphic is to give readers information in ways that text alone cannot. Because humans have a visual sense, we can communicate with each other through images. That allows us to present some things more directly, as with the classic example of showing a picture of a spiral staircase rather than trying to describe it in words. Some things are simply much easier to explain with an image than with text.

Nor should we forget the second part of the educational maxim—to delight. The major reason to use graphics may be to instruct, but combining understanding with pleasure is a powerful combination for winning over your readers.

The Main Types of Graphics

Before we discuss solving rhetorical problems with graphics, let's look at the most common kinds of graphics that professional writers use.

Photos: Showing It Exactly

Photographs are essential when you need to show the reader exactly what an object or person looks like. For example, Figure 4.1 shows us two girls.

Figure 4.1
Using photographs to show exact appearances

While it's certainly possible to describe these girls in words, it would not be simple. Even more difficult would be finding the words that convey the precise differences between them. (One is darker, one has longer hair, and so forth—but by how much?) The more alike the two girls are, the more difficult it would be to express their differences.

Similarly, consider the two textures in Figure 4.2.

Figure 4.2
Photographs that show variations in texture

While the textures undoubtedly differ, expressing that difference is far easier with pictures than with words. The same is true for colours. In a painting, an artist might use many shades of one colour; again, words simply would not be sufficiently powerful to convey the differences.

The message is clear: the more we wish to communicate exactly what an object looks like, the more we need photographs.

Finding and Using Photographs

Having decided that you need a photo, you have four main ways of getting one into your document:

- Purchase a stock photo from a commercial supplier; their catalogues often include thousands of pictures in both electronic and hard-copy versions. You're not guaranteed, of course, to find exactly what you want.
- Take the picture yourself and literally paste it onto a printout of your document. This won't work, of course, if you plan to distribute the document electronically. Further, the results likely will be amateurish, and certainly inconvenient and expensive if you need more than a few copies.
- Take the picture yourself, digitize it with a scanner, and paste the electronic version into your word-processed document. The price of scanners has fallen

---

WORKING SMARTER

Clip Art and Stock Photos

Clip art generally refers to simple line drawings or cartoons of common objects or activities—for example, computers, telephones, or people at work. Clip-art images are usually small, as are their file sizes. Although they are often professionally drawn, their quality varies tremendously, some being little more than crudely drawn doodles. They are distributed mostly via CD-ROM or as downloads from the Web; purchasing clip art gives you the right to use it in your own work, although there may be copyright limitations.

Clip art comes in different file types, and not all file types display on all computers. Macintosh machines, for instance, generally use PICT files, and Windows and DOS machines use BMPD files. GIFs and JPEGs files are cross-platform formats and are generally used on Web pages. Be sure to know what kind your computer platform accepts.

Stock photos, like clip art, are created by professionals and their quality also varies. A stock photo file is generally bigger than a clip-art file. Again, file types vary and not all file types display on all platforms.

Both clip art and stock photos are convenient, especially if you're lucky enough to find what you need. But because they are off-the-shelf solutions, you may not find the image you want. Also, you may not want your work to look like everyone else's.

dramatically in the past few years; you can buy quite acceptable ones for less than two hundred dollars.

- Take the picture yourself with a digital camera and paste it into your document. The price of digital cameras also has dropped in the last few years, although a good one still costs considerably more than a comparable film camera or a good scanner.

Whether you scan pictures or take them with a digital camera, you must choose a resolution (that is, the number of dots per inch) appropriate to the way that you'll distribute the final document. If you plan to distribute your document only electronically, for example, note that a typical computer screen can show only 72 or 96 dots per inch. Graphics at higher resolutions will be huge files whose detail won't be displayed. Hard-copy documents, on the other hand, require at least 600 dots per inch for good results. Therefore, choose the resolution of your graphic according to how you'll distribute your document.

Taking a picture yourself may be the only way to get exactly what you want, but not everyone can take a good picture. As with other sorts of graphics, hiring a professional may be desirable but impractical. Expect to live with trade-offs between quality and cost.

Diagrams: Showing the Essentials

There are times when being faithful to the original makes a reader's task harder. Too much detail can obscure what you want the reader to see. In such cases, you need a diagram—that is, an image that shows certain features of an object and deliberately omits others.

What you show depends on what you deem essential for the document you're writing. For example, suppose you were explaining how the human eye works. A photograph reproducing a human eye exactly shows only what's normally visible. On the other hand, the diagram in Figure 4.3 (page 58) shows what normally *can't* be seen and just as importantly hides what isn't necessary to explain how the eye works. With diagrams, therefore, you must first decide what readers need and what's irrelevant.

The diagram of the automobile in Figure 4.4 (page 58) also lets readers look inside an object, seeing what would otherwise be impossible or impractical to see. This diagram of an automobile's fuel system deliberately discards most other information about the car. You would have to literally dismantle a good part of the car to see what the diagram reveals.

The diagram does not pretend to represent a fuel system exactly, only its essentials as the writer conceived them for this point in the text. By excluding some things, therefore, the diagram provides a better view of others—and certainly is more convenient than dismantling the car.

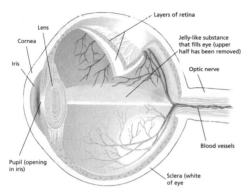

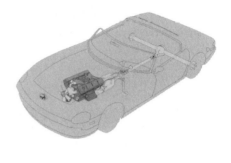

Figure 4.3
Seeing what otherwise couldn't be seen

Source: Carlson, Buskist, Enzle, and Heth,
Psychology: The Science of Behaviour
(Scarborough: Allyn and Bacon Canada, 2000)

Figure 4.4
A diagram showing appropriate detail

Source: Autoshop online <www.autoshop-
online.com/auto101/fuel.html>

Using diagrams underlines a point common to all writing: Before you can design a diagram, you must first be clear in your own mind about what you want your audience to understand. Otherwise, you have no way of knowing what parts of an object to show and what parts to leave out.

Simple Diagrams

Creating diagrams like the ones above requires considerable skill. For many writing situations, however, simple line drawings work well enough. For example, suppose you wished to show how the placement of two actors on the stage affects the action. In Figure 4.5, a stick diagram shows the bad guy (in the black hat, of course) saying nasty, ironic things about the good guy, while standing behind him and out of earshot. If you wanted to show the effect of placing the characters face-

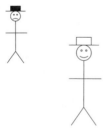

Figure 4.5
Simple diagram showing the effect of
placing the villain behind the hero

Figure 4.6
Simple diagram showing the effect of
placing the villain beside the hero

to-face, you could complement your discussion with Figure 4.6. While no one would mistake these two diagrams for art, they do help illustrate how placing actors affects the play.

Creating Diagrams

As with using an existing photograph, you can scan a hard-copy diagram and paste the resulting file into your document. However, many applications (including word processors) can themselves create simple diagrams. There are two main types of graphics programs:

Paint programs create images pixel-by-pixel (a pixel being the smallest picture element on a computer monitor). These images are flexible but create large files.

Drawing programs create diagrams by recording information about shapes and lines. While they lack the flexibility of paint programs, they produce much smaller files. They are especially good for diagrams based on common shapes like circles and squares. Both stick-figure diagrams above were done in a few minutes with a word processor's built-in drawing program. Again, they are not art, but their context doesn't require art.

Tables: Presenting Information Concisely

Tables require no artistic ability; you simply enter information. You arrange information in columns and rows, thereby significantly reducing the number of words you'd otherwise need. For example, Figure 4.7 displays the essay marks and averages for three students.

The table makes it very easy, for example, to find the second student's second mark or the third student's average. Without the table, readers would have to make their way through something like this:

> On his first essay, Tom received a mark of 84; on his second essay, he received a mark of 83; on his third essay, he received a grade of 75. Tom's average for the three essays was 80.6. On Dick's first essay . . .

Name	Essay 1	Essay 2	Essay 3	Average
Tom	84	83	75	80.7
Dick	85	86	68	79.7
Harry	66	70	75	70.3

Figure 4.7
Table with numerical data

Even with relatively little information to convey, the paragraph quickly becomes tedious and unwieldy. Worse, trying to find a specific item (Harry's average, for instance), forces the reader to go through everything that comes before. Tables, by contrast, help readers locate information quickly, especially when there is a lot of it.

Tables can include more than numbers. For example, Figure 4.8 tells potential car buyers about some key options.

Make and Model	CD/FM/AM	Anti-Lock Brakes	Air Bags
Ford Taurus	Standard	Standard	Standard
Honda Accord	Standard	Standard	Standard
Toyota Tercel	Optional	Optional	Optional
Yugo	N/A	N/A	N/A

Figure 4.8
Table with textual data

If you wished, you could also insert graphics into some of the cells. However, tables have their limitations:

- They don't emphasize specific comparisons between two elements, for example, whether Tom did better than Harry or the Taurus has more features than the Yugo.
- They don't show trends such as whose grades got worse over the semester.

Creating Tables

Two mainstream computer applications create tables:

Spreadsheets are tables in which individual cells hold values; those values themselves can be linked to values in other cells. For example, a cell that holds the total for a column of numbers will change automatically when values in the column change. Spreadsheets are convenient because you need only cut-and-paste information from them into your document. Most importantly for professional writers, spreadsheet programs also generate tables and graphs based on cell values. Figure 4.8 was created that way with just a few mouse clicks.

Word Processors include powerful and flexible tools for formatting tables. These tools are ideal for creating easy-to-read, non-numerical information and are your only real choice for embedding graphics within the table. However, they generally do only very simple mathematical calculations, making them less useful than spreadsheets when you want to present complex numerical relationships.

Line Graphs: Showing Trends

A line graph shows how a value changes over time. For example, Figure 4.9 shows average essay grades improving from the start of the semester to its end.

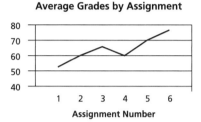

Average Grades by Assignment

Figure 4.9
Line graph showing increase in grades over the semester

The line graph lets readers quickly see the trend of somewhat better grades as the semester progresses. However, although they show trends well, line graphs obscure the exact value of any particular item. In Figure 4.9, for example, you cannot tell how any one student did on any one assignment.

Line graphs can also distort information. For example, Figures 4.10 and 4.11 use the same data about stock market prices; however, simply changing the scale makes that data can look very different. Figure 4.10 emphasizes the volatility of stock market prices—that is, their continual rise and fall. Figure 4.11 (page 62), however, elongates and flattens the line, thereby reducing the

Freedonian Stock Prices 2000

Figure 4.10
Line graph showing volatility

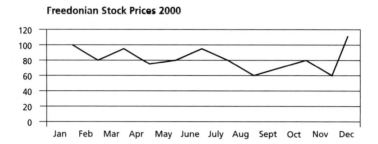

Figure 4.11
Line graph reducing the appearance of volatility

apparent volatility. The old maxim that "Figures lie and liars figure" obviously applies to graphs too.

Creating Line Graphs

You can plot a line graph on paper, scan it, and then paste the file into your document. However, using a spreadsheet program is much easier because it will generate graphs once you have entered data. If you change that data, the application automatically updates the graph, a real convenience.

Column and Bar Graphs

A column graph—sometimes called a bar graph—compares values at a particular time. For example, Figure 4.12 shows the sales of five different products in May.

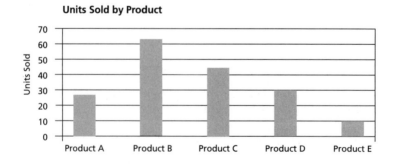

Figure 4.12
A simple column graph

At a glance, you see the best and the poorest performers. The exact numbers for each product, however, are less clear. For example, it is clear that Product A's sales were the second lowest, but we would have to measure the graph carefully to know if those sales were 26, 27, or 28 units. Deciding to use a column graph, therefore, depends on whether you need to show precise values.

A column graph can also behave like a line graph and display trends. Figure 4.13, for example, shows how National Hockey League salaries rose over six years.

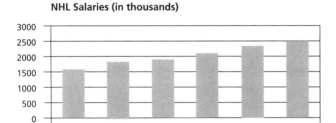

Figure 4.13
Column graph showing a simple comparison

You can also stack information on each column to display how much each component contributes to the total value. In Figure 4.14, for example, each column shows the total salaries paid to major-league players for one year. However, each column also displays how much was paid to players at different positions (pitchers, infielders, and outfielders).

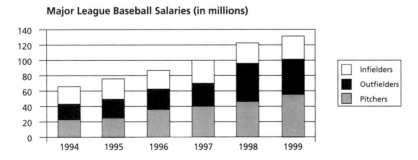

Figure 4.14
Stacked column graph

As with a line graph, the easiest way to create a column graph is to let your spreadsheet application generate it.

Pie Charts: The Part and the Whole

A pie chart shows how much an individual element contributes to the whole, but each segment focuses on a single value (not several, as does a stacked column graph). For example, Figure 4.15 shows how much each quiz, essay, or exam contributes to a student's final grade in a business-writing course:

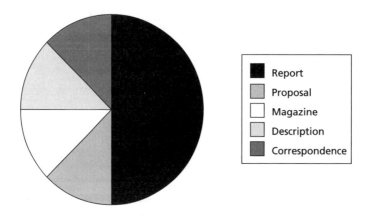

Figure 4.15
Pie chart showing how components make up the total

At a glance, readers know that the report is the largest component of the grade and that the correspondence and description assignments are the smallest. Again, pie charts are most easily done with spreadsheets.

Flow Charts: Showing a Process

A flow chart shows a sequence of events, such as a process. What makes them particularly helpful is that they also show the decision points in a process, that is, where actions may be taken based on some pre-established criteria. Figure 4.16, for example, shows that a bomb-disposal expert may choose one of two possible actions, depending on the situation.

A flow chart's rectangles show various actions while the decision diamonds pose questions (generally answered with "Yes" or "No"). Flow charts can illustrate paths through highly complex processes with a great many actions and decisions.

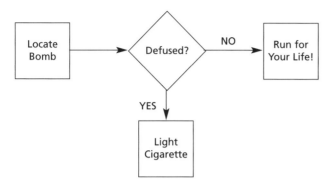

Figure 4.16
A flow chart with decisions

There is special software to create flowcharts but, unless you use them often, you may not get back your investment in buying an application and learning to use it. Drawing programs work well, but for occasional use, it's often faster to simply draw the flow chart on paper and scan it into your document.

Organization Charts: Showing Hierarchy

An organization chart shows an organization's hierarchy and who reports to whom. For example, Figure 4.17 illustrates the top three levels of a mythical corporation. The higher (literally) someone appears on the chart, the more authority he or she has. An organization chart also indicates who has jurisdiction over different functions and how authority flows. What such a chart cannot show, however, is political reality, that is, the extent to which a job title reflects the person's power to effect change. Although there are specialized applications to produce organization charts, a simple drawing program is generally all you need.

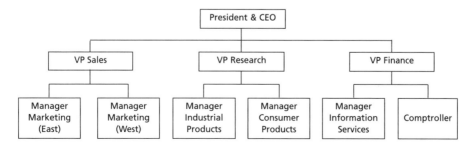

Figure 4.17
An organizational chart

Other Kinds of Graphics

The graphics we've discussed so far constitute the majority of what professional writers use. In the course of your work, you will no doubt encounter many variations and styles, as well as much more elaborate renderings than appear here. With all graphics, however, the critical issue is how well they convey information to the reader. That's the issue we'll look at next.

Persuading With Graphics

A picture is worth a thousand words—but only sometimes: It depends on which picture and which thousand words.

A graphic is one way a document's persuades. To the degree it does its job, a graphic *is* worth a thousand words—or a hundred or a million or none at all. That is, its mere presence doesn't guarantee that readers will be any more convinced. A graphic, therefore, is just another tool, not necessarily better than any other. Before you insert a graphic into your document, you must first ask the same questions you do when making other choices:

- What information does the audience need to know?
- What problem am I having in presenting that information?
- How will a graphic help?

If you can't answer these questions and then verify your answers with a touchstone reader, you have no reason to include a graphic.

Complex and Simple Information

Including a graphic obviously requires you to be able to visualize something. Generally, the simpler the information to convey, the less likely it warrants a graphic. Conversely, the greater the information's complexity, the greater the reason to consider a graphic.

Suppose, for example, you wanted to show that quarterly profits increased by 300% over one year. You could show quarter-to-quarter growth with the line graph in Figure 4.18. The graph says that profits for the first quarter were about $5000 and profits for the last quarter were about $20 000. But it adds little if your main point is simply "Quarterly profits quadrupled from the first to the final quarter." The idea isn't sufficiently complex to ask the reader to examine the graph.

However, suppose you wanted to emphasize that, while a company's profits were only slightly lower at the end of the year than at the start, the profits were

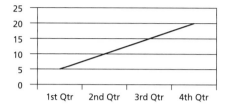

Figure 4.18
A line chart with too little information

Profits in 2000 (in thousands of dollars)

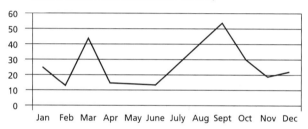

Figure 4.19
A line chart showing complexity

volatile, with some months being very bad and others very good. Figure 4.19 shows this wide range by plotting the profits monthly rather than quarterly. A reader would quite rightly want to know what accounted for the volatility.

A text version of Figure 4.19 would have to specify the amount of profit or loss for each month and underline the variability from one month to the next. For example:

> In January, the profit was about $26 000. The next month, it dropped to about $12 000. In March, it rose to $45 000 . . .

Such writing quickly gets tedious and obscures the main point about volatility. Figure 4.19, on the other hand, conveys the volatility at a glance and so warrants inclusion, while Figure 4.18 does not.

Here's another example where a picture isn't worth a thousand words. Suppose you ask preschoolers if they like broccoli and then learn (big surprise) that most don't. The pie chart in Figure 4.20 would add little to your presentation.

The Broccoli Preference of Kids

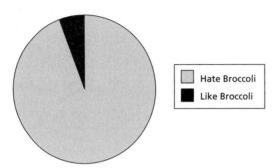

Hate Broccoli
Like Broccoli

Figure 4.20
A pie chart adding little information

Why Kids Won't Eat Broccoli

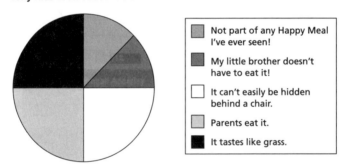

Not part of any Happy Meal I've ever seen!

My little brother doesn't have to eat it!

It can't easily be hidden behind a chair.

Parents eat it.

It tastes like grass.

Figure 4.21
A pie chart with more information

However, if the information were more detailed and represented broccoli haters by the kind of responses they gave, a pie chart like Figure 4.21 would be helpful. Again, the information conveyed is sufficiently complex to warrant the graphic. So merely adding a graphic does little good—in fact, it can do harm— unless the graphic does some useful work.

That's not to suggest that a graphic itself must be complex; quite the opposite. The purpose of a graphic is to present complexity—not embody it—so that you render ideas without oversimplification or distortion. Let's examine how that applies to non-numerical information.

Making the Abstract Concrete

We frequently must write about abstractions, and readers often struggle with them because they are by definition something we can't see or touch. But if we can find a visual expression for an abstract idea, our readers will be better able to comprehend it.

An Example From Logic

Here is an example of this from introductory logic:

> All A is part of B
> All B is part of C
> Therefore, all A is part of C

Although this syllogism doesn't present difficulty for most people, Figure 4.22 makes it easier to (literally) see.

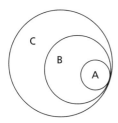

Figure 4.22
An example from logic

The smallest circle (A) is part of the second smallest (B), itself part of the largest (C). We therefore have visual evidence that A is also part of C. Readers can not only follow the logic of the conclusion—*all A is part of C*—they can also see it.

An Example From Psychology

Here's a second example, this time from the study of perception:

> We not only see, we look for.

This says that humans impose a pattern on what they see, rather than being merely passive receptors. Figure 4.23 helps make the point.

Most people looking at this graphic soon alternately see a goblet and two faces in profile. Once they know both images are there, they generally can summon up one or the other at will.

Figure 4.23
We not only see, we look for

Source: Carlson, Buskist, Enzle, and Heth, Psychology: The Science
of Behaviour *(Scarborough: Allyn and Bacon Canada, 2000)*

A psychologist would say that what we see at any moment depends on what we are looking for—the goblet or the faces. The power of the graphic is that it makes concrete an abstraction about perception. The graphic doesn't replace the text but complements it, letting readers see—again, literally *see*—what they otherwise couldn't.

An Example From Algebra

The two previous graphics demonstrate how we can express complex ideas parsimoniously, that is, in fewer words. This does more than simply save paper: The fewer words we use, the less our readers have to work.

To illustrate the value of such parsimony, consider the following abstraction, found in any introductory algebra text:

> The square of a binomial equals the sum of the squares of its two terms plus twice their product.

Even assuming readers know terms like "binomial," the sentence doesn't make it particularly easy to see that one thing (the square of a binomial) equals another (the sum of the squares of a binomial's two constituents *plus* twice the first constituent multiplied by the second). Things get somewhat simpler for readers who understand mathematical notation:

$$(a + b)^2 = a^2 + b^2 + 2ab$$

Compare, however, either expression of the idea to its graphical representation in Figure 4.24.

The figure permits us to quickly grasp the equality because we can see with our own eyes that the large square—$(a + b)^2$—is the same size as all the other rectangles combined. That is, $(a + b)^2$ has exactly enough area to hold all the smaller rectangles. (Better yet is letting the reader manipulate the squares or

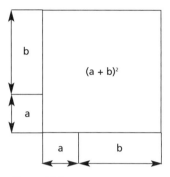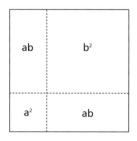

Figure 4.24
The visual representation of algebraic ideas

showing animation in which the small rectangles move one by one into the large square). The highly abstract original statement becomes concrete and so easier to understand.

Helping the Reader See the Graphic

These last three examples show how we can help our readers understand abstractions. This does not mean, however, that graphics should replace text. Rather, the two must work together, each providing information the other can't.

Including a graphic, however, isn't enough; you also have to help the reader look at it. Here are some ways:

Help the reader locate the graphic: Refer to graphics by their names (like *Figure 1*); this is technically known as a callout. Then tell readers what they're seeing and why it's important. For example:

> The pie graph in Figure 1 shows how much each department contributed to the company's profit.

> Figure 2 illustrates the working of a four-cylinder engine and how power is transmitted to the rear axle.

> Figure 3 shows the texture and colour of the aquatint finish.

Place the graphic as close as you can to the first text that refers to it, so that your reader doesn't have to hunt through the document. And unless you have absolutely no other option, keep the graphic on the same page as its callout.

Help the reader through the graphic: Although a graphic should be self-contained, some explanation is usually helpful. After you've shown the graphic, therefore, lead readers through it, highlighting its key elements. If there is a part of the graphic that is more important than other parts, point that out and explain its significance. Do the same for other parts. For example:

> As you examine Figure 4.23, alternately look for either the goblet or the faces. As your expectations change, so should what you perceive.

> In Figure 4.24, notice that the large square has enough area to hold each smaller shape.

> In Figure 4.21, we see that children won't eat broccoli not only because of taste but because they perceive their parent's unfairness.

Saying only "See Figure 1" likely will leave readers not knowing what they're looking at or why it deserves their attention.

Give credit where credit is due: Unless you yourself have created the graphic from scratch or are licensed to use it without credit, tell your reader where it comes from. Respect copyright, in other words, just as you would when you quote secondary textual sources. Doing so is both ethical and helpful to readers pursuing their own research.

Overdoing a Good Thing

We've looked at line and pie graphs (Figures 4.18 and 4.20) whose persuasive value simply didn't justify their presence. But even a useful graphic can be overdone. For example, the three-dimensional bar chart in Figure 4.25 makes it harder to see the basic idea about sales.

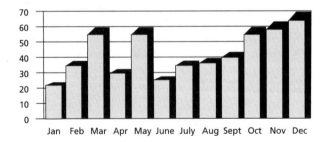

Figure 4.25
Embellishing and obscuring information

Much software makes it easy embellish graphics, showing them in three dimensions, for example. If such embellishments add no information, they should be cut. Similarly, you've no doubt waited—and waited—for an image to download on the World Wide Web. When it does finally appear, it adds little or nothing.

Including one or two graphics like this isn't terrible and does add a little visual interest. But using graphics just for their own sake can undermine your credibility and lose your readers' attention. Figure 4.26 illustrates a similar problem.

You have probably seen documents with a host of fonts and styles. Computers have made it very easy to create **graphics**, perhaps *too* easy. The result can be graphics that call **attention** to *themselves*.

Figure 4.26
Too many fonts and styles

As you read a paragraph like this, everything calls out for attention. Each change in font style, size, or colour, however, cancels the others; very soon, you stop paying attention both to the fonts and to the writer's ideas. This overdone example goes well beyond what most people would produce. However, it does show how mere embellishment can interfere with meaning.

ACTIONS

Because there are so many ways to create graphics, it's not possible to provide step-by-step advice for every type with every possible application. Instead, the following sections give advice about when and how to use graphics, as well how to integrate them into your text. Throughout, we assume that you already know how to use your software.

Step 1: Decide Whether to Use a Graphic

A. Answer this question:

What is the key idea I wish to communicate at this point in my document?

You must have a clear sense of what readers should understand. For example, you might answer "I want readers to see where this process breaks down" or "I want readers to compare Object A and Object B."

B. Next answer these questions:

> *Does the key idea I wish to communicate require many words?*
> *Can I myself visualize it?*

If you answer "Yes" to both questions, continue.

Step 2: Choosing the Kind of Graphic

A. Does the key idea involve a physical object, either mechanical or natural, that needs to be shown exactly as it is?
   No: Go to Step 2B.
   Yes: Use a photo and go to Step 3A.

B. Does the key idea involve a physical object, either mechanical or natural, for which a photograph will *not* show what you wish?
   No: Go to Step 2C.
   Yes: Use a diagram. Emphasize those parts that best answer the questions in Step 1. Then go to Step 3A.

C. Does the key idea involve a set of items, all of which can be categorized in a similar way?
   No: Go to Step 2D.
   Yes: Use a table, mixing numbers, images, and text as appropriate. Then go to Step 3B.

D. Does the key idea involve a numerical relationship showing how a series of values changes over time?
   No: Go to Step 2E.
   Yes: Use a line graph. Go to Step 3C.

E. Does the key idea involve a numerical relationship comparing several items with each other?
   No: Go to Step 2F.
   Yes: Use a column graph. Go to Step 3C.

F. Does the key idea involve a numerical relationship comparing several items with each other and showing how each item is itself made up of other items?
   No: Go to Step 2G.
   Yes: Use a stacked column graph. Go to Step 3C.

G. Does the key idea involve a numerical relationship showing how various values contribute to the whole?
   No: Go to Step 2H.
   Yes: Use a pie chart. Go to Step 3C.

H. Does the key idea involve a process?
   No: Go to Step 2I.
   Yes: Use a flow chart. If there are decision points in the process, include decision diamonds. Go to Step 3D.

I. Does the key idea involve a social relationship between members of an organization?
   No: Go to Step 2J.
   Yes: Use an organizational chart. Then go to Step 3E.

J. No standard graphic is appropriate. Use text instead.

Step 3: Preparing the Graphic

A. Photographs or diagrams:
   1. If an electronic version of a stock graphic is available and sufficient to your needs, insert it directly into your document.
   2. If a hard-copy version of a stock graphic is available and sufficient to your needs, scan it and insert it into your document.
   3. If there is no suitable stock graphic available, create the graphic yourself:
      • Photographs: Take a picture with a camera and then insert it into your document.
      • Diagrams: If the diagram consists mostly of basic shapes (lines, rectangles, circles, and polygons), use a drawing program and insert the file into your document. Otherwise, draw the diagram on paper and then scan it into your document.

B. Tables:
   • If the data consists of numbers, prepare the table with a spreadsheet program and then copy it into your document.
   • If the data consists of text and/or images, use the tables feature of your word processor.

C. Line, column, or pie charts:
   Prepare these graphics with a spreadsheet program.

D. Flow charts:
   • If a specialized flow chart application is available and you are proficient with it, use the flow chart application and copy the chart into your document.
   • If you're proficient with a drawing program, use it.
   • Otherwise, create the flow chart on paper, and then scan it into your document.

E. Organizational charts:
- If you're proficient with a drawing program, use it.
- Otherwise, create the organizational chart on paper, and then scan it into your document.

Step 4: Integrating the Graphic Into Your Text

A. Position the graphic as closely as possible to the text that refers to it for the first time. Do not put it on a different page unless you have no alternative.

B. Label the graphic with its figure number and title. Place labels for tables above them; you may place labels for other graphics either above or below.

C. Number the graphics consecutively. If there is more than one chapter, start a new sequence for each chapter (for example, "Figure 1-1" or "Figure 3.5"). Some organizations' style guides require that tables and other graphics be numbered separately; check the appropriate guide or ask your supervisor.

D. If the graphic is taken from a secondary source, give credit after the caption.

Step 5: Writing the Callout

Refer to the graphic by its name and give a brief idea of what the reader will see (for example, "Figure 1 shows ABC Inc.'s profits for the last year").

Step 6: Guiding Your Reader Through the Graphic

Guide your readers through the graphic. Don't merely say "See Figure 1" and go on to your next point. Instead:

A. Provide a context (for example, "Figure 1 illustrates how a transmission works" or "The line graph in Figure 1 shows the how grades improved during the semester").

B. Direct your readers to the first part of the graphic to which you want them to pay particular attention (for example, "On the upper left of the diagram, we see the backing plate"). This is especially important with diagrams.

C. Say what is significant about that part of the graphic (for example, "The backing plate provides the unit's stability; without it, extreme vibration would occur and cause premature failure").

D. Move to the next important part of the graphic, again saying what is significant. You do not have to discuss each segment of the graphic, only those parts that are important to the point you're making.

Step 7: Testing the Graphic

Think of a real person who will read your document; this person will be your touchstone reader, that is, the person whom you will have in mind as you test your graphic. If you can't name such a person, think of the attributes of someone typical. Ask a colleague or friend to play the part of your touchstone reader, asking for responses to the following:

- Did the graphic help you visualize the topic being discussed?
- Did the text make clear the reason for looking at the graphic?
- Did you know what to look at in the graphic?
- Did the graphic show all the necessary information to supplement the text? If not, what was missing?
- Was the graphic itself clear and its text readable?

CHAPTER SUMMARY

Employers increasingly expect writers to incorporate graphics into their documents. Even though results may not be fully professional, they can still be sufficient. Graphics, however, are not mere embellishments but tools for solving communication problems.

As a professional writer, you need to know about the various types of graphics and how to use them appropriately. Photographs, diagrams, tables, graphs, and charts all have their own particular strengths. Used properly, all can persuade your readers by making complex information—even abstractions—easier to understand.

However, you can't simply insert a graphic into your document; you must also lead the reader through it, pointing out its most important features. And although graphics should delight as well as instruct, you must resist the temptation to overdo your graphic for its own sake.

Before deciding to use a graphic, you must articulate what it will contribute. Only then will you know what kind to choose, how to prepare it, and how to integrate it into your text. As with every document, you must test your graphic's effectiveness with touchstone readers.

CHECKLISTS

AUDIENCE ANALYSIS

- [ ] Who is my touchstone reader?
- [ ] What does my reader need to know?
- [ ] What is the problem in helping them see that information?
- [ ] How will a graphic help?
- [ ] Is my graphic appropriate to the level of my audience's technical sophistication?

CHOOSING A GRAPHIC

- [ ] Is the information complex enough to warrant a graphic or can text convey it better?
- [ ] Have I used a photograph because I need to show something exactly as it is?
- [ ] Have I used a diagram because I need to show what cannot be seen or what would be obscured in a photo?
- [ ] Have I used a table because I need to show a set of items that can be classified into groups?
- [ ] Have I used a line graph because I need to show a trend or changes over time?
- [ ] Have I used a column graph because I need to compare and show changes over time?
- [ ] Have I used a pie chart because I need to show how different items contribute to the whole?
- [ ] Have I used a flow chart because I need to show a process, especially one with decision points?
- [ ] Have I used an organization chart because I need to show relationships among organization members?

PREPARING THE GRAPHIC

- [ ] Is a suitable graphic available in an electronic version from stock sources?
- [ ] Is a suitable stock graphic available in a hard-copy version that can be scanned?

Is software available to create the graphic at a reasonable cost of time and money?

Must the graphic be prepared as hard copy and scanned in?

PLACING THE GRAPHIC IN THE TEXT

Is there a statement that tells the reader why the graphic is important?

Is the graphic close to the first reference to it in the text?

Is the graphic numbered consecutively and labelled?

Is the graphic's source acknowledged?

Is there a callout?

Is the reader guided through the graphic by the text?

Your additional comments:

EXERCISES

Exercise 1

Describe three topics (like the relative growth of two companies over five years) that would benefit significantly if you included a graphic. Describe three more (like a list of phone numbers) that would not benefit significantly.

Exercise 2

Which kind of the graphics discussed in this chapter would you use to illustrate the following?

a.   How water transfers energy inside a steam engine

b.   The portion of government revenues that comes from personal income tax

c.   Warnings to people working in nuclear plants

d.   A nation-wide alert about an escaped murderer

e.   Someone's unsuccessful history of dieting

f.   Weekly airplane schedules for three airlines leaving Toronto for Winnipeg

g.   Instructions for installing a computer home network with either two or three machines

h.   The result of recent changes to a school board's administration

i.   The total number of goals First- and Second-Team All-Star forwards have scored, showing how many goals were scored against each team in the NHL

Exercise 3

Write a sentence or two justifying each answer in Exercise 2 and include a rough sketch of what your graphic would look like.

Exercise 4

Write callouts for each of the graphics in the Exercise 2, providing the necessary context. Then direct your readers' attention to the graphic's key parts.

Exercise 5

Prepare graphics that best present the following information:

a.   Last year, Amalgamated Consolidated Incorporated's canned fruit division sold the following number of cases of each product: 2 343 272 pears; 3 000 543 peaches; 1 891 875 apricots; 2 356 421 pineapple; 600 472 cherries; 200 050 mangoes; 650 321 passion fruit. The total number represents a gain of 12.5% from the previous year. The CEO wants know the contribution of each product.

b.   Three major manufacturers—Ace, Boing, and Charming—have been in a fierce battle for several years to control the dental floss market. The shareholders in all three companies want to know how each of their products is doing and how their company stacks up. Each company makes several different kinds of floss. Here are the sales figures for each product (in metres) for 1997, 1998, and 1999:

Acme Regular: 1 234 658, 1 081 042, 1 431 098; **Acme HeavyDuty:** 1 296 390, 1 113 473, 1 231 274; **Acme Waxed You Need It:** 1 061 210, 1 146 877, 1 328 464; **Acme PlaqueHappy:** 100 270, 1 111 283, 1 353 156.

Boing Regular: 1 500 734, 1 216 722, 1 375 877; **Boing TasteeYum:** 1 275 771, 1 253 223, 2 007 188; **Boing Trust Me:** 1 254 559, 1 090 820, 1 891 769; **Boing SuperTuff:** 1 337 287; 1 329 545, 1 598 030.

Charming Regular: 1 824 152, 1 869 431, 1 945 889; **Charming Morning Glade:** 1 615 359, 1 510 514, 1 631 015; **Charming BigDate** 1 011 127, 1 452 830, 1 815 186; **Charming Emergency:** 1 111 684, 1 496 414, 1 612 249

c.   Show how to parallel park—assume your reader is both novice and nervous.

d.   The shares of Pete's Pizza have been worth the following: Q1 1998: $2.42; Q2 1998: $2.67; Q3 1998: $2.21; Q4 1998: $1.91; Q1 1999: $1.67; Q2 1999: $1.99; Q3 1999: $2.46 Q4 1999: $2.67.

e.   Here are some people and their job titles at Omega University: Brock Loopy, Dean of Fine Arts; Edgar Pistol, Academic Vice President; Sam Slogg, Dean of Engineering; Nelson Fripp, Associate Vice President; Topaz Gemstone, Chancellor; Frank Frankness, President; Artur Anderskonk, Vice-President of Finance; Roper Waey, Dean of Science.

CHAPTER

5

Document Design

What This Chapter Covers

Ideas

Why Documents Have to Look Good
Less Is More
House Styles
Planning Your Document's Appearance
Using a Grid
      Creating Grids With a Word Processor
White Space: Nothing Is Something
      White Space and the Relationships Among Ideas
      White Space and Paragraph Length
      White Space and Lists
Grammatical Parallelism in Lists
Headings: Previewing Information
Choosing Fonts
Styled Text
Using Colour
A Computer Isn't a Typewriter

Actions

Step 1: Check for a House Style
Step 2: Visualize What Your Document Will Look Like
Step 3: Write or Revise Headings
Step 4: Create Lists
Step 5: Create White Space With Paragraph Length
Step 6: Insert Emphasis
Step 7: Use Computer Conventions
Step 8: Test for Usability and Revise

Chapter Summary

Checklist

Exercises

**Learning
Objectives**

At the end of this chapter, you will be able to explain:

- How a good document design helps readers
- How to use house styles
- Why design begins with planning the most common elements
- How grids help you lay out your document
- Why white space is important
- How lists organize information
- How paragraph length affects readability
- How informative headings help readers
- How to use fonts, styled text, and colour

**At the end of this chapter, you will be able to design a
document by:**

- Checking for a house style
- Visualizing your document before you start writing it
- Creating headings
- Creating white space
- Emphasizing content with styled text
- Using computer conventions
- Field testing and revising

I D E A S

Why Documents Have to Look Good

A well-designed document makes reading easier. Like a good road map, a good design helps readers find what they're looking for. It also shows them which places along the way are most important and which are secondary. A good design, furthermore, sends the subtle but powerful message that you care about even the smallest detail. Your design decisions, therefore, are part of how you persuade readers.

Changes to a document's design may be small and subtle, but taken together, they give you a competitive advantage. All other things being equal, an attractive document is more persuasive. Readers will assume that a clear presentation signals clear thinking.

As with creating graphics, document design is no longer left solely to specialists. The marketplace requires that costs be controlled, which means that writers themselves must know how to do basic design. The results, even though not fully professional, can still be entirely satisfactory. The necessary hardware and software are affordable and usable.

This chapter won't make you into a professional page designer. It should, however, help you produce pages that make your readers more receptive to your message. Other chapters—such as those on Web design, instructions, and proposals—deal with design issues for those specific documents.

Less Is More

A word of caution: Less truly is more with document design. Computers have made designing documents relatively painless, so it's easy to over-design. That is, rather than helping readers find their way through a document, writers often add flourishes that serve no purpose other than showing that the writer likes to play with software. Over-design—too many fonts, too many colours, and too many embellishments—come between your reader and your message. Unless you can articulate a reason why a design element will persuade readers, leave it out.

House Styles

In some cases, you will have few design choices. Many organizations insist on a house style, that is, a set of rules for how documents must look. Those rules can specify everything from the colour of the document's binding to the font size in its index. A house style always takes precedence over your own preferences.

Organizations use house styles so that everything they generate has a consistent and (hopefully) professional look. A single style also saves time and money because design decisions need to be made only once. However, house styles won't spell out every detail, so you will still have some latitude. How you use it reflects your professionalism and credibility.

Planning Your Document's Appearance

Just as you need to know your ideas and your audience, you need a clear picture of your document's eventual appearance before you prepare your final draft. (Again, this assumes that you are not completely bound by a house style.) Start with those decisions that will affect every page of your document. We will discuss those decisions in more detail as we go through the chapter, but here is a preview:

- What will be the basic layout of the document? Will pages be divided into columns? If so, how many and how wide?
- What size margins will you use? If you use columns, what will the margins be between them? What margins will you set for quoted material, lists, and graphics?
- Will headings appear above body text or to the left?
- How will text be aligned?
- Where will you position page numbers? Will they be part of a page header with other information (such as your name and the document's name)?
- What font will you use for text and what font for headings? What size will they be? What colour? What style?
- How much colour do you need? How much can you afford? (It can be expensive.)

By planning and then applying your choices, your document will have a consistent appearance. And that makes it easier for readers to find information.

Using a Grid

An important device to make page layout consistent is a grid, that is, a table in which you place recurring page elements such as headings, body text, and graphics. Each element has its own attributes (for example, typeface, type size, colour, and alignment). Grids help readers by ensuring consistency. But they also help you because when you use the same grid throughout a document, you don't have to design every page anew.

Figure 5.1 (page 86) shows a simple two-column grid. In this grid, the left column (about 25% of the page width) is reserved for headings and the right column is reserved for text. Each cell in a column has the same attributes (that is,

Heading 1	Text for Heading 1. Text for Heading 1. Text for Heading 1. Text for Heading 1. Text for Heading 1. Text for Heading 1. Text for Heading 1. Text for Heading 1. Text for Heading 1. Text for Heading 1. Text for Heading 1. Text for Heading 1.
Heading 2	Text for Heading 2. Text for Heading 2. Text for Heading 2. Text for Heading 2. Text for Heading 2. Text for Heading 2. Text for Heading 2. Text for Heading 2. Text for Heading 2. Text for Heading 2. Text for Heading 2. Text for Heading 2.
Heading 3	Text for Heading 3. Text for Heading 3. Text for Heading 3. Text for Heading 3. Text for Heading 3. Text for Heading 3. Text for Heading 3. Text for Heading 3. Text for Heading 3. Text for Heading 3. Text for Heading 3. Text for Heading 3.

Figure 5.1
A simple two-column grid

its alignment, font style, font size, and colour). The headings in the left column are right-justified to tie them together with the text they introduce.

A grid is like a scaffolding used to construct a building; when the job is done, you remove the scaffolding. Removing the grid lines before printing produces a book-like, professional appearance as shown in Figure 5.2.

Grids can be more complex, however, especially when you include graphics. Professional designers, for example, will often use four to eight columns, merging them and varying their widths as needed. Figure 5.3 is an example of a more complex grid.

Heading 1   Text for Heading 1. Text for Heading 1. Text for Heading 1. Text for Heading 1. Text for Heading 1. Text for Heading 1. Text for Heading 1. Text for Heading 1. Text for Heading 1. Text for Heading 1. Text for Heading 1. Text for Heading 1.

Heading 2   Text for Heading 2. Text for Heading 2. Text for Heading 2. Text for Heading 2. Text for Heading 2. Text for Heading 2. Text for Heading 2. Text for Heading 2. Text for Heading 2. Text for Heading 2. Text for Heading 2. Text for Heading 2.

Heading 3   Text for Heading 3. Text for Heading 3. Text for Heading 3. Text for Heading 3. Text for Heading 3. Text for Heading 3. Text for Heading 3. Text for Heading 3. Text for Heading 3. Text for Heading 3. Text for Heading 3. Text for Heading 3.

Figure 5.2
A simple two-column page with grid lines removed

Text here. Text here.	
Text here. Text here. Text here. Text here. Text here. Text here. Text here. Text here. Text here. Text here. Text here. Text here.		Text here. Text here. Text here. Text here. Text here. Text here. Text here. Text here. Text here. Text here.
		Text here. Text here. Text here. Text here. Text here. Text here. Text here. Text here. Text here. Text here.

Figure 5.3
A more complex grid with text and graphics

For most business and professional documents, however, two columns—one for headings and one for text and graphics—are adequate.

Creating Grids With a Word Processor

Major word processors ship with excellent tools for creating tables. You can readily change column width, spacing, and alignment. By assigning styles—that is, a collection of attributes that define how text looks—to a table's columns, you will have a template to reuse on every page. You may not achieve the same results as a professional page designer who uses professional layout tools; what you will achieve, however, will be adequate for most documents.

Once you have a grid that you like, save it as a template file, that is, a read-only or stationery file. You can open and reuse that file as many times as you wish; you can't accidentally overwrite the original.

White Space: Nothing Is Something

Using a grid also makes it simpler to include adequate white space, that is, any part of your page without content. (White space doesn't have to be white, just blank.) Despite its seeming status as "nothing," white space is critical because it reduces visual clutter, giving each element breathing room. That makes reading easier.

Margins are the most common (and overlooked) kind of white space. Usually, they are set to one inch for the top, bottom, and right, and an inch and a half at the left (the inside margin) to allow the document to be bound. When a document is to be printed on both sides of the paper, however, the inside margin alternates between the left and right pages, as shown in Figure 5.4.

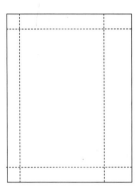 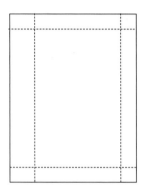

Figure 5.4
Wider margins on alternate pages allow for binding

Set your word processor to automatically handle this formatting detail.

The right margin for body text can be either justified (that is, aligned) or ragged. Right-justified text looks more book-like but requires extra spaces to be inserted between words; these spaces can produce uneven gaps, making the text harder to read. A ragged right margin, on the other hand, guarantees even spacing between words. Further, a page with a ragged margin, has more white space and a lighter appearance, which again improves readability.

White Space and the Relationships Among Ideas

Another important use of white space is to show readers where one logical element leaves off and another begins, as Figure 5.5 demonstrates.

The white space—above, below, and at the sides—provides important visual clues to the structural logic of the discussion. Widgets as vitamins and widgets as pets, for example, are equally important topics. The care of pet widgets is a sub-topic of widgets as pets and is set off accordingly.

Although a numbering scheme can reinforce the structure, the white space does the real work. Figure 5.6 shows what happens when we remove the white space.

Widgets in History

People of many nations have used widgets for centuries. King Rebgert of Luxania would often call his court together on important occasions and make two points:

1.1: Widgets provide an important source of vitamins and minerals. A good widget, for example, has twice the iron as in a pound of calf's liver.

1.2: Widgets make fine pets. They are especially fond of children, although accidents do happen.

1.2.2: Pet widgets require no special care, other than plenty of fresh straw and lots of water.

Widgets in History People of many nations have used widgets for centuries. King Rebgert of Luxania would often call his court together on important occasions and make two points: 1.1: Widgets provide an important source of vitamins and minerals. A good widget, for example, has twice the iron as in a pound of calf's liver. 1.2: Widgets make fine pets. They are especially fond of children, although accidents do happen. 1.2.2: Pet widgets require no special care, other than plenty of fresh straw and lots of water.

Figure 5.5
White space showing the structure of ideas

Figure 5.6
Ideas presented without white space

Without the white space, we have to read through the whole discussion to understand the relationships among its ideas. With the white space, we take these relationships in at a glance.

White Space and Paragraph Length

A paragraph is both a logical and a visual unit. Although a paragraph should be about a single topic, it should also help readers assimilate information. When readers come to the end of a paragraph, they have the chance to pause and reflect on what they've just read—or simply rest. Very long paragraphs don't provide enough of those opportunities.

Despite your concerns for unity, split paragraphs when they appear as long, unbroken chunks of text. For example, here are the opening paragraphs of this chapter merged into one:

A well-designed document makes reading easier. Like a good road map, a good design helps readers find what they're looking for. It also shows them which places along the way are most important and which are secondary. A good design, furthermore, sends the subtle but powerful message that you care about even the smallest detail. Your design decisions, therefore, are part of how you persuade readers. Changes to a document's design may be small and subtle, but, taken together, they give you a competitive advantage. All other things being equal, an attractive document is more persuasive: Readers will assume that a clear presentation signals clear thinking. As with creating graphics, document design is no longer left solely to specialists. The marketplace requires that costs be controlled, which means that writers themselves must know how to do basic design. The results, even though not fully professional, can still be entirely satisfactory. The necessary hardware and software are affordable and usable.

Although the single long paragraph is about one topic—why documents have to look good—there is simply no visual clue where one part of the topic stops and another starts. The page so jammed with text that readers have to wait too long to rest or assimilate what they've read.

On the other hand, a series of very short paragraphs—especially the one-sentence paragraphs common in newspapers—makes your writing choppy.

They force readers to connect your ideas from one paragraph to the next.

As a result, readers have to work harder than they should and you lose your credibility.

As these last four paragraphs show.

White Space and Lists

The principle of using white space to show logical units also applies to lists. Because lists have white space built-in, they conveniently show discrete units of information, as in this example:

> Here are the cars in your price range:
> * Honda Civic
> * Toyota Tercel
> * Chevrolet Nova

The bullets indicate that no one item is more important than another—the Nova is as good a candidate as the Honda. Numbered lists, on the other hand, show hierarchy or sequence, as in these two examples:

> **Recommendations to Reduce Cars Speeding on Spruce Street**
> 1. Put in speed bumps.
> 2. Widen sidewalks and reduce lane width.
> 3. Introduce photo radar.
> 4. Arm the neighbours.

Starting Your Car on a Cold Day
1. Check that the transmission is in Park.
2. Depress the gas pedal to the floor and keep it there.
3. Insert the ignition key.
4. Turn the ignition key and hold it until engine starts, then release the gas pedal.
5. If the car doesn't start within 15 seconds, wait 15 seconds and try twice more.
6. If the car still doesn't start, call for road service.

In the first list, the numbers indicate the priority of the recommendations. In the second, the numbers indicate the order in which the tasks must be carried out.

WORKING SMARTER

Automatic Lists

You can create a list manually by hitting Return after typing each item. However, any subsequent changes (like adding a new item or altering alignment) will force you to reformat the entire list. Word processors, on the other hand, reformat automatically.

For example, if you were to insert a new item in the middle of a numbered list, the entire list would be automatically renumbered. If you were to add words to a list item so that it would extend beyond one line, the software would automatically align those extra words with the word above (rather than with the left margin), as shown below:

- This item is just one line long.
- This item is also just one line long.
- This item will not fit on one line but continues on. Regardless, it lines up under the first word of first item, not its bullet. That white space makes the list more readable.

Grammatical Parallelism in Lists

Lists must be grammatically parallel, that is, all items must have the same grammatical form (such as noun, verb, or phrase). The first item in a list determines the form of all the rest. If the first element were a noun, for example, the others must be nouns too:

Consider all the following factors when you buy a car:
- Safety
- Value
- Performance

If the first item were an imperative verb (that is, telling you to do something), the items that follow must also be imperative verbs:

> How to Make a Long-Distance Call
> 1. Pick up the phone.
> 2. Listen for the dial tone.
> 3. Dial 1 + the area code + the number.

This grammatical parallelism signals the reader that all elements are equal in content as well as form. But that signal isn't sent in a list with faulty parallelism, as in this example:

> Consider all the following factors when you buy a car:
> • Safety
> • Value
> • How it performs

"Safety" and "Value" are nouns; "How it performs" is a subordinate clause. The change in form obscures rather than clarifies the equality of all items, and readers must transform the last item.

A final note: Lists need introductions so that readers have a context in which to understand its items. "Consider all the following factors when you buy a car" makes it unequivocally clear that the writer is talking about cars and nothing else.

Headings: Previewing Information

Headings also add white space and help readers find what they're looking for. More importantly, headings tell readers about what they are going to read.

The psychologist David Ausubel has shown that advance organizers—brief explanations that precede a chunk of information—make it easier for people to learn. For details, see Ausabel's *Educational Psychology: A Cognitive View* (New York: Holt, Rinehart, and Winston, 1968). Headings are like advance organizers in that they preview information, giving readers a sense of what is to come and a context in which to understand it.

A heading, therefore, must carry real information, not merely say the obvious—for example, that what comes at the beginning is the "Introduction" and what comes at the end is the "Conclusion." The heading for this section, for instance, announces the section will be about headings and their chief function.

Headings must have a consistent appearance. Changing how a heading looks signals that what follows is of a different order of importance. Once you establish a heading's appearance, therefore, you must continue with the same typeface, type size, colour, and alignment wherever the heading occurs.

Moreover, the higher the heading level (that is, main, secondary, etc.), the more visible it has to be. To again use this book as an example, chapter headings are set in a large size of bold type. Headings that precede each section are also bold but are smaller. And headings in the body text are smaller yet. A heading's relative size, therefore, indicates its importance.

WORKING SMARTER

Using Styles for Headings

The best way to achieve consistency with your headings is with your word processor's style feature. A style is a collection of attributes that indicate how text should look.

For example, a style for a main heading might be Arial, red, and 14 points. A secondary heading may be Arial, blue, and 12 points. Once you've defined styles for different levels of headings, you simply select text and apply the style. All the selected text will take on the attributes of the style.

If you later decide to modify one or more attributes of a style (for example, its font size or colour), your word processor will automatically make the change wherever you've used that style. That saves finding and editing each instance.

Choosing Fonts

Fonts come in many varieties, but most can be divided into two main groups, serif and sans serif. Figure 5.7 illustrates the difference between these two groups.

Figure 5.7
Serif and sans serif versions of the same letter

The A on the left is a serif font, that is, one with short lines that extend from the letter. The A on the right is a sans serif font, or one without extenders.

Generally, most designers use serif fonts for body text because their extenders lead the reader's eye across the page. Serifs also make it easier to identify each letter. San serif fonts, however, stand out more and are common for headers and warnings, whose purpose is to grab attention. A common rule of thumb is to limit yourself to one serif and one sans serif font per document. Using more can create visual noise and distractions.

Font choice is a matter of taste, and your readers' taste may not be yours. Don't alienate them with idiosyncratic choices but stay with the most common fonts (for example, Times or Palatino for serifs and Arial or Helvetica for san serif). Specialized fonts like *this* or *this* are difficult to read for more than a few lines; if overused such fonts annoy many readers.

Styled Text

You can, however, create visual interest and emphasis by varying the size, style, and colour of your two basic fonts. Less, however, is again more because too much emphasis generates noise, not interest. Everything clamours for attention, as in this example:

> **Important Note:**
>
> **All** *cashiers* **must** *report* to the **Assistant Manager** at the **beginning** and **end** of their shifts. **There can be no exceptions.**

Because so many words are emphasized, nothing stands out.

The most common ways to emphasize text are with bold, italics, size, and colour. Bold words obviously stand out more, as do italics. However, long strings of italics are problematic because readers have to view at them at a slight angle. They are particularly hard to read on a computer monitor. Italics, therefore, should be reserved for these special instances:

- Indicating titles (*Ideas Into Action*, the *Globe and Mail*)
- Calling attention to a word used as a word ("*And* is a conjunction.")
- Marking a word from another language ("In Montreal, corner stories are called *depanneurs*.")
- Indicating a particular tone of voice ("I'd *love* to come to the meeting.")
- Marking a word that you consider particularly important ("Why should I care *now*?")

Other kinds of styled text are available such as shadow, embossed, or ALLCAPS. But they call attention to themselves, not the content, and shouldn't be used at all.

Using Colour

As with other elements, colour should not merely embellish your document but solve design problems. For example, colour can evoke cultural associations. Red and green (at least, in Western societies) tell people to stop or go, and using them can reinforce the content of a message. Thus you might set "Warning: Read instructions before using this appliance" in red and "Go to the next step" in green.

A dash of colour for its own sake can make your page attractive. But colour has to be used sparingly for these reasons:

*   Colour is expensive for print documents (although inexpensive on a computer).
*   Not everyone has the same colour tastes, and yours may alienate some of your readers.
*   Too much colour—like too much emphasis—creates noise, not information.

The safest choices are the standard ones—a white background and black type for body text. Save other colours for headings, taking care to apply them consistently for all heading levels.

A Computer Isn't a Typewriter

Typewriter conventions are not appropriate for word processors. Instead, use the following:

*   Real bullets (for example • or ☐), not asterisks (*)
*   Em dashes (—), not two hyphens (--)
*   Symbols (like ©), not spelled-out words (like "copyright")
*   *Italics* for titles, not underlining
*   Real quotation marks (" "), not double hatch marks (")
*   One space between sentences, not two

ACTIONS

The following steps make up a general strategy for designing documents. Use them as you prepare your final draft. Other chapters discuss the design of specific types of documents.

Step 1: Check for a House Style

Is there a house style, that is, the organization's prescribed way of presenting information?

No: Go to Step 2.
Yes: Follow it exactly. For issues not covered by house style, go to Step 2.

Step 2: Visualize What Your Document Will Look Like

Using a grid, create a template for your document. Specify the following:

- Placement of headings
- Serif font for body text
- Sans serif font for headings
- Font sizes for body text and all heading levels
- Margins for the whole document, as well as particular elements such as columns, quoted material, lists, and graphics
- Alignment for the whole document, as well as particular elements such as columns, quoted material, lists, and graphics
- Text justification
- Placement of page numbers and other information in headers
- Amount of colour you need and can afford

    Save the template as a read-only document for future use.

Step 3: Write or Revise Headings

- Insert one heading about every two or three paragraphs.
- Write meaningful text that previews what is to come.
- Set off headings and subheadings with adequate white space.
- Apply the appropriate style to each heading.
- Ensure that a heading's style is used at the correct level (for example, main headings and first-level subheadings).

Step 4: Create Lists

- Locate text that discusses three or more discrete items, all with equally important content. Create a bullet list for them.
- Locate text that discusses a sequence of actions or a hierarchy of objects. Create a numbered list for them.

- Introduce each list with a statement to set the context for the list.
- Make lists grammatically parallel, that is, use the same grammatical form for all list elements.

Step 5: Create White Space With Paragraph Length

- Locate paragraphs that appear as long, unbroken chunks of text.
- Split them into shorter paragraphs while maintaining their basic coherence.
- Avoid a series of one-sentence paragraphs.

Step 6: Insert Emphasis

Use the following text styles for emphasis:

- Bold for information you want to stand out, especially warnings
- Italics for titles, words used as words, foreign words, a particular tone of voice, or a particularly important word
- Colour to reinforce messages

  Don't overuse emphasis.

Step 7: Use Computer Conventions

Use the following computer conventions rather their typewriter counterparts:
- Real bullets (not asterisks)
- Em dashes (not two consecutive hyphens)
- Symbols (not words)
- Italics (not underlining)
- Real quotation marks (not double hatch marks)
- One space between sentences (not two)

Step 8: Test for Usability and Revise

Briefly try out your basic design with sample members of your intended audience. Ask a colleague or friend to play the role of your touchstone reader (that is, the real person who you are imagining as you prepare the document). If no one is available, play that role yourself. Focus on these issues:

- Which headings help the reader understand what will follow? Which don't?
- Which pages have adequate white space? Which need more?
- Which paragraphs are broken up into readable units? Which aren't?
- Which sections have text that would work better as lists?
- Which lists are grammatically parallel? Which aren't?
- Which text is emphasized? Which text needs more emphasis? Which text has too much emphasis?
- Which pages have colour that helps the reader? Which pages have colour that distracts?

CHAPTER SUMMARY

A well-designed document helps readers find what they're looking for, showing them how you've structured information. A good design also persuades readers that you've taken care down to the smallest detail.

Organizations often use house styles to specify how documents must look. When there is no house style, you yourself must impose a consistent appearance on every page of your document. That frees readers from having to readjust their expectations on every page.

Software makes it easier to produce good designs. With a word processor, for example, you can readily insert grids, white space, and lists, as well as select fonts, text styles, and colours.

Designing a document requires planning. In the absence of a house style, you have to visualize your document's final appearance, choosing (among other items) the alignment, margin sizes, and text justification. You must also write headings, create lists, and apply text styles. Finally, since design is often a matter of taste, you must field test your choices to ensure that your document's appearance helps rather than hinders readers.

CHECKLIST

House style followed

Templates created as needed, covering basic layout, margins, heading style, alignment, fonts, and colour

Headings preview information that follows

Adequate white space inserted (margins, justification, and paragraph length)

Lists (bullet and numbered) created with parallel structure

Appropriate emphasis included (such as bold or italics)

Computer conventions followed

Tested for usability

Your additional comments:

EXERCISES

Exercise 1

Working in groups, look through a magazine or a professional journal and describe its design. List three of its strengths and three of its weaknesses.

Exercise 2

Working in groups, write specifications for your own house style. On a piece of paper, draw a grid (about 5 x 5) and place the elements that would appear on every page of a document (for example, headers and footers). Decide on margin widths, placement of headings, alignment, fonts (serif and san serif), and colour. Explain your choices.

Exercise 3

Working individually, pick three headings in this chapter that could be improved and rewrite them.

Exercise 4

Working individually, make the following grammatically parallel:

a.   I came, I saw, and I was able to defeat my enemies.

b.   I re-examined all my ideas of war and bravery when I saw the destruction, the mass graves, and when I saw the sadness of the survivors.

c.   Three key virtues for all people are faith, hope, and giving money to those in need.

d.   Open Door A, Locate Switch B, and then Switch B should be set to 9.

e.   The plane was sleek, fast, and it cost millions to buy.

f.   The tasks were to power up the computer, launch the word processor, and to load a file.

g.   The coach had us work on shooting from the foul line, how to dribble with either hand, and blocking shots.

h.   The truck was old, battered, and many people had owned it.

PART

2

What Professional **Writers** Produce

6 Correspondence

7 Writing Instructions

8 Writing Proposals

9 Reports

10 Writing Descriptions

11 Writing for General Readers

C H A P T E R

6 Correspondence

What This Chapter Covers

Ideas

Conversations at a Distance
Respect, Honesty, and Brevity /'breviti/ n. 简短
Imagining the Audience
The Language of Correspondence
Your Credibility 可信,可靠性
Why People Correspond
Types of Correspondence
  Memos
  Routine Messages
  Bad News: Saying No Without Saying Goodbye
  Covering Letters
  Correspondence Format
  E-mail
  Voice Mail

Actions

Memos
Routine Letters
Bad-News Letters

Chapter Summary

Checklists

Exercises

Learning Objectives

At the end of this chapter, you will be able to explain:

- How a letter is a conversation
- Why what you say and how you say it depends on the social situation
- Why you must use language that is respectful, honest, and brief
- Why you must maintain credibility by attending to every detail of form
- How memo writers and recipients share the same context and why that affects the memo's content, form, and length
- Why routine messages to people outside an organization should carry information directly and briefly
- How to give bad news without losing the social relationship with the recipient
- Why e-mail and voice mail require different manners than traditional correspondence

At the end of this chapter, you will be able to write memos, routine messages, and bad-news letters by:

- Determining the purpose of the message
- Describing its audience
- Drafting the opening, body, and closing
- Following conventional formats
- Testing and revising

I D E A S

A letter is a conversation—or rather, a part of one. As with other conversations, how people treat each other is critical, so the rules that govern social behavior also apply to correspondence. However, unlike face-to-face conversations, you cannot use the other person's voice and facial expressions as guides to how well they understand you or like what they hear. You have to imagine that and act accordingly.

There are techniques, however, to make that kind of imagining more likely to work. Since much correspondence shares the same purposes and strategies (although obviously with quite different content), you can create re-usable templates that will save you time in the future when you need to produce something similar. This chapter shows how.

Respect, Honesty, and Brevity

When you're writing someone, it's easy to forget that you're engaged in a social act even though you may be alone. Just as in a regular conversation, the other person judges you—how nice you are, how smart you are, how credible you are. But there is a delay between when you write and when the other person reads; that means if you make a bad impression, it can take a long time to correct it. Letter writers, therefore, must always remind themselves of three key principles:

*   The reader is as worthy as I am; therefore, I will give respect.
*   The reader is as smart as I am; therefore, I will be honest.
*   The reader is as busy as I am; therefore, I will be concise.

You still try to persuade the reader to see things your way, but you must do so without sacrificing respect, honesty, and brevity. Altruism isn't your sole motive (as important as it may be); respect, honesty, and brevity make you credible and your content more persuasive.

Imagining the Audience

Like all writing, correspondence works best when you know for whom you're writing. That's fairly easy when you write to friends and colleagues. But in professional or business situations, correspondence is often the first or second contact you have with someone. You must, therefore, look carefully at those initial contacts in order to know how best to respond.

In general, correspondence is part of a transaction, that is, an exchange of goods, services, or information. Those transactions are usually one of two kinds:

- Someone needs information about a product or service; someone else imparts that information.
- Someone has a complaint or an opinion; someone else acts or at least listens.

Regardless of which side of the exchange you happen to be on, respect, honesty, and brevity are the starting points. Whether you're asking for something or being asked, you're in a relationship that you want to maintain.

If you are doing the asking or the complaining, you must imagine the recipient. For example, is the recipient:

- Overloaded by similar requests or complaints?
- The right person to help you?
- Going to benefit by helping you?

You won't get much help by figuratively snapping your fingers and treating recipients as if they exist solely to do your bidding. Similarly, going into great detail with the wrong person won't get results. Failing to show a benefit—like continued business or even just acknowledgement of the recipient's effort—won't motivate anything more than a perfunctory response.

If you are receiving a request or a complaint, you must imagine the sender. To start with, ask yourself if the sender:

- Offers a relationship worth maintaining
- Has a reasonable query or complaint
- Has tried without success to get help elsewhere

For example, if a sender is a good customer—or could become one—you clearly want to make him or her happy. You won't earn gratitude by rebuffing legitimate queries or otherwise being dismissive.

Regardless of the particulars, you always must get beyond the content of the letters and imagine the senders. This does not mean you must necessarily act as they want you to. It does mean that you have to understand their needs and talk to them appropriately—for your benefit as well as theirs.

That raises the issue of the language you should use, and we'll consider that next.

The Language of Correspondence

How formal should your language be? That depends on the social situation. With people you know well, you can be quite casual. With strangers, however, you must be careful not to offend by appearing flip or aggressive. Nor do you want to be too effusive. Your tone—that is, your attitude towards your readers—will either drive them away or make them receptive.

There are conventions that most people expect when you write them, and not using these conventions will signal readers that you don't know how to behave. So starting with "Howya Doin', Mr. Jones?" and closing with "So long" may do the same work as the usual forms but will very likely cost you your credibility.

Convention, however, is a moving target that changes with circumstances. The elaborate flourishes of yesterday ("I am, as always, your humble servant") are now not so much wrong as out of place, the conventions of another culture. Equally out of place, however, are slang, vulgarity, or overfamiliarity (such as "Dear Bob" written to someone whom you've never met). The language of the street belongs in the street, not in the culture of business and the professions.

Contemporary readers also expect you to speak plainly, and you can achieve much of that by being respectful, honest, and brief. We cover Plain Language more fully in Chapter 3, but here are a few important concepts that apply to correspondence:

Be plain. The reader is as busy as you are. Use simple words rather than fancy ones whenever you can (*walk* rather than *perambulate*, *speak* rather than *utter*, and *think* rather than *ponder*). Get rid of warm-ups and throat-clearers.

Be direct. Use verbs to convey action, rather than nouns derived from verbs. For example, write "She decided" rather than "She made the decision" and "We were interested in X" rather than "X was of interest to us." Put the main point of a paragraph in the first sentence, so someone reading quickly won't skip over it. Get rid of words that don't do necessary work.

Be brief. Break up long sentences by locating prepositions and conjunctions. A sentence isn't long because it has a particular number of words; rather, it's long if there are too many relationships to untangle.

Your Credibility

Credible writers are those readers trust. When you take care of the smallest detail in your writing, you signal that you'll take care of the smallest details everywhere else. Respect, honesty, and brevity contribute to your credibility, as, of course, does getting your facts straight. But writing correctly—spelling, grammar, punctuation, etc.—also plays an enormous part. Readers who are unsympathetic to your ideas will use your mechanical mistakes to confirm—fairly or not—their hostility.

Although that's true with all writing, it's especially true here. Correspondence is a conversation that takes place at a distance, so you don't have the chance to immediately correct mistakes or rephrase as you do when dealing in person. To quote a dandruff-shampoo commercial: "You don't get a second chance to make a first impression."

Why People Correspond

Let's turn from readers to specific kinds of correspondence. Letters can have many purposes. Here are the most common ones:

- Facilitating routine transactions (ordering, inquiring, etc.)
- Providing information
- Giving good or bad news
- Complaining
- Introducing people
- Transmitting (reports, brochures, etc.)
- Applying for jobs

Types of Correspondence

We can classify correspondence as internal or external, that is, sent to people either within or outside an organization. Because writing to people within an organization is somewhat easier, we will start with memos, the most common type of internal correspondence.

Memos

Memos make information clear and timely for people within the same organization. 通知 Because writer and reader share the same context, what might have to be explained to an outsider can be taken for granted. For example:

> The Hodgkin's planning committee will meet on Tuesday, April 19 in the boardroom. The main item on the agenda will be Ned Wilkens' suggestion to approach Conners to supply extruded aluminum for the project. We'll also consider alternatives to the Eliot estimate for half-ton trucks. Please bring your calendars so we can also set a date for the field trip to Acme.

The writer doesn't have to provide background about whatever Hodgkin is, where the boardroom is located, who Wilkens is, and so on. Anyone receiving the memo would already know or else would be privately brought up-to-speed.

Organizations also use memos to confirm understanding. For example, a meeting can cover a range of issues, some of which can easily get forgotten. A memo gives writers a chance to express their understanding of what went on at a meeting and ask for clarification if they've misunderstood. That's what the following memo does:

> As we discussed at our meeting of November 3, the new policy on photocopying will be as follows:

Each department will be responsible for monitoring photocopying by its own members, and it can choose whatever method works best for it (personal codes, tally sheets, etc.). In addition, departments will pay for their own paper, cartridges, and normal maintenance. However, the company will continue to pay for repairs.

Please let me know by November 10 if you have any corrections.

So despite being at the meeting, the writer wants to make sure everyone agrees on what was decided.

Memo Format

Most organizations have their own specific formats for memos, but in general these formats include:

- The company logo (but not its address)
- The originating department's name (optional)
- The word *Memo* (or *Memorandum*)
- A *To* line
- A *From* line
- A *Subject* line
- A *Date* line
- A horizontal bar that separates the heading from the body (optional)
- The body

Figure 6.1 shows a typical memo format.

```
Acme Explosives!

MEMO

    To:        Hodgkin Planning Committee Members
    From:      Dave Harrison
    Subject:   Next Meeting
    Date:      October 26, 2000
    _____

Our next meeting will be ...
```

Figure 6.1
Memo format

Memo Length

A memo should convey information quickly. Although there is no specific limit to a memo's length, most are a page or less. Memos can exceed that length, but generally writers communicate more complicated information in a report format, as discussed in Chapter 9.

Routine Messages

Memos carry routine messages to people within an organization, but most organizations must also routinely send messages to people outside. Again, there is a wide range of content—anything from processing orders to dealing with complaints to responding to job applications.

Routine messages require no particular rhetorical strategies—other than clarity, brevity, and honesty, of course. The recipients want information, so routine messages should be direct, starting with the main idea or question, followed by an explanation or amplification and ending with a friendly closing. Figure 6.2 is an example of a routine letter.

Horvath Construction
123 Billings Way
Victoria, BC V8W 4Y1
(250) 555-5555

November 3, 2000

Customer Service
Acme Explosives
555 WistaVista Way
Eglinton, Ontario M5M 5M5

Dear Customer Service:

Our construction company would like information about your line of blasting caps and dynamite. We frequently have to remove boulders about three to five feet in diameter.

We are also interested in using plastic explosives, if they are appropriate for the job.

We expect to need explosives starting in January. Please forward product desciptions and a price list.

Yours truly,

Polly Horvath
General Manager

Figure 6.2
A routine letter

Like a memo, a routine letter is brief without sacrificing any necessary information. The letter in Figure 6.2 gets to the main point immediately, then devotes a separate paragraph to each issue. Here is a possible response:

> Thank you for your letter of November 3 in which you inquired about Acme's product line. As you requested, I'm enclosing a catalog and a price list. The blasting caps and dynamite listings are on pages 5-7 and the plastic explosives are on page 19.
>
> Note that the MegaCap on page 6 (Item #27321) is backordered, and we don't expect a new shipment until February. The MiniCap, however, may be enough for you; you'll find its specifications on Page 5.
>
> Acme's range of products is both extensive and well tested; I'm sure you'll find something that meets your needs. Please call me directly at 1-800-555-5555 if you need further information.
>
> Yours truly,
>
> Blair Adams
> Customer Service Representative
> Phone: 1-800-555-5555

Adams starts with the context (Horvath probably writes many letters and might need reminding) and immediately directs her to where she'll find the information she asked about. He does so in relatively few words, signalling that he knows her time is valuable. Again, there is no absolute correct length for such a letter, but shorter is better than longer. Adams amplifies only what will help Ms. Horvath.

Of course, even routine responses offer a chance to do some marketing. That's legitimate, as long as the marketing doesn't obscure the information. For instance, Adams ends by briefly reminding Horvath of Acme's excellence, but more importantly, he offers help without imposing himself. In brief, he adheres to the basic principles of respect, brevity, and truthfulness. Horvath may not buy from Acme, but it won't because of Blair Adams.

Sending a neutral message or granting a request is relatively straightforward; but what happens when you have to say *no*? That's what we'll look at in the next section.

Bad News: Saying *No* Without Saying *Goodbye*

All too often, we must deliver bad news: A client's request for a refund isn't reasonable, a job applicant doesn't get the job, or a product isn't available. In such cases, our goal is to say *no* while still maintaining the relationship. Bad news does not have be the last news you give.

Sending bad news requires the same three principles we've been discussing—respect, honesty, and brevity. For example, if you fail to give respect and dismiss a request as foolish or unreasonable, recipients will assume that you're saying *they* are foolish and unreasonable, with the obvious consequences for you.

Similarly, being dishonest—or even evasive—about a refusal won't win you any friends either. Regardless of how much you sugarcoat your *nos*, eventually you'll run out of sugar. At that point, readers are doubly angry—first, for being refused and second, for being treated as if they were too stupid to know that they were being refused.

Finally, taking a long time to say *no* is also a bad strategy because it forces readers to spend much time reading for no payoff. You don't have to cut to the refusal instantly—bluntness will be read as disrespect—but neither should you delay excessively.

A Strategy for Saying No

Here is a four-part strategy to say *no*:

1. Begin by finding something both you and your reader can agree on.
2. Explain the facts as you see them.
3. Refuse gracefully, linking your *no* to the explanation you've offered. Try to find a benefit or alternative for the reader.
4. Look to future transactions with the reader.

For example, suppose your retail store has received a letter from a customer asking for a refund on a one-year-old electric shaver that stopped working after he dropped it into the bathtub. The customer writes that he had been very happy with the razor up until then, and, in fact, he had bought another as a gift. Here's what you might say:

> Dear Mr. X:
>
> Thank you for your letter of October 25, 1998 in which you ask for a refund for the shaver that you purchased a year ago at our Main Street store.
>
> The WhiskerOff shaver you purchased is built to perform under the normal conditions of everyday wear and tear. It carries a one-year warranty against all manufacturing defects. As you said in your letter, the shaver worked properly for one year, and it stopped when it was dropped into your bathtub.
>
> Under these circumstances, it isn't appropriate to refund the purchase price. If we did offer refunds when such unfortunate accidents occur, we couldn't continue to provide our customers the lowest possible prices.
>
> We do carry a full line of shavers from WhiskerOff and other leading manufacturers as well. Please ask for me when you come by our store, and I'd be happy to demonstrate them.

The letter opens with a neutral statement with which the customer should agree. It doesn't give false signals ("I'm always very glad to hear from customers") or signal the refusal immediately ("I'm sorry, but I can't refund your money"). The second paragraph provides a clear and reasonable context for the refusal that follows—the warranty covers only manufacturing defects.

The third paragraph (which contains the core of the refusal) doesn't hide behind policy or say the writer is just following orders ("The company's practice won't allow me to . . ."). It doesn't patronize ("A shaver is a delicate instrument . . ."), harangue ("You shouldn't have dropped the shaver") or dismiss ("We can't stay in business by giving away products"). Instead, it shows a benefit (lower prices) and offers an alternative (come in for a personal demonstration). Most importantly, it assumes a continued relationship.

If your business could offer future discounts as goodwill gestures, everyone would be pleased. But sometimes that's just not possible, and your goal is to refuse in such a way that there is some chance the customer will return. To repeat, say *no*, not *goodbye*.

Covering Letters

A covering letter (also called a letter of transmittal) provides the necessary context for documents you send out. Reports, proposals, and price lists are some examples of documents that need separate covering letters. As the first item a reader of your long document will see, the impression a covering letter makes is crucial.

A covering letter generally has a three-part structure:

The context that introduces the subject and purpose of the document the letter accompanies (for example, "As we agreed, here is the my proposal for improving golf services at the Pleasant Valley Golf Course.")

A brief statement of one or two key points in the document, often something about the problem the longer document addresses or about your recommendations (for example, "The driving range at the golf course does not meet expectations because . . . ")

A plan of action—the reader's next step—and a courteous closing (for example, "If you have any questions about this proposal . . .")

Write a covering letter only when you've finished completely writing the longer document; only then can you introduce it to the reader.

Correspondence Format

As with other aspects of correspondence, convention dictates format. Typically, letters use a block format as in Figure 6.3.

Fenton Investigation
37 Hardy Road
Bayport, Ontario N0N 0N0
Phone: (616) 555-5555 Fax: (616) 555-5556
www.fenton.com

January 3, 2000

Jonathan Owen
2515 Maple Street
Toronto, Ontario M5M 5M5

Dear Mr. Owen:

Thank you for your letter of December 25, 1999 in which you asked for our rates for locating reindeer and other cloven-footed creatures.

Unfortunately, we cannot help you since we limit our work to locating human beings. I suggest you contact your local SPCA or the provincial wildlife association.

However, if your future needs do involve humans, please call on us. I'm sure we can help.

Sincerely,

Franklin W. Dixon
Account Manager
Fenton Investigation

Figure 6.3
Correspondence format

The block format aligns everything to the left margin, leaving a space between paragraphs. Here are the elements that you must include:

* Letterhead with contact information including street address, phone and fax numbers, and e-mail and Web page addresses (if available)
* Date
* Recipient's name and address
* Greeting
* Body text

- Closing
- Signature
- Sender's name and job title

If you don't know the name of the person who will read your letter, use the department's name. It's no longer acceptable to say simply "Gentlemen"; you risk alienating any female who receives your letter.

WORKING SMARTER

Boilerplate Files

A boilerplate is a file that you use whenever you have to enter the same text over and over. It is most often used for correspondence but can, in fact, be used for any kind of document. Boilerplates consist of prepared and preformatted text. Typically, you just change only parts of the file (like the recipient's name or the date).

Once you've have chosen a format, make an electronic copy to use it as a boilerplate, changing the contents as needed. To make a boilerplate, first create a file with the text you want and placeholders for the portions of the text that you will have to change. Then save the file as read-only (in Windows) or as stationery (on a Mac). When you open the file in the future, you will work with an untitled copy of your prepared file, which you then save under a different and appropriate name. You cannot, therefore, accidentally overwrite your original.

Refer to the documentation that came with your application and operating system.

E-mail

An e-mail message is like any other business or professional message except for the way it's sent. The rules of respect, honesty, and brevity apply as much to e-mail as to any other communication.

The major strength of e-mail—its speed—can also be its major drawback. Once you click the Send button, your message is on its way. That's true, of course, of a regular letter once you drop it into a mailbox, but a message you mail gives you more time to reconsider and revise before it becomes irretrievable. To guard against the possibility of sending something you later regret, you need to develop good e-mail habits.

In the early days of the Internet, most e-mail was sent among friends, and people took a pretty casual attitude about what they wrote. Writing to friends encouraged a conversational tone, often accompanied by jokes and expressions of feelings. But feelings expressed via e-mail without the added dimension of face-to-face contact were sometimes difficult to interpret. Writers soon began to add emoticons, that is, little keyboard graphics made up of characters that showed happy or sad faces such as :-) or :-(.

But with e-mail now a standard tool of business, the easy-going ways of the past are inadequate. There is simply too much at stake to risk readers misinterpreting messages. So in addition to respect, honesty, and brevity, here are some useful practices to follow when sending e-mail:

- Spend the same amount of time composing, revising, and copy-editing e-mail as you would with hard copy. Don't confuse the speed the message travels with the haste of its writing. For example, use the spell checkers that now come with many e-mail programs.
- Don't depend on emoticons. If you're unsure of the impression you're making, rewrite until you get it right.
- Reply to the right person. This is especially true with listserv e-mail (that is, where messages are sent to a group of persons, not just one). Pressing the Reply button will send your message to everybody, not just the originator. At best, that will waste the time of the unintended recipients; at worst, the wrong people will read your confidential messages.
- If you can, wait a few hours to reply, especially if a message includes or will generate strong feelings. It's easy to click the Send button but impossible to unclick it. Under no circumstance should you *flame* recipients—that is, attack them personally. If the matter is serious enough, phone or meet them in person.
- Don't attach files unless recipients expect them; otherwise, you tie up their computers and interfere with their workflow. If you do attach a file, say so in the subject line and perhaps add the length of the file ("Jones.doc attached (52K)"). In the body of the message, say what application the recipient needs to open the file. Give the attached file a meaningful name; "draft2.doc" won't help people with lots of files on their systems.
- *Never* attach an executable file—that is, one that doesn't just contain data but can actually run—without clearing it first with the recipient. Executable files can transmit viruses, and even harmless executable files cause concern.

Voice Mail

Large organizations use voice mail because it automates much of what humans would otherwise do. Most clients, however, loathe voice mail because it can take too much time or be too impersonal. Since the technology isn't going away, here are some good voice-mail practices:

- Be brief in your welcoming announcements; assume callers are as busy as you are. Say who you are, when you're available, where they can find immediate help, and when you'll return their calls. You don't have to tell callers to wait for the beep; voice mail isn't uncommon anymore.
- Don't use a message that says that you're busy helping someone else. That doesn't help the caller.
- Don't record clever announcements with sound effects and jokes. They may work the first time—maybe—but not after that.
- If there is a range of choices ("Press 1 for Technical Support, Press 2 for Sales . . . "), keep them all very brief. Don't create too many levels where the caller has to keep entering numbers.
- If pressing 0 will redirect the caller to a live person, say so early in the message.
- If you're preparing an automated message, avoid empty statements like "Your call is important to us." If it really were important, you'd hire more staff.
- When you leave a message on voice mail, don't start by saying, "Hi, it's me" unless you're calling your mother. You might be surprised by whom the word "me" brings to mind.
- When you have to leave a message, be prepared. Formulate your response while waiting for the inevitable beep.

Memos

Step 1: Determine the Purpose of the Memo

Write a one-sentence summary of the most important information you wish to convey.

Step 2: Describe the Audience

A. Name at least one person who will receive your memo.
B. Write a one-sentence summary of what that person already knows.
C. Write a one-sentence summary of what that person needs to know.

Step 3: Draft the Opening Paragraph

A. Say why you are sending this memo in the first sentence.
B. Set the context; tell readers what they need to know to understand the memo.

For example:

I'm writing to inform you of the new policy regarding travel expenses.

I have reviewed your request to re-evaluate your travel expense claim.

Step 4: Draft the Body of the Message

- For each main idea, use a separate paragraph.
- Open each paragraph by stating the main point of that paragraph.
- Limit sentences to no more than two main clauses and one subordinate clause.
- Where possible, use bullet lists when your points are equally important.
- Use numbered lists where items are either ranked or sequenced.
- Use graphics sparingly, especially when you'll send the memo via e-mail.

Step 5: Draft the Closing

A. Briefly restate the key point in the message. For example:

> Unless we follow the actions outlined above, the Hodgkin's project may not be profitable.

B. End by saying what must be done and by whom. For example:

> Please send your revised expense report by Tuesday morning.

Step 6: Test and Revise

Since there won't be enough time to test the memo with sample recipients, play that role yourself:

A. Let a few minutes pass (an hour, if possible), then try to paraphrase the main point of the memo. If you can't, revise.

B. Check for clarity, Plain English, and short sentences.

Step 7: Check the Format

Revise the memo so that it conforms to the appropriate format. It should have:

- The company and/or department name
- The word *Memo*
- A *To* line
- A *From* line
- A *Subject* line
- A *Date* line
- The Body

Step 8: Copy-Edit

Read the memo aloud and check for:

- Missing or added words
- Grammar and punctuation errors
- Spelling errors, especially people's names

Maintain your credibility; don't give the recipient the chance to reject your ideas because of writing errors.

Routine Letters

Step 1: Determine the Purpose of the Letter

Write a one-sentence summary of the most important information you wish to convey.

Step 2: Describe the Audience

A. Name at least one person who will receive your letter.
B. Write a one-sentence summary of what that person already knows.
C. Write a one-sentence summary of what that person needs to know.

Step 3: Draft the Opening Paragraph

A. Say why you are sending this letter.
B. Set the context; tell readers what they need to know to understand to the letter. For example:

> As we discussed on the phone last Tuesday, I am sending you the specifications for the Magnus 401 tractor.

> Thank you for your letter of October 30 in which you asked about shipping costs to Alberta.

Step 4: Draft the Main Message

- For each main idea, use a separate paragraph.
- Open each paragraph by stating the main point of that paragraph.
- Limit sentences to no more than two main clauses and one subordinate clause.
- Where possible, use bullet lists when your points are equally important.
- Use numbered lists where items are either ranked or sequenced.
- Use graphics sparingly, especially when you'll send the letter via e-mail.

Step 5: Draft the Closing

A. Briefly restate the key point in the letter. For example:

> The Magnus 407 has most of the features you inquired about and is priced well below our other models.

B. Maintain the social contact. For example:

> I hope these specifications are clear. If I can provide you with further information, please call me directly at 555-5555. I look forward to hearing from you again.

Step 6: Test and Revise

Since there won't be enough time to test the letter with sample recipients, play that role yourself:

A. Let a few minutes pass (an hour, if possible), then try to paraphrase the main point of the memo. If you can't, revise.
B. Check for clarity, Plain English, and short sentences.

Step 7: Check the Format

Revise the letter so that it conforms to the appropriate format. It should have these items:

- Letterhead (with contact information)
- Date
- Recipient's name and address
- Greeting
- Body
- Closing
- Your signature, name, and job title
- Your contact information

Within the body, make the letter easy to read by using white space and lists as appropriate.

Step 8: Copy-Edit

Read aloud and check for:

- Missing or added words
- Grammar and punctuation errors
- Spelling mistakes (especially proper names)

Maintain your credibility; don't give the recipient the chance to reject your ideas because of writing errors.

Bad-News Letters

Step 1: Determine the Purpose of the Letter

Write a one-sentence summary of the most important information you wish to convey.

Step 2: Describe the Audience

A. Name the person who will receive your letter. List whatever information you have about him or her.
B. Write a one-sentence summary of what that person already knows.
C. Write a one-sentence summary of what that person needs to know.

Step 3: Draft a Neutral Opening Paragraph

Do:
- Find the common ground between you and the reader; ask "What can we agree on?"
- Use a neutral, uncommitted tone

Don't:
- Give false signals ("I was very interested to read your very reasonable request . . .")
- Express your pleasure ("I'm very glad to reply to your letter of . . . ")
- Signal your refusal too early ("Dear X: I cannot accept your request . . .")

Step 4: Draft the Second Paragraph to Set Forth the Context

Do:
- Set out the facts of the circumstances objectively
- Draft a separate sentence for each fact
- Limit sentences to no more than two main clauses and one subordinate clause

Don't:
- Apologize excessively ("I'm really upset that we cannot refund . . .")
- Hide behind policy ("As much as I'd like to refund your money, it is not our policy . . .")
- Patronize ("These matters are very complicated . . .")

Step 5: Draft the Refusal

Do:
- Say *no* explicitly
- Show there is a benefit in your saying *no*
- Offer an alternative

Don't:
- Emphasize the refusal ("There is simply no way that I can refund your money.")
- Blame the recipient ("Had you handled the blender properly, it would still be working.")
- Be blunt ("We can't stay in business by giving away blenders.")

Step 6: Draft the Closing

Do:
- Be upbeat
- Assume there will be a future transaction

Don't:
- Refuse again ("To repeat, I can't refund your money.")
- Apologize ("I'm very sorry for my refusal.")
- Resort to clichés ("Service is our most important product.")

Step 7: Test and Revise

Although there won't be much time to test the letter with sample recipients, ask a colleague or play that role yourself:

A. Let a few minutes pass (an hour, if possible), then try to paraphrase the main point of the memo. If you can't, revise.
B. Check to ensure you have the four key elements:
- Opening middle ground
- A statement of the facts
- The refusal
- The future transaction

C. Check for clarity and Plain English.

Step 8: Check the Format

Revise the letter so that it conforms to the appropriate format, including:

- Letterhead (with contact information)
- Date

- Recipient's name and address
- Greeting
- Body
- Closing
- Your signature, name, and job title
- Your contact information

Within the body, make the letter easy to read using white space and lists as appropriate.

Step 9: Copy-Edit

Read aloud and check for:

- Missing or added words
- Grammar and punctuation errors
- Spelling mistakes (especially proper names).

Maintain your credibility; don't give the recipient the chance to reject your ideas because of writing errors.

CHAPTER SUMMARY

Correspondence is a conversation held at a distance rather than face-to-face. Like all conversations, you have to be acutely aware of the social situation, being sure to observe the appropriate conventions of form and language. You must recognize that your reader is as worthy, smart, and busy as you are, and your writing must therefore be respectful, honest, and brief.

A common kind of professional correspondence is the memo, written by and for people within the same organization. Memos convey information similar to routine messages sent to people outside an organization; however, because memo senders and recipients share the same context, there's less need for long explanation. Bad-news letters, also a common type of professional correspondence, try to maintain a social relationship with the person whose request the writer is refusing.

Writing any kind of message—good news or bad, electronic or hard copy—requires you to determine its purpose and know your audience before starting to write. Like other professional documents, you should test and revise correspondence before sending it out, although time constraints can make that difficult.

CHECKLISTS

MEMOS

Opening paragraph states main purpose of the memo.

Each main idea is in a separate paragraph.

Each paragraph opens with its main point.

Sentences have no more than two main clauses and one subordinate clause.

Lists are the appropriate type: bullet for equally important items and numbered for items that are either ranked or sequenced.

Ending briefly restates main point.

Ending says what must be done and by whom.

Plain English is used throughout.

Format is correct: company and/or department name; *To, From, Subject*, and *Date* lines; and body.

Memo has been tested and any necessary revisions have been made.

Copy-editing has corrected missing words, repeated words, misspellings, and grammar and punctuation errors.

ROUTINE LETTERS

Opening paragraph states main purpose of the letter.

Each main idea is in a separate paragraph.

Each paragraph opens with its main point.

Sentences have no more than two main clauses and one subordinate clause.

Lists are appropriate type: bullet for equally important items and numbered for items that are either ranked or sequenced.

Closing briefly restates main point.

Closing maintains social contact.

Plain English is used throughout.

Format is correct: letterhead, date, recipient's name and address, greeting, body, closing, your signature, name, job title, and contact information.

Document format uses white space and bullets to improve readability where appropriate.

☐ Letter has been tested and any necessary revisions have been made.

☐ Copy-editing has corrected missing words, repeated words, misspellings, and grammar and punctuation errors.

BAD-NEWS LETTERS

☐ Opening paragraph finds common ground.

☐ Opening paragraph has neutral tone.

☐ Opening paragraph *does not* give false signals, express pleasure, or refuse.

☐ Second paragraph sets out facts objectively.

☐ Second paragraph *does not* insult reader's intelligence, hide, or apologize.

☐ Third paragraph states the refusal explicitly.

☐ Third paragraph tries to find a benefit.

☐ Third paragraph tries to offer an alternative.

☐ Third paragraph *does not* emphasize the refusal, blame the reader, or use blunt language.

☐ Closing assumes a future transaction.

☐ Closing *does not* refuse again, apologize, or resort to clichés.

☐ Sentences are limited to two main clauses and one subordinate clause.

☐ Plain English is used throughout.

☐ Format is correct: letterhead, date, recipient's name and address, greeting, body, closing, your signature, name, job title, and contact information.

☐ Letter has been tested and any necessary revisions have been made.

☐ Copy-editing has corrected missing words, repeated words, misspellings, and grammar and punctuation errors.

Your additional comments:

EXERCISES

Exercise 1

Rewrite Bob "Buzz" Deacon's memo below, being sure to include only the relevant information. Present it so that it's accurate, brief, and clear about the message he wants to communicate. By the way, Buzz is a lousy speller, makes basic errors, and doesn't know much about format. His manners are also questionable.

Acme Circuits Inc
8787 Yellow Point Road
(555) 477-1234

Interoffice Memo

From: Bob "Buzz" Deacon, Office Manage

To: All Employees

Subject: New Xerox Policy

There are a number of questions regarding company policy that I would like to discuss with you. It is agreed that all employees who work for Ace Circuits should note the following change in policy. All company Xerox machines that we use will soon (we hope within three days but not more than a week or two at most) have a log book beside them which people must record in the various things that they copy. There has been a good deal of copyright violation as well as abuse of Xeroxing privaliges. My immediate boss, the Director of Office Services, has asked me to inform you of a new proceedure for keeping tabs on how Xerox machines are used. John Green of Green Semiconductors in Port Black have tried a similar approach, and it works very well. All employees will have a page in the log book with there names on them. Its essential that if an employee copies alot of material for their personal use, she must write down the number of copies made in the log's second column. In order to be handy, the log book will be beside each Xerox machine. If the copies are for other departments, the record has to be made in the third column. Finally, if the copies are made for the person's own department, it must be recorded in the log's first column. The reminder is made by The Director of Office Services to everyone is that the company can be sued when employees make illegal copies. He has told me confidentially that Blue Fish Wrapping Inc. will be sued by the publishers of English Simplified. This may cost them 1000s of dollars, although it probably won't happen to us at all. The new policy will go into effect on December 15, 1994. The Director of Office Services is Harold Bloom, who has been in his position for five years. Let's all think about this one. Thanks.

Exercise 2

Write a routine memo informing colleagues of your company's new vacation policy. Here's the relevant information (in no particular order):

- Employees must make arrangements within their departments for colleagues to take over their most critical duties and notify of you who will be doing what.
- Employees must choose a three-week vacation period between June and August, a one-week period between September and December, and another between February and May.
- They must inform you of their choices for the coming year within two weeks.

Exercise 3

Write a routine letter to Michael Cullen, a minor-league hockey coach, who has requested information about your sporting goods store's pricing and products for hockey equipment.

Exercise 4

Write a bad-news memo based on the following case. You have received a memo from Les Morely (one of your sales reps) that says this:

> Last week, I visited Applied Pigskin, one of my accounts, bringing with me two briefcases filled with samples and brochures. When I got home, I realized that I had left one of the briefcases there; I called them but no one has been able to find it. This briefcase was a Christmas present ten years ago from my wife. It cost $200 then and $300 today, and I'd like to be reimbursed. Our company policy says (and I quote) "Employees will be reimbursed for all reasonable costs incurred when carrying out their assigned duties." I'd appreciate the $300. I enclose a page from a catalogue, showing the current price.

You have the authority to make whatever decision you wish. Les is productive, works long hours, and services his accounts very well. And he's right about the company policy being worded as it is. Still, he was careless, something similar happened once before, and you would like to keep costs down.

In the end, you decide not to grant his request.

Exercise 5

Write a bad-news letter based on the following case:

> You are your Gridley University's chief financial officer, and one of your responsibilities is campus parking. Over the years, it has become an increasing problem as more people drive to Gridley and more buildings compete for land.

A private company maintains the parking lots, and when the contract was signed years ago, you were able to subsidize parking to all staff and students. Your rationale then was that people often had to be on campus after buses stopped running; their safety and well-being was worth the cost to Gridley. However, a number of things have changed over time. For example, the private company is increasing its charges, the government is cutting back operating grants, more and more people are parking on campus, and space is needed for three new buildings.

You have therefore decided to charge everyone the real costs for parking. Fees will increase 25% to $250 a year. Moreover, you will reduce the number of parking spots available by 20%. You will have to restrict parking permits only to staff and full-time third- and fourth-year students. Even then, not every student who qualifies will be able to get a permit. The new policy begins in January.

Campus Security (7255) does have a computer listing of people interested in carpooling, and Ace Transit has increased its scheduled service until 11:00 PM weeknights.

Write Jane Smith, President of the Gridley Student Association, PO Box 1234, Sesame Hall, Gridley University. Inform her of the new policy and ask for her support in explaining it to students. Include whatever reasons you consider legitimate and that would help convince this particular person. Don't invent things such as "Quicksand has been found under the parking lots" or "All muggers have been apprehended"; instead, think of good and plausible reasons for this situation.

CHAPTER

7

Writing Instructions

What This Chapter Covers

Ideas

What You Need to Know About Content
       Telling How
       Two Sample Instructions
       Knowing How, Who, and Why
       How Much Does the Writer Need to Know?
Task Analysis: The Content You'll Teach
       Why Task Analysis Is Important
       Doing a Task Analysis
       Representing Expert Knowledge With a Flow Chart
       Keeping in Touch With Your Expert
Audience Analysis: The People You'll Teach
       Differences Among Readers
       Doing an Audience Analysis
Making It Easy to Use
       Plain Language
       Making Graphics Inform
       Document Design
Testing Your Instructions
       How Much Testing Is Enough?

Actions

Your First Draft
Usability Testing
The Final Draft

Chapter Summary

Checklists

Exercises

CHAPTER—7

Learning Objectives

At the end of this chapter, you will be able to explain:

- What are the key ideas about instructions
- Why you must know both how to do a task and who will learn it
- Why you must perform a task analysis and what are the key questions to ask when you do one
- How a flow chart can represent an expert's knowledge
- Why you must perform an audience analysis and what key questions you must ask when you do one
- What are the basic principles of presenting instruction
- What are the basic principles for using graphics
- Why you must carefully design the appearance of your instructions

At the end of this chapter, you will be able to write instructions by:

- Performing task and audience analyses
- Drafting a brief overview of the task
- Describing the entry-level skills your audience needs
- Formulating warnings and cautions
- Listing necessary materials to complete the task
- Estimating the time to complete the task
- Sequencing the steps
- Inserting warnings and assurances into the sequence of steps
- Explaining technical terms
- Concluding with an overview
- Testing for usability and revising

What You Need to Know About Content

Telling How

Technology can't be helpful unless we know how to use it. Showing people how to operate the complex things that surround them, therefore, is a critical task of the professional writer. Indeed, in no other kind of writing is success or failure so obvious: Your readers either can or cannot do what you teach.

However, not everything can be taught. For example, while you can show people how to set the aperture on a camera, you can't necessarily to teach them how to take an aesthetically pleasing picture. Similarly, you can teach people how to operate a microwave oven; you can't necessarily teach them to become great chefs. Or you can show them how to do the buck-and-wing but not how to become great tap dancers. When you write instructions, therefore, you have to be reasonably sure that your topic is one that you can teach.

Like teachers, professional writers instruct—how to operate a fax machine, how to use software, how to complete a tax form. And like teaching, simply knowing how to do a task yourself isn't enough to impart it to someone else. You must also know about the audiences who will actually use your instructions and the ways to test and revise your work. All this calls for a set of techniques that combine teaching with writing.

The basic ideas are straightforward:

only how ·

Instructions tell readers how to carry out some procedure in such a way that they always accomplish their task. That is, instructions don't teach *knowledge about* but *knowledge how.* Your readers, for example, might want to know how to use a microscope but not want to learn about optics. They might want to know how to make toast but not want to learn about heat transfer. Or they might want to use a VCR's remote without learning about infrared transmission. Your job is to show them each step so they can do just what they want.

sequential

Instructions are always sequential. Readers need to know what to do first, second, and so on. They will keep asking "What do I do next?" until they complete the task.

*explicit
direct*

Instructions are always explicit. Writers should never merely imply what to do next, nor should readers ever have to infer. Instructions must be complete and direct. There is no room for ambiguity.

stand-alone

Instructions are stand-alone. While it would be ideal to have a live, knowledgeable human beside your readers while they learn, that usually does not happen. You must write instructions, therefore, so that someone can complete them without needing another person to be there, even when things go off the rails.

Instructions have to be field-tested. A critical part of writing instructions is the tryout-feedback-revision cycle with testers who are typical of your intended audience. You need to gather information from them about what's working and what isn't and then revise accordingly.

field–tested

Two Sample Instructions

The examples in Figures 7.1 and 7.2 show these ideas at work. The first teaches users of a word-processing application how to create a complex table; the second shows users of a wet/dry vacuum how to operate the machine as a blower.

In each case:

- Someone working alone has enough information to complete the task.
- The writer assumes users have the appropriate entry-level skills.
- The instructions walk users through a sequence of steps, some of which are themselves made up of smaller steps.

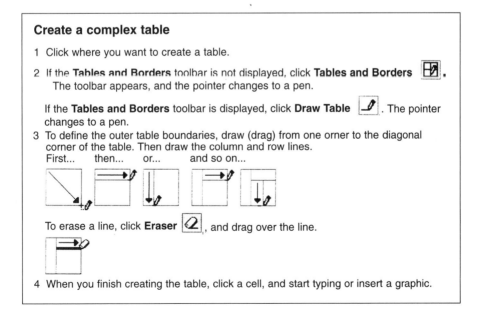

Figure 7.1
Creating a complex table

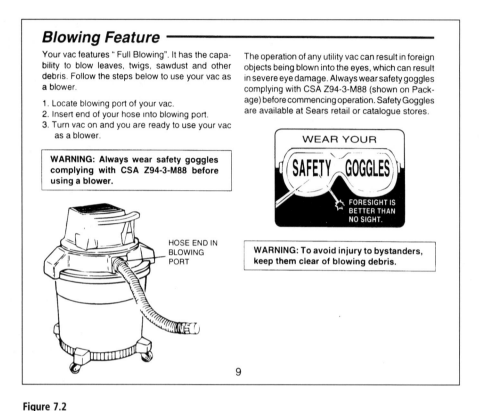

Blowing Feature

Your vac features " Full Blowing". It has the capability to blow leaves, twigs, sawdust and other debris. Follow the steps below to use your vac as a blower.

1. Locate blowing port of your vac.
2. Insert end of your hose into blowing port.
3. Turn vac on and you are ready to use your vac as a blower.

WARNING: Always wear safety goggles complying with CSA Z94-3-M88 before using a blower.

The operation of any utility vac can result in foreign objects being blown into the eyes, which can result in severe eye damage. Always wear safety goggles complying with CSA Z94-3-M88 (shown on Package) before commencing operation. Safety Goggles are available at Sears retail or catalogue stores.

WEAR YOUR

SAFETY GOGGLES

FORESIGHT IS BETTER THAN NO SIGHT.

HOSE END IN BLOWING PORT

WARNING: To avoid injury to bystanders, keep them clear of blowing debris.

9

Figure 7.2
Using the blower feature

Source: Shop-vacuum manual (Sears Canada stock no. 29044), 9.

- Actions are stated explicitly (for example, "Click where you want to create the table" or "Insert end of your hose . . .").
- Graphics supplement the text.

And although we have no direct proof that these particular instructions have been tried out with potential users, major corporations do test their documentation as a matter of course.

Knowing How and Who—and Also Why

Writing instructions requires knowledge of both how to do a task and who will learn it. You can think of writing instructions as continually solving a central problem of teaching: *Given this particular body of knowledge and this particular audience, how do I bring the two of them together?* Put another way, you ask what strategies will work best to teach this task to this audience.

You also have to know *why* someone should learn a task. There are many worthwhile things to know in the world, but only some of them are relevant at any particular time. For example:

- Knowing how a computer stores data is interesting; however, it doesn't help someone wanting to know just how to increase font size with a word processor.
- Knowing how a thermometer works is also interesting; but it doesn't help if all you wish to know is how warm it is outside.
- Knowing hydraulics has many virtues; but when you want to stop your car, all you want to know is where to find the brake.

When learners know why something is important for them, they're more likely to be motivated to master it. After all, why should people bother to study a skill that they will never use?

How Much Does the Writer Need to Know?

How much to know

Instruction writers usually face an immediate problem: They either know too little or too much about the subject. Knowing too little is an obvious problem, but knowing too much is a more subtle one.

If you know a task very well—say, getting home from the other side of town—some parts of it will be so automatic that you'll barely think of them. As a result, when you tell someone how to get to your house, you may overlook what you do without thinking—like being in the right-hand lane at a certain corner, noting that a particular building marks the halfway point, or knowing at what time of day traffic is most congested. Just because you know these details doesn't mean that they will be obvious to others.

Moreover, there is often more than one way to do things. For instance, because you know your neighborhood well, you may take a rather tricky route that saves ten minutes. But a longer way may well be better for a stranger if it is easier to follow.

Experts do many complex tasks seemingly automatically—throwing a curve ball, executing a pirouette, dividing a five-digit number with two decimal places by a six-digit number with four decimal places. But different experts may do the same task different ways. Instruction writers must know those different ways and then choose the appropriate one for their readers. That's a matter of informed guessing followed by real-world trial-and-error testing.

Task Analysis: The Content You'll Teach

Why Task Analysis Is Important

Before you can teach something, of course, you have to be able to do it yourself. Observing an expert is a good way to both learn and analyze the task in question.

That expert can sometimes be you, as long as you scrupulously observe yourself in action and record what you are doing. In many instances, of course, you will have to observe another person. However, all experts have to be slowed down so

---

WORKING SMARTER

Electronic Outliners for Sequence

Mainstream word processors now include electronic outliners that can automatically arrange your work as numbered and/or bullet lists:

1. Heading 1
    a. main step here
        sub-step here
        sub-step here
2. Heading 2
    a. main step here
        sub-step here
        sub-step here

Outliners are especially useful when you're trying out different sequences of material because these programs let you conveniently move entire sections. If you decide, for example, that you want to reverse the order of steps, you need move only the heading; everything associated with it will automatically follow. You can move text manually, of course, by cutting and pasting; however, an outliner is safer, faster, and easier.

An outliner also allows you to collapse headings, that is, show only certain levels of an item. For example:

1. Heading 1
    a. main step here
2. Heading 2
    a. main step here

You can show even less:

1. Heading 1
2. Heading 2

You can expand the information as necessary with a single click. You can easily vary your perspective of the material from an overview of only the largest elements to the detail of the smallest points. That's helpful because different junctures in your writing process will demand different perspectives.

that you can identify each step they perform. One way to do that is to have them speak as they do a task, explaining what they are doing and why.

A task analysis also helps you choose or narrow a topic. Watching an expert in action should demonstrate whether you could, in fact, teach a particular skill to the audience you have in mind. For example, most able-bodied persons can change a flat tire, but many people with various physical limitations cannot. Most math skills require prior knowledge that some students have but others lack. And following a recipe in a cookbook demands being able to read. A task analysis will show you whether there is a good fit between what you want to teach and who will learn it.

Doing a Task Analysis

The tools for a task analysis can be as simple as a notebook or as elaborate as a camcorder. Regardless of what you use, you must answer these questions:

What is each step in the sequence? What does the expert do first, second, and so on? Take nothing for granted because experts may do some things so quickly that their actions are almost invisible—perhaps even to themselves.

Why does the expert do a specific step at any given point? When in doubt, stop and ask so that you'll be able to convey the answer to your readers. If you needed to know, so will they.

Are there points where an expert's action depends on some condition being satisfied? For example, think of using a telephone:

> • If you hear a ringing signal, then wait until someone answers.
>
> • If you hear a busy signal, then hang up and try later.

You need to identify both the various conditions users may encounter and the actions they would then have to take. Otherwise, you could well leave them hanging in mid-task.

What parts of the task require a prerequisite skill? Some prerequisites may be difficult to recognize because they are too obscure or too obvious. An example of an obscure prerequisite would be having to know the Lorenz equations in order to fully grasp Einstein's theory of relativity. An example of an obvious prerequisite would be knowing that even if you hear a ringing signal after you've dialed a number, no one may answer. Such specifying of entry-level skills is absolutely critical for both you and your audience.

Does the expert cluster several steps in one larger one? If so, what are they? For example, someone may appear to just pick up the telephone and then start dialing. In fact, two preliminary steps occur: (1) picking up the telephone and (2) listening for a dial tone.

Are special materials or tools necessary? For instance, hanging risers for shelves requires the right size of screws, changing a car's oil filter requires a specific type of wrench, and embroidering requires special needles. Find out what users will need and advise them to have it on hand before they begin.

Where are the danger points that require warnings? Danger can be either actual bodily harm or an action that causes the operation to fail. For example, using a lawn tractor requires eye and ear protection or injury can occur. Installing doors demands careful measurement or they won't hang properly. And baking cookies means keeping track of the time unless you like your cookies burnt. You have to know the danger points in order to warn users where they can either hurt themselves or get off track.

What are the signs of success? How do experts know when they've done something right? Telephone experts listen for dial tones, busy signals, and voices. Furniture assemblers look for edges to be aligned. Lab technicians watch for chemicals to change colour. When you know these signs, you list them for your readers to assure them that they're on the right track.

For which steps will pictures help? Graphics often convey information more directly than words. For example, try writing a description of the scroll in Figure 7.3. Your text and the image may both convey the same information, but the graphic would probably do so more elegantly.

Figure 7.3
A difficult object to describe

As you observe your expert, therefore, imagine a picture that would illustrate each step. Do quick sketches as you go. (You do not need to be a great artist; stick figures or simple diagrams will do). You might not use all of your sketches, but having them available will make writing easier.

Representing Expert Knowledge With a Flow Chart

Experts must make decisions as well as perform actions. A flow chart is a good way to represent that combination because this kind of chart shows not only

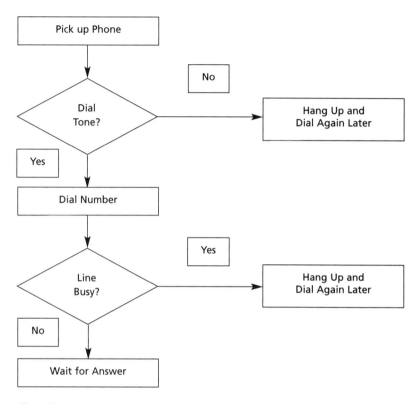

Figure 7.4
Dialing a number

specific tasks in sequence but also the various points at which experts decide what to do next. Figure 7.4 shows a flow chart for dialing a number.

In addition to helping you represent for yourself the full range of events an expert might encounter, a flow chart can also help your audience. That assumes that flow charts aren't themselves impediments to learning—some non-technical audiences may find them intimidating. The only way to determine how an audience will react, of course, is to test.

Keeping in Touch With Your Expert

It's a good idea to arrange a follow-up with your expert, in case you later discover a step that needs clarifying or one that you've misunderstood completely. Later in this chapter, we'll discuss **usability testing,** that is, having real people try out your instructions to see whether your steps and their sequence and execution are correct. However, having your expert review your work can save you and your audience much frustration.

Audience Analysis: The People You'll Teach

Differences Among Readers

An audience for instructions differs from others you'll encounter because they not only *read* but *read and do*. That is, they generally don't read for *knowledge about* something (like a company's products). Instead, they read for *knowledge how* (like performing a task) and usually apply that knowledge right away. They're focused on one specific problem like connecting a stereo or changing a spark plug. They can't afford to waste time either by having to reread simply to understand what you meant or by getting distracted by irrelevancies.

Individual members of your audience also differ from each other, like students in a class. They all bring their own backgrounds, motivations, and skills. You need to know as best you can, therefore, for whom you are writing. Just as telephone instructors wouldn't talk about area codes unless they knew their students were numerate, you first have to find out what your readers already know and why they might be interested in your topic. Only then can you decide what *further* things they need to know.

Doing an Audience Analysis

Doing an audience analysis requires no more than a notebook and access to persons typical of your intended audience. Here are the key questions to answer:

What do they need to know? You can't teach everything at once, of course, so you have to focus on the specific task that your audience must learn *right now, right here*. People learning to format text in a word processing program clearly need to know the commands for bold, italics, and font size. They do not need to know how to save a file or print it out—instructions about that would only distract them. Someone changing engine oil does not want to learn how to top up brake fluid now. A person setting up a VCR isn't interested in changing the contrast on the TV screen until later, if at all. Make sure, therefore, that the tasks you teach are the ones your audience needs *at that moment*.

What do they already know? Specify if your intended audience is made up of rank beginners or of experts in a related topic on which they can build. If they are somewhere in between, what skills do they have? Do they have problems with reading? Do they have physical limitations? Do they know enough math? The more you can describe your audience in terms of what you plan to teach, the better your chance of producing a helpful set of instructions.

What do they need to master before starting your instructions? Instructions have to specify an entry level, that is, the minimum skills someone must already have in order to do a task. Learning to parallel park, for example, requires first knowing how to put a car in reverse. Hanging pictures requires first knowing about hammers. Formatting text on a word processor requires first knowing how to enter text.

Why do they need to know it? People are motivated when they know why learning something is important. Video game players learn about trajectory because they need to blast aliens. Amateur mechanics learn car maintenance because they want to save money. And novice telephone users learn about long-distance calls when they want to speak to somebody out of town. When you understand what motivates your audience, you can use that to focus them on completing the task.

For all these issues, begin with some informed guesses and then supplement them with explicit questions to your test audience. In some instances, you may have to draft and administer a test to reveal the specific skills your target audience already has or needs to learn.

Making It Easy to Use

Plain Language

A plain writing style makes reading easier. Plain English doesn't mean oversimplifying your instructions but rather making them as clear and as straightforward as possible. Chapter 3 talks about Plain English in much more detail, but here are the important points for writing instructions.

Keep sentences short

Generally include only one or two small steps in each sentence. Break up long sentences into separate steps so readers can *read and do* without losing their place in the instructions. For example, look at this pair of instructions:

> ***Weak:***
> Before exiting the program, make a backup of your file by first saving your work, then selecting "Save As" from the file menu, adding "Bak" to the end of the file name, and clicking OK before quitting the program.

> ***Better:***
> Before exiting the program, make a back up file:
> 1. Save your work.
> 2. Go to the File Menu and select Save As.
> 3. Add "Bak" to the end of the file's name and click OK.
> 4. Quit the program.

The first example requires readers to hold several steps in mind or go back and forth from the page to the task, finding their place in a relatively long sentence each time. The better example, on the other hand, isolates each step for the reader by putting main actions in separate sentences and separate list items. Each main step starts on a new line, providing readers with a visual cue as they move back and forth between the instructions and the task.

Short, simple sentences will not make your writing sound simple-minded; they will instead make your content clear.

Be conversational

Imagine real live people—with real names, preferences, dislikes, etc.—right there in front of you. Address them as *you*, speaking directly to them as if you were really there. Instructions are a conversation between a teacher and a student, so don't erect language barriers.

List Steps in Order

Present steps in the order the reader will do them. For example:

> **Weak:**
> Choose Save from the File Menu.

> **Better:**
> Go to the File Menu and choose Save.

The first reverses the order in which the task is actually done (that is, it tells the reader to choose Save before going to the File menu). Because your readers will *read and do*, an incorrect sequence of actions will force them to start over.

Explain Unfamiliar Terms

Replace technical or otherwise unfamiliar words with simpler ones or insert brief explanations. For example:

> **Weak:**
> Check your computer's internal mass storage device regularly for excessive fragmentation.

> **Better:**
> Check your hard drive regularly for *fragmentation*—that is, segments of your files that aren't stored next to each other, reducing the speed at which your computer can retrieve them.

The first sentence uses a less-familiar term ("internal mass storage device") that is better replaced by "hard drive," an expression most people already know. The sentence also assumes that all readers will know the meaning of "fragmentation." The better example, however, appends a brief and fairly unobtrusive explanation. If you have a great many words to explain, create a separate glossary in addition to explaining each term the first time you use it.

WORKING SMARTER

Version Control

As you revise instructions and other documents, you should hang on to the older versions as backups. The latest version may not necessarily be the best. For example, you may have cut something that a few days later you would want to use. However, keeping several different versions of the same document can cause confusion. Further, when you collaborate on a document (as when one person acts as the general editor and others contribute), tracking changes to the different versions gets complicated.

Here are a few ways to reduce this confusion:

- Use descriptive file names, saving the file, for example, with the date and the writer's initials. "ModemInstructMar9Ak.doc" would indicate that the document teaches about modems and was updated on March 9 by AK. (To make the file name easier to read, use lowercase letters except for the first letter of words.) You can use other kinds of notation such as Vers1, Ver1A, etc., if you find that easier.
- At the start of every document, insert a brief statement with relevant information—the title and subject of the document, the date it was created, the date of the last modification, the writer's names and contributions. You will, of course, remove all this from the final draft.
- If your word processor has a summary feature, enter relevant information there.
- If several people comment on a single document, have them append their initials to each comment. You can also assign each person a different colour with which to make comments on the document.

Major word processors automate a number of tasks for version control such as tracking changes and formatting comments. Consult your documentation.

Making Graphics Inform

Graphics shouldn't be mere embellishments (or "eye-candy," as they are called in the trade) but ways of conveying information. For many tasks, a combination of text and graphics is essential, especially when a picture can simplify, clarify, or supplement the text. For example, if you're teaching word processing, reproduce the icons a user would find on the toolbar. If you're teaching how to assemble a mechanical device, show how the parts fit together. If you're teaching how to use a craft kit, show the tool that comes with it. Chapter 4 goes into more detail about the different kinds of graphics you can use.

Document Design

Document design refers to how you arrange your page to help readers follow your ideas. Chapter 5 discusses white space, layout grids, and other design techniques. These are critical for instructions because, as we've seen, readers will continually move back and forth between the instructions and the task. Each time they return to the instructions, they need to quickly locate the start of the next step.

White Space

Your basic tool is white space—that is, parts of the page with neither text nor graphics. White space gives your readers visual breathing space and lets them find their way more readily through the steps. Compare the two presentations in Figure 7.5.

Step 1: lordo colloquia pastantem quid ovidus rach **Step 2:** lordo colloquia pastantem quid ovidus rach lordo colloquia pastantem quid ovidus rach	**Step 1:** lordo colloquia pastantem quid ovidus rach **Step 2:** lordo colloquia pastantem quid ovidus rach lordo colloquia pastantem quid ovidus rach

Figure 7.5
Using white space

Both have the same information; the one on the left, however, has few visual clues to indicate how that information is organized. The version on the right breaks the information into manageable chunks with the white space as boundaries.

Imagine using the first set. You would read Step 1, trying to determine how much to take in before going to the task. When you do go to the task and then return, you may have to read from the beginning in order to find where you left off.

Other Visual Markers

In addition to white space, you can also change your fonts and their appearance to signal how you have organized the material. Figure 7.6 shows some examples.

In addition to visual markers, make your headings informative, that is, briefly preview what they introduce. We cover that more fully in Chapter 5.

Styled Text (Bold, Italic, Size)	*Step 1:* lordo colloquia pastantem quid ovidus rach *Step 2:* lordo colloquia pastantem quid ovidus rach
Different Fonts for Headings and Text	Step 1: lordo colloquia pastantem quid ovidus rach Step 2: lordo colloquia pastantem quid ovidus rach

Figure 7.6
Visual markers

Making Your Graphics Easy to Find

Put text and accompanying graphics close together; never force readers to search for a picture, as Steps 1 and 3 do in Figure 7.7.

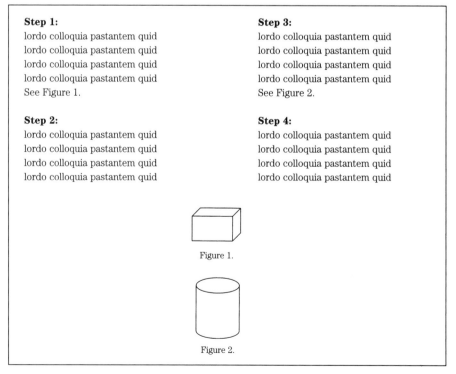

Step 1:
lordo colloquia pastantem quid
lordo colloquia pastantem quid
lordo colloquia pastantem quid
lordo colloquia pastantem quid
See Figure 1.

Step 2:
lordo colloquia pastantem quid
lordo colloquia pastantem quid
lordo colloquia pastantem quid
lordo colloquia pastantem quid

Step 3:
lordo colloquia pastantem quid
lordo colloquia pastantem quid
lordo colloquia pastantem quid
lordo colloquia pastantem quid
See Figure 2.

Step 4:
lordo colloquia pastantem quid
lordo colloquia pastantem quid
lordo colloquia pastantem quid
lordo colloquia pastantem quid

Figure 1.

Figure 2.

Figure 7.7
Poor layout for instructions

It's far easier for the reader if you place the graphic right beside the text, as in Figure 7.8.

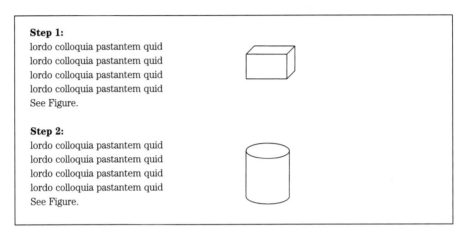

Step 1:
lordo colloquia pastantem quid
lordo colloquia pastantem quid
lordo colloquia pastantem quid
lordo colloquia pastantem quid
See Figure.

Step 2:
lordo colloquia pastantem quid
lordo colloquia pastantem quid
lordo colloquia pastantem quid
lordo colloquia pastantem quid
See Figure.

Figure 7.8
Better layout for instructions

Again, your goal when you lay out your instructions is to provide visual clues for how you've ordered information. Chapter 5 covers this issue more fully.

Testing Your Instructions

Once you have a draft, you're ready to test your instructions. Usability testing is a crucial part of writing instructions because you need real-world responses in order to revise. Moreover, testing will be an ongoing cycle of trying out your work with touchstone readers—people who are typical of your intended audience—and then using what you've learned to make the necessary changes. Testing is a data-gathering exercise that answers this question: *What do I need to know in order to prepare the next draft?*

Observe your touchstone readers smiling or frowning as they follow your instructions. At times, you will be frustrated with their responses; what seemed clear to you will confuse others. It's human nature to be upset when people criticize your work, but do your best to maintain a professional distance. Remind yourself that this is about what you've produced, not who you are. It won't always be fun; it will always be necessary.

How Much Testing Is Enough?

We never have world enough and time; nonetheless, deadlines have to be met and product has to be shipped. Moreover, after a while, the law of diminishing returns sets in and tryout costs exceed any benefits. Your first few field tests should yield the most information and subsequent tests will produce less—as long as you're truly making changes based on what you're seeing.

A C T I O N S

Your First Draft

Once you have completed your analyses of the task and of the audience, you can begin writing. Your goal in the first draft is to get the material out into the world where it can be tested and revised. You are moving from the expert's covert knowledge (which you can't see) to the users' overt responses (which you can).

In what follows, we'll walk through the steps for producing a draft. Of course, what you come up with here will be only a first try, which is certain to need revision and refinement.

Step 1: Show the Big Picture

Draft a brief overview of the task—the traditional twenty-five words or less—that tells *what* your instructions will teach and *why* that's important. Readers shouldn't waste their time on subjects in which they have no interest.

Step 2: Say What Users Must Already Know

Tell readers what skills they require before starting, being as specific as you can. They shouldn't waste time on subjects for which they're not ready.

How specific must you be? That depends on how well you know your audience. If you're confident, for example, that you are writing for intermediate computer-users, then you don't have to say that they should know how to turn on their machines. Your early drafts should err on the side of caution, however; you can always remove information if your testers tell you that it's unnecessary.

Step 3: Issue Warnings and Cautions

At the very outset of your instructions, explicitly warn of any dangers, such as materials that are combustible, parts that are sharp, or data that could be lost. For example, a driver who has to change a flat tire must know that the car cannot be on a hill. A homeowner operating a power lawn mower must know about eye protection. A person using a strong chemical must know to avoid inhaling the fumes. You have to be concerned both with the well-being of your readers and your own liability for any injury or loss they might suffer. A doctor's first rule is *do no harm*. That goes for instruction writers too.

You should also warn readers at the places where they can make common mistakes. For example:

- If a part should be oriented in a particular position before assembly
- If flour must be sifted before being added to other ingredients
- If a software application conflicts with others

Make these warnings stand out with larger type, colour, boxes, highlighting, or conventional danger icons. For example,

CAUTION!   DANGER!

Repeat the warnings just before the steps where they are relevant.

Step 4: List Materials

Be explicit about the materials, parts, or tools that users will need to complete the task. Put this information at the beginning of the instructions. Again, err on the side of caution and include as much as you can in the first draft (you can always remove superfluous items later). For example:

- If users will fix a tire, list the jack, the wrench, *and* an inflated spare.
- If users will assemble a patio swing, list all parts from the largest segments of the frame to the smallest screw.
- If users will need to solder, tell them before they start the task.

Step 5: Say How Much Time

How long will the operation take? Give an estimate of the total time needed unless it's only a few minutes. Don't let users find themselves in the middle of a task they don't have time to complete.

Step 6: List the Steps in Sequence

Present the steps in sequence, breaking them into separate sub-steps as necessary. If your testers later tell you that the instructions are disjointed, you can combine steps. But, at the start, go slowly and ensure that every step is there. Wait until you have a better sense of how effective your instructions are before you consolidate.

It's impossible to state categorically the optimum number of steps required for any particular task. You are making your best guess at this point, one that you will test and revise.

Step 7: Warn and Assure

Issue warnings immediately *before* the steps where they are relevant. Do the same for commonly made mistakes. For example:

Be sure to wear your safety goggles and ear protection before starting your tractor!

Place assurances immediately *after* each step—that is, state how things will be if the action has been correctly followed.

If installation was successful, you'll see the following message:
Installation successful. You must now restart your computer.

Step 8: Explain Difficult Terms

Briefly define technical words or jargon the first time you use them. If there are many such terms, compile a glossary so readers won't have to search for previously encountered words whose meaning they've forgotten.

Step 9: Provide the Big Picture Again

After you've listed all the steps in the task, conclude by showing the big picture one more time. Tell readers what they have accomplished and what the finished product should look like. If you know, also tell them what other tasks logically follow this one and where they can find instruction.

Usability Testing

It's difficult to know exactly how many testers you need, but a minimum of three is a good rule of thumb. Here's why: What happens with a single person may be merely an accident; what happens with two may be a coincidence; but what happens with three is a pattern. If everyone says that Step 5, for example, isn't clear, it isn't.

Step 1: Pick Your Subjects

Field testing works only when your subjects come from the same audience as you intend to teach. In some cases, it's relatively straightforward selecting them, as when institutions use job classifications or grade levels. In other cases, you have to depend on more vague descriptions like *novice, intermediate,* or *expert.* In more difficult situations yet, you may have to devise and administer a test of some kind. Your object is to use testers who are typical of your target group in terms of background, motivation, and entry skills. The better you can analyze your audience, of course, the better can be your choice of testers.

Step 2: Establish the Right Distance

When you field test, you observe without intervening as a user follows your instructions. Here are some guidelines:

- Assure your tester that you're looking for an honest opinion and that your feelings will not be hurt by criticism.
- Resist the temptation to hover; maintain the necessary distance to observe what's going on without intruding.
- Let the user follow the instructions as they are written without any additional help from you.
- Speak up only when the user explicitly asks for help or when a disaster is about to happen.
- *Never* dispute your user's comments or otherwise argue.
- Record exactly what and where things went wrong so that you'll know how to focus your revisions.

Step 3: Debrief

After the testers have finished, debrief them, that is, have them reconstruct the experience and then give you comments and suggestions. Ask them to start by completing these general statements:

> What I liked best about this was...
> What I liked after that was . . .
>
> What I wanted some immediate clarification about was...
> What I also wanted some clarification about was...

The first two statements will help you find successful strategies that you can replicate elsewhere. The last two statements show you the problems that particularly troubled the tester.

Request that testers point to specific things in the instructions rather than make vague comments like "It wasn't clear" or "I liked it." Again, assure them that your feelings won't be hurt by criticism and that you are, in fact, grateful and appreciate their honesty.

Step 4: Keep Careful Records

Use the same checklist each time you test in order in order to keep your records consistent and ensure that you cover all important issues every time. Here's an example of such a checklist (which you can download from our Web site at **<www.pearsoned.ca/keller>**):

Task Being Taught:_____

Date of Tryout:_____

Version Number:_____

Tester's Name:_____

Which steps have the following weaknesses?

• Contains inaccurate information:

• Lacks clarity or otherwise required rereading:

• Is not sufficiently explicit:

• Requires a list or otherwise needed be better structured:

• Fails to warn of dangers or mistakes:

• Fails to give assurances that step was done correctly:

• Fails to define technical terms:

• Has confusing layout or typography:

• Lacks graphic or graphic isn't helpful:

Which specific parts of the instructions worked well?

Additional comments:

Step 5: Ask for Expert Advice

Two other types of testers can help you: someone who knows the task and someone who knows how to write instructions. Their help differs from that of your touchstone readers because you ask them to cast a professional eye on your work, to validate your content and suggest how to better communicate it. Here are some of the things they can look for:

• Missing warnings or cautions
• Materials needed
• Sequence of presentation
• Sentence clarity
• Graphics
• Layout

Ask them to concentrate on your content and its clarity rather than on typographical errors. Proofing is what you do during the last revision.

Again, you want to know what must be done in the next draft. You can reject some suggested revisions, but you should see each one as a warning flag that requires your consideration.

Preparing the Final Draft

As we've said, at some point, you'll have to send your instructions out into the world. But before you declare your work done, ensure your presentation is as professional as you can. Copy-editing is the last stage of writing and rids the work of what can both distract readers and damage your credibility. Read your work aloud and, if possible, get a colleague to help.

Edit for Plain English, document design, and graphics. Copy-edit for typos, misspellings, and missing or extra words. See Part I of this text for details.

CHAPTER SUMMARY

Well-written instructions tell readers how to carry out a procedure in such a way that the readers always succeed. Instructions must be sequenced, explicit, and stand-alone. When you write them, your first step is to analyze the task you wish to teach so that you yourself know it thoroughly. To do this, you observe and question experts (which can include you), noting what they do, why they do it, and what can go wrong. You must also analyze the particular group of people whom you'll teach, finding out their current skills, what they want to learn, and their motivations.

The instructions your audience sees should begin with an overview of the task, a statement of prerequisite skills, a list of necessary materials, and any warnings about potential dangers or common errors. Your language must be plain and the steps must follow the sequence in which learners will do them. Graphics should inform rather than merely embellish, and your document's design should make it easy for readers to go from the page to the task and back again. Technology can help you do this work more efficiently.

Always test instructions with touchstone readers. Conduct these tests scrupulously, maintaining the appropriate distance, debriefing your subjects, and keeping careful records. If possible, consult experts to double-check that your information is correct.

CHECKLISTS

TASK ANALYSIS

Work with your expert to:

☐ List all steps and sub-steps in the sequence

☐ Identify which large steps need to be broken down into smaller ones

☐ Prepare a flow chart that traces the expert's actions

For each step, determine:

☐ The reasons why the expert does it

☐ The prerequisite skills

☐ The conditions that must be satisfied before action is taken

☐ Any danger points that require warnings

☐ The signs of success to assure users that they are doing things correctly

☐ Any special materials or tools required

Arrange with your expert:

☐ A way to communicate in case you later have to check your understanding of something

☐ A time and place to validate your instructions once they are in draft form

Your additional comments:

AUDIENCE ANALYSIS

Identify:

☐ What your target audience needs to know (in general terms)

☐ Why they want to know how to do the task

☐ Which of the entry-level skills noted during the task analysis the audience has and which they lack

Determine any other important characteristics of your target audience:

☐ Language or reading skills

☐ Previous experience

☐ Attitudes

☐ Age

☐ Other (specify)

Your additional comments:

ORGANIZATION

Make sure you have included the following items and check if any of them still need editing:

- A brief overview of the entire task
- A statement early on of what skill(s) users require before starting
- A list of all materials
- A statement of approximately how long the entire operation should take
- Any necessary warnings at the start of the instructions
- Emphasis such as larger type, colours, boxes, or icons to make warnings easily visible
- Repetition of any applicable warnings before each step
- Assurances so readers know when they've done something correctly
- A glossary of technical terms

Also check that:

- All steps and sub-steps are numbered
- All technical words are defined within the steps
- Readers can easily find the start of the next step as they go back and forth from the instructions to the task

Your additional comments:

LANGUAGE

Make sure that you have used the following techniques throughout your instructions:

- Plain language that avoids unnecessary big words, passive sentences, and buried verbs
- Sentences that stress the actions the user takes
- Addressing the reader as "you"
- Conversational language that is addressed to a live member of the audience
- Listing actions within steps in the order in which the user will perform them

    ☐ Sentences that include no more than two steps or relationships that readers must keep in mind

    ☐ Brief explanations for technical terms the first time you use them

Your additional comments:

GRAPHICS

Check the following:

    ☐ Diagrams or photographs inserted where needed

    ☐ Illustrations show what readers will see when they perform the task

    ☐ Text supplements the graphics

    ☐ Graphics placed where users can easily locate them

    ☐ Graphics labelled and titled

Your additional comments:

DOCUMENT DESIGN

Check for the following and locate the places that still need editing:

    ☐ Ample white space

    ☐ Styled text that shows readers how you've organized the materials

    ☐ Bold

    ☐ Italics

    ☐ Colour

    ☐ Special fonts

    ☐ Informative headings

Your additional comments:

USABILITY TESTING

Ensure that your testing follows these guidelines:

    ☐ Draw testers from the same pool as your potential users.

    ☐ Use at least three qualified testers.

    ☐ Maintain appropriate distance from your testers.

Give assurances to your testers that you are looking for an honest opinion.

Intervene only to respond to explicit requests or to prevent disaster.

Do not dispute testers' opinions.

Keep thorough records and record all relevant issues in the same way for all testers.

Elicit additional comments from testers.

Debrief users, asking them to list both the strengths and weaknesses.

Your additional comments:

FINAL DRAFT PREPARATION

Check for:

Spelling errors

Missing or extra words

Grammatical errors

Manuscript conventions

Your additional comments:

EXERCISES

Work in groups of three or four to do the following exercises.

Exercise 1

a. Analyze a particularly weak set of instructions (for example, for something you bought) and highlight the areas that need revising.

b. Analyze a particularly strong set of instructions (for example, for something you bought) and highlight the areas that were particularly helpful.

Exercise 2

Analyze and revise these instructions:

graphic
add internal steps
feel free to add information
problems involve

a.   Assembly of The Rear Wheel of a Bicycle

Hold it up so that it is taught and grab the chain. Then holding chain and by sliding into the slot on the stays, attach the rear wheel. Then drop chain onto teeth of rear sprocket. Put some oil on bolt and slide bolt into center of wheel, while aligning the bolt with the mark you had previously made on the slot. Then tighten bolt. You may have to re-bolt. Notice that where the rear wheel is bolted in this slot determines how centered the wheel is when it spins. You want to bolt the wheel so that it rotates freely, not rubbing against either the frame of the bike nor the brakes. Re-bolt if necessary. There may also be a wobble in the wheel but this may be due to the wheel itself. If the wheel wobbles more than quite a bit, take it to a bike mechanic. It could possibly be dangerous.

b.   Draining Engine Oil

- TURN THE OIL FILLER CAP AND REMOVE.

  THE OIL FILTER CAP IS THE BLACK ONE ON

  THE ENGINE MARKED "OIL".

- USE A SOCKET WRENCH TO TURN THE DRAIN PLUG. TO REMOVE IT POSITION SELF BENEATH VEHICLE, LAYING ON YOUR BACK.

  THE ENGINE AND ENGINE OIL MAY BE HOT ESPECIALLY IF THE CAR HAS BE ON FOR A LONG TIME. SO BE CAREFUL WHEN TOUCHING OR HANDLING PARTS OF THE CAR.

Exercise 3

Perform an audience analysis of one or more of the following:

a.   Members of your class (to teach them how to change a flat tire)

b.   Your parents or grandparents (to teach them how to connect a computer, monitor, printer, and modem)

c.   A kindergarten class (to teach them how to operate a CD player)

d.   A Grade 6 class (to teach them how to play a video game of your choosing)

Exercise 4

Do a task analysis for one or more of the following topics. Use a flow chart to represent an expert's actions. When you're finished, list the necessary skills readers must have before starting, the materials they need, and any special terms they should know.

a.   Getting from where you are now to the nearest restaurant

b.   Making a collect call from Halifax, Nova Scotia to Winnipeg, Manitoba

c.   Setting a VCR to record a one-hour program at 2:00 AM next Tuesday and a thirty-minute program tonight at 6:00 PM

d.   Copying a file from a hard drive to a floppy disk

e.   Connecting to the Internet from home

f.   Putting gas into your car's tank at a self-service station or changing the oil

Exercise 5

Using the task analyses from Exercise 4, issue warnings and cautions for places where users could either hurt themselves or make mistakes.

CHAPTER

Writing Proposals

What This Chapter Covers

Ideas
Asking for Resources
Why People Write Proposals
Internal or External
Solicited or Unsolicited
A Sample Request for Proposals
Proposals and Persuasion
      Who Will Read Your Proposal?
      Showing a Problem Exists
      Showing the Problem Is Worth Solving
      Showing You Can Help
      How Will You Do What You Are Proposing?
      How Will You Measure Effectiveness?
The Formal Components of Your Proposal

Actions
Step 1: Introduce Yourself and the Problem
Step 2: Describe the Problem
Step 3: Say What Should Be Versus What Is
Step 4: Say How Your Technical Plan Will Solve the Problem
Step 5: Write a Management Plan That Says Who and When
Step 6: Prepare the Budget
Step 7: Create an Appendix
Step 8: Write the Executive Summary
Step 9: Write the Covering Letter
Step 10: Prepare a Table of Contents
Step 11: Create the Title Page
Step 12: Design the Document
Step 13: Review and Revise
Step 14: Copy-Edit
Step 15: Deliver the Proposal

Chapter Summary

Checklists

Exercises

Learning Objectives

At the end of this chapter, you will be able to explain:

- How a proposal must persuade its reader to provide resources
- Why people write proposals
- What are the various types of proposals
- What is a formal request for proposals
- Who are the different audiences for the same proposal and why you must shape your message for them
- Why you need to measure the outcomes of your proposed solution
- How you must demonstrate that a problem exists, that it is worth solving, and that you are the one to provide its solution
- What are the formal components of a proposal

At the end of this chapter, you will be able to write and test a proposal that includes:

- A description and analysis of the problem you are considering
- A statement of what is and what ought to be
- A technical plan that states how you will solve the problem
- A management plan that states what tasks will be carried out when and by whom
- A budget that shows the costs incurred to solve the problem
- Other components such as an appendix, an executive summary, a covering letter, and a title page

I·D·E·A·S

Asking for Resources

It's easy to know if a proposal works; you either get the money or you don't.

Proposals must be the most persuasive of documents. In them, you try to convince the reader to give you resources, in exchange for which you will solve a problem. This is a much more difficult task, obviously, than merely wanting the reader to tacitly agree with you—for example, that the world needs cleaner air or that technology displaces people. A proposal fails when it doesn't result in the reader actively engaging the writer to do something.

Proposals should always focus on a problem the reader wants solved, that is, a situation where there is a clear discrepancy between *what is* and *what should be*. Many times, a potential client will already know the problem intimately and put out a general call for suggestions to solve it. Other times, clients will have only a vague sense of the problem, and you will need to help them define it.

But it is not enough merely to state the problem: you must also convince the reader that you have the knowledge and the means to solve it—and at a price that makes sense.

Usually, your proposal will compete against others. That means you must convince your client not only that you have good ideas but that they are better than anyone else's. Think of a proposal as a sales tool in which you try to convince the reader to buy your product, in this case, you and your ideas.

Proposals, therefore, call upon the full range of tools and techniques that professional writers must have. Research and planning must be sound, organization and argument must be clear, and presentation must be impeccable. This chapter discusses those tools and techniques.

Why People Write Proposals

Organizations continually face problems. At times, they solicit help by explicitly issuing a request for proposals (RFP), which invites interested parties to suggest solutions. Other times, however, proposals are unsolicited and come from someone offering to solve problems whose full extent the organization may not have recognized. In all cases, a proposal can offer products, services, advice, or some combination of the three. Here are some common reasons people write proposals:

Products must be bought. What organizations use must be periodically upgraded. For example, local computer networks may no longer be fast enough to handle current traffic. Manufacturing equipment may become outdated or break down too often. A university's new teaching building may require audiovisual equipment.

A policy no longer works. Organizations may sometimes falter because of a changing environment. A company's range of products, for example, may no longer keep up in the marketplace. A service organization's way of dealing with minorities may no longer fit social realities. A software company may no longer be able to give free technical support.

A policy needs incremental improvement. Very often change can be simple and cheap instead of dramatic and expensive. For example, decreasing the size and weight of paper used for mass mailings will reduce costs without compromising the effectiveness of the message. Rearranging the equipment in a restaurant kitchen will decrease the number of people getting in each other's way. Using recycled photocopier cartridges rather than new ones will save money.

Research funds have to be secured. Government and private groups often have money available to researchers. For example, a social agency might want to know how to improve the diet of the poor. A software company might want to know how its product could be used in primary schools. Or a government department charged with encouraging basic research might fund any innovative project in its area.

In all these instances, an organization becomes aware that something is not as it should be. That awareness can come from individuals within the organization, from outside consultants, or from an organization systematically monitoring its operations. When problems become sufficiently acute, organizations seek solutions and invite proposals.

Internal or External

Proposals may come from inside or outside an organization. Suppose you're working for a small-town newspaper whose printing schedule is often delayed because last-minute advertisements need to be inserted. If you drew your supervisor's attention to the problem, you might get permission to go ahead and prepare a proposal to solve the problem.

The format of an internal proposal can be simply a memo. More extensive internal proposals—asking for more extensive resources—may need to be as fully detailed as external ones. The advantage you have writing an internal proposal is that you share a context with your reader—you don't have to learn or explain as much. The possibilities for internal proposals are, of course, as varied as the problems within organizations.

External proposals come from outside an organization. If a company lacks the necessary expertise or materials to solve a problem from within, it must look elsewhere. A government agency, for example, may need training for its staff. A manufacturer may need to improve its quality control. A small office may need a new and faster printer.

Solicited or Unsolicited

In addition to coming from inside or outside an organization, proposals can be solicited or unsolicited. Solicited proposals, as we've said, result from a request for proposals. Organizations often do this publicly, for example, through ads in newspapers or trade journals. They may also do it privately, seeking out companies they have dealt with before or know by reputation. Unsolicited proposals may come from an outsider who recognizes an organization's problem and hence an opportunity to win business.

In all cases, the organization will adjudicate the proposals it receives, looking for the one that makes the most sense in terms of how the company operates and what it can afford. That adjudication may be relatively informal (especially if the requested resources aren't big) or done quite rigorously (especially when public money is spent). Organizations are under no obligation to accept any particular proposal regardless of who wrote it or how it came through the door.

A Sample Request For Proposals

Although names have been changed, the request for proposals in Figure 8.1 originates with a real medium-sized municipality.

If you wished to respond to this request for proposals, you'd face a number of difficulties: Although the RFP gives some information, it doesn't provide everything you need, and you would have to call the Town Manager. That's a critical step because your proposal must show that it understands Happy Vale's situation. For example, the municipality's RFP tells you the following:

- The town doesn't have a particular service in mind—"golf services" could mean a better driving range, practice greens, lessons, minigolf, or something else entirely.
- There is already a restaurant and a pro shop, so proposals for them won't have much chance.
- Whatever service is proposed must satisfy existing customers and bring in new ones.
- The course is open eight months a year, and that makes it difficult or impossible to keep staff year-round.

The Municipality of Happy Vale
666 Blissful Road
Happy Vale, British Columbia V5V 5V5

Request for Proposals
Reference #2000-24
Business Opportunity
Pleasant Ridge Golf Course

The Municipality wishes to enter a business arrangement with an interested party to develop and operate golf services in the area currently established as the driving range at the Pleasant Ridge Golf Course at 3400 Smiley Avenue. These services must be designed to support existing customers who frequent the golf course and/or generate new interest from the public or other users.

The golf course has 18 holes and operates eight months a year. On average, there are 90,000 rounds of golf per annum. The course is located in a residential area on the border of a neighbouring municipality and is within a short driving distance of most areas of the Metro region. A new clubhouse was opened in 1997 with full restaurant services and pro shop.

Interested parties may contact the Town Manager (at 555-5555) for more details. The closing date for proposals will be Wednesday, September 30, 1999 at 3:00 PM.

Edward L. Smith
Town Manager

Figure 8.1
A request for proposals

A number of questions are left answered. How many different persons, for instance, play those 90,000 rounds? Who are they? What do they think about the current services? How open are they to change? What kind of service would keep them and attract new customers, given the location? You can no doubt think of other questions.

Before you could write a proposal, therefore, you would have to spend some time learning about the specific context of Happy Vale. That requires an investment that might not pay off. However, a proposal has a better chance if it demonstrates a tailor-made solution, not a one-size-fits-all proposition.

Proposals and Persuasion

The object of a proposal is to convince real people to give you resources—time, money, or materials. That requires that your proposal must be not only compelling on its own terms but better than its competitors. Persuading your reader of that, however, does not mean including hyperbole or inflated promises. Instead, you work towards a reasoned and professional presentation that shows that you both grasp the client's problem and can solve it. As with other kinds of professional writing, the place to start is with your audience.

Who Will Read Your Proposal?

Depending on the size of the organization and the significance of the problem, you'll likely have two kinds of readers:

Decision makers: This is, of course, your main audience. Expect them to be knowledgeable and skeptical; they will, after all, be paying the bills. Assume that they'll instantly recognize a factual error and recoil from exaggeration; they will see each lapse as a mark against your credibility. Every unnecessary word will annoy them. In short, you have to assure them at every turn that that you care about the details and go the last step. Why should they give resources to someone who didn't?

Advisors: The people who make final decisions usually depend on others for advice. Some will be gatekeepers who will read all proposals to check that there is a basic fit with the company's needs. Technical advisors will verify the expertise you claim. Advisors may read only portions of your proposal or, at least, read only some portions closely. Those sections, however, will get careful scrutiny. Advisors, after all, know how much their own careers depend on providing sound advice.

You should, therefore, describe your audience to yourself before you do much writing. Can you learn who will read your proposal? Their qualifications and biases? What they already know and what they want to know? The better you describe your audience, the better you can shape your message to appeal to them.

Knowing your audience prepares you to focus on how to present content—specifically, these key points:

- A problem exists.
- It is serious enough to warrant seeking a solution.
- You can help.

Let's look at these issues in more detail.

Showing a Problem Exists

That a problem exists may seem obvious, especially if the client has already said so. In many cases, however, clients have only a general sense that things are not working as they should.

Your proposal, therefore, must give concrete examples of the client's problem, using your own words to demonstrate that you really have thought about it. Simply repeating an RFP suggests a quick and dirty, cut-and-paste job. Your own words best demonstrate that you know the company and how it functions.

You have several potential sources for concrete examples:

The request for proposals: The document that the company produces includes the company's own sense of itself and what it considers important. These must always be your starting and ending points. However, the RFP generally isn't enough. For example, the Pleasant Ridge RFP says what services are available, how many rounds of are played, and so on. But, as we've also seen, it doesn't give you everything. For that, you need to talk directly to people.

The people in charge: An organization's managers can tell you what they didn't include in the RPF. Moreover, getting to know them provides invaluable information about their preferences, enabling you to better shape your message for them.

The people on the ground: Yogi Berra once noted that you could see a lot just by looking. If you also talk to the people who live with the problem every day, you're likely to have no trouble finding concrete examples to include in your proposal. (Indeed, if they can't give you examples, there may not actually be a problem.) For instance, the staff at Pleasant Ridge Golf Course—groundskeepers, golf pros, office staff—will know much that official documents don't mention.

The literature: A company's own reports, the reports of its competition, and the trade or professional journals can also help. The company may have previously tried solving the problem. Trade journals may offer anecdotes about similar problems. Suppliers' brochures may give you ideas too. From a persuasive point of view, citing the literature demonstrates your credentials as a knowledgeable professional.

To repeat, the purpose of gathering concrete information before you start writing is so that you don't produce a one-size-fits-all solution. If you're going to persuade, you'll need examples that illustrate the specifics of the client's problem. A proposal that does not continually refer to the client's context has little chance.

Listening to people and reading literature takes time, however, and that will cost you money you may not recover. (You have to be sure that there is a potential payback for the time you spend.) However, once you've decided to write a proposal, you will have a real advantage over your competition if you show that you genuinely know your potential customer.

WORKING SMARTER

Research Using the Web

The World Wide Web complements the research you do in a library but does not replace it. The Web is excellent when you need to find current information, especially from business, the professions, and the news media. Many journals also now publish both Web and print versions. Various professions—like computer science—publish almost exclusively on the Web. For books and other kinds of information, however, the traditional library remains important.

Finding Material on the Web

Unless you already know which Web publications likely have the information you need, you'll have to use a search engine. Although there is some overlap, search engines results fall into three basic types:

A list of sites: Search engines like Yahoo or Excite return a list of sites that their editors have visited and categorized. This is particularly helpful for preliminary research.

A list of pages: Search engines like AltaVista or Northern Lights return a list of specific pages that contain the terms you looked for. You need to have a pretty good idea of what you want so you can supply a narrow list of terms to look for. Otherwise, you'll receive an overwhelming number of irrelevant pages.

A list of results from several search engines: Metasearch engines like MetaCrawler and AskJeeves return the results from several other search engines, saving you the trouble of visiting each one yourself. This is especially helpful when the information you need may be classified and described in diverse ways. Because the various search engines have different ways of finding information, each one may find some pages and overlook others. Using a metasearch increases your chances of locating most of the relevant URLs.

Checking the Credentials of Web Authors

Just because a document gets into print doesn't mean it's reliable. That's especially true on the Web, where people can easily post whatever they want. Before you use Web-based information, therefore, you have to evaluate it. For example:

- What are the writer's credentials? Is the writer a recognized authority? What is the writer's affiliation (for example, with a company, a university, a professional association)? Is the writer known for peculiar ideas or a political, economic, or social bias?

- Who is the audience for the information? Professionals in a field? Interested amateurs? General readers? People with a political, economic, or social bias?
- Whose imprint is on the page? Is the organization reputable? Does the organization have a political, economic, or social bias? Is other information on the same site reliable?
- Does the page link to other pages that are themselves trustworthy?
- How current is the information? Can you determine when it was created and/or updated?
- Does the information follow accepted standards for using information from other sources? Does it give credit where credit is due or otherwise respect copyright?

This is not to imply that you should dismiss writing not done by famous authorities and put out by famous publishers. But the credibility of the details of publication usually indicates the reliability of the information.

Copying Information From the Web

As with other electronic publications, it's convenient to copy material from a Web page and paste it into your document. There are a several ways to do this, depending on how much information you require:

Do a regular cut-and-paste. This works best when you need a short piece of text.

Save the Web page as text. This works best if you intend eventually pasting it into a word processing document. You will need to remove extra spaces, change the fonts, etc. to match your own document. Typically, you copy an entire page for your own reference in the early part of your research when you're unsure how much you'll need.

Save the Web page as "Source" (that is, as an HTML file). This works best if you intend to paste the material directly into a Web page. Again, you would do this in the early part of your research when you're unsure how much you need. Note that graphics on a Web page must be saved one by one. If you want them to display, you'll have to change the references in the HTML code.

Drag and drop information. This works best when you're copying a URL or a small amount of text.

Copyright

You may quote parts of a Web page, as long as you cite it properly. The same copyright rules apply to Web-based material as to print; these rules cover graphics, sounds, and animations as well as text. You must give credit where credit is due. Appendix II provides more information about citing your sources.

Very often, however, the page you're citing will itself not have respected copyright. That does not exempt you from doing so. You must get written permission to use intellectual property of any kind. it. In some instances, you will have to pay a fee. If you can't reach a legitimate understanding with the owner of the copyright, don't publish the material; provide a link to it on your Web page instead. These caveats do not apply when you are citing work to make an argument.

Citation Format

Several professional associations like the Modern Language Association (MLA), the American Psychological Association (APA), and the International Organization for Standardization (ISO) maintain Web sites about how to cite Web sources. As with print, which style you choose depends on the document you're citing and for whom you're writing.

In general, however, you will need the usual information about the author, the title, the year of publication, and so forth. In addition, you'll need the URL, that is, the place on the Web where your reader can see the document. The URL should be enclosed in a pair of angle brackets like this:

<http://maplesquare.com>

Any closing punctuation should come after the second angle bracket so that a reader won't confuse it with ending of the URL.

Since URLs can be long and tricky to type, the best way to copy them is from the site itself. Once the page is displayed, copy its URL directly from your browser's Location field and then paste it into your citation.

Alternately, you can do this:

1. Go to a site that links to the page you want
2. Hold down your mouse button until the browser pops up a menu
3. Select the Copy URL option
4. Paste it into your citation.

Before using this method, however, verify the link by trying it yourself with your browser.

Showing the Problem Is Worth Solving

Not every problem is worth solving. Therefore, your proposal must show that what you identify affects the organization seriously enough to warrant its attention. Again, you must provide concrete instances of how serious a problem is and for whom. Merely listing general reasons won't convince; you need specifics.

For example, you can't just assert that money, time, or goodwill is being lost; you have to say how much, naming names and providing numbers. Here are three examples of this:

- Membership in the Pleasant Ridge Golf Club is down 40% in the last year.
- More than half of customers surveyed indicate that many staff members seem uninterested in helping.
- Spot testing of customer requests for help shows an average waiting time of 20 minutes (as opposed to our main competitor's 5 minutes).

The more you can measure, the more convincing your case will be. When figures aren't available, you'll need to estimate them. Base your estimates on reasonable assumptions and make those assumptions clear so you don't seem to be inventing facts.

Showing You Can Help

From a purely selfish perspective, your next persuasive task is convincing readers that you—and only you—offer the best solution. You have to do that both explicitly and implicitly. You must be clear about what you will do and about your qualifications to do it—your experience and professional credentials. Implicitly, what establishes you as the right person is your grasp of the client's needs and the quality of your presentation.

How Will You Do What You Are Proposing?

In addition to solving a problem or otherwise meeting a need, your reader will also want to know how you will manage your solution, that is, how you will put your ideas into practice. You need to cover three main issues:

When will things be done? You must prepare a critical path or timeline, that is, a schedule that identifies each major event of your solution and the date by which it will be done. A critical path also tells readers how your plans dovetail with theirs. In addition, it allows the reader to assess both if you have thought of everything and if you've allotted it a realistic amount of time.

Who will do what? You must also list the credentials of those who will carry out each task; that assures your reader that you and your associates have a reasonable expectation of success. You need to strike a balance between hype and modesty since too much of either will doom your proposal.

How much will it cost? The budget, of course, is essential. You have to account for the money the client will spend. Again, your numbers must demonstrate your credibility.

How Will You Measure Effectiveness?

Your readers also will want to know how you will ensure quality. An RFP often will be explicit about how the organization will evaluate the implementation of a proposal, and you must echo that evaluation. With unsolicited proposals, however, the onus is yours to explain how you will know when your solution works. It's important, therefore, to speak about how you will ensure quality. For example:

- If you're proposing a product, say how you will test that what gets delivered will meet specifications.
- If you're proposing a service, say how you will monitor how well the service helps its target group (for example, you will use written questionnaires or interviews).
- If you're proposing a study, say how you will ensure its validity (that is, that you measure what you say you measure) and reliability (that is, that your results don't vary from day to day).

Again, by showing how you will measure the effectiveness of your solution, you enhance your credibility and make your proposal more persuasive.

The Formal Components of Your Proposal

Proposal formats vary, but you must scrupulously follow any format described in the RFP. Indeed, many government agencies cannot even consider proposals that don't follow their prescribed formats. They are not being arbitrary but simply ensuring that what's important to them gets full coverage. Moreover, evaluating proposals is much easier when all follow the same format.

Obviously, when organizations don't ask for a specific format or when you submit an unsolicited proposal, you have more latitude. Regardless, your proposal should include the following items in this order:

- Covering letter
- Title page
- Executive summary
- Table of contents
- Problem discussion
- Technical plan
- Management plan
- Budget
- Appendices (as necessary)

The technical plan is the core of your proposal, the place where you get to the specifics of your solution. A text like this can't give you the expertise to solve a problem; it can tell you only about strategies for presenting your expertise.

As we'll see, you won't prepare these components in the order readers will see them. In what follows, we go step-by-step through their creation.

ACTIONS

This section takes you through the first draft of your proposal. As with the other documents this book deals with, a number of general techniques apply—Plain English, document design, graphics, and so on. They will be mentioned only in passing unless they have a special role to play in proposals. Please refer to the appropriate chapters in Part I for full discussions of these techniques.

The procedures in this section assume that you have already determined that you can deliver the expertise you promise and can also live with the fees you'll charge. The focus here is what you put down on paper once you have decided to submit a proposal.

Step 1: Introduce Yourself and the Problem

Your goal in the introduction is to keep readers reading. That's because readers who have several proposals in front of them want to know immediately who you are and if your proposal addresses their problem. Briefly do three things:

Demonstrate that you've grasped the essence of your reader's problem. State it as succinctly as you can. Rephrase rather than merely repeat the RPF or what you've learned elsewhere. For example: "The driving range at Pleasant Ridge Golf Club requires rethinking if it is to contribute to the company's profitability."

Present your qualifications. Readers don't want to waste time reading a proposal from someone without the background to do what's necessary. For example: "I am now working on my degree in business and have worked as an assistant manager at the Far Ridge Golf Club's pro shop in Arnprior, Ontario."

State what you will deliver. Indicate whether your solution is a product, advice, service, or some combination of the three. For example: "I will deliver a detailed business plan for a combination minigolf and child-care service."

In some instances, you may want to add a note that the information you include in the proposal is proprietary—that is, it belongs to you and you alone. You ask readers to keep your proposal confidential. Keep your tone neutral, of course, not confrontational. You simply are telling the reader that you have much invested and must protect your intellectual property.

Step 2: Describe the Problem

Whether the proposal is solicited or unsolicited, external or internal, start by describing and analyzing the problem. Do not offer a generic discussion; make sure that all your examples are drawn from the client's world so that you demonstrate how well you are tailoring your work to his or her needs. For example:

- Pleasant Ridge's driving range has lost 30% of its customers in the past year.
- Customer service reports complaints from 20% of customers.
- Maintenance equipment no longer meets industry standards for safety.

How much you write here depends on how much context you share with the reader. When you draft, it's better to err on the side of including too much detail rather than too little; you can always remove unnecessary information. The best test is to try out the proposal with a colleague, as we'll see later.

Next, offer *three* concrete examples of the problem, saying for whom it is a problem and its severity. (Chapter 1 discusses why you should give three examples.) Use some kind of measurement such as hours, customers, or revenue lost. For example:

- The driving range should bring customers to the restaurant and to the pro shop, but both have seen revenues drop by 12% in the past year.
- Staff who work at the driving range also work in other parts of the club; without sufficient business at the range, 20% of personnel may have to be laid off.
- In the past ten years, the driving range has contributed 19% of the course's profits; in the last year, it produced a 2% loss.

Your goal is to persuade readers that you are aware of the specifics of the organization.

Step 3: Say What Should Be Versus What Is

Having established *what is*, turn your attention to *what ought to be*. Again, provide three concrete examples of what the organization would be like if the problem were solved. Be specific about who benefits. For example:

- Driving range staff would not have to be laid off, thereby reducing difficulties in hiring and training when more staff is needed. Morale would improve, making it easier for managers to get better performance from staff.
- Both the restaurant and the pro shop would have a larger pool of potential customers.
- Overall profitability would improve.

Once more, your goal is to establish that yours is a solution tailored for this organization and no other.

Step 4: Say How Your Technical Plan Will Solve the Problem

Having established that you have a good sense of the problem, you must describe how you will solve it. For that, you need a technical plan that says what you'll do and how you'll do it.

Say what you'll do: Offer your solution, again in specific terms. If a discussion becomes too technical for general readers, move those parts to an appendix. The technical plan is, as we've said, the heart of your proposal, and only you can produce it. But to present it effectively, do the following:

* Describe in detail your deliverables, that is, what services or products you'll supply.
* State why your deliverables will solve the problem.
* Outline other possible solutions and why the one you've chosen is best. Think of what your competitors may offer and say why their solutions won't work as well. (Don't exaggerate, of course.)
* Anticipate and address readers' objections and concerns.

Say how you'll do it: Outline what you will actually do. For example:

* If you are proposing purchasing a product, specify the make and model.
* If you are proposing a service, describe what particular tasks you'll perform.
* If you are proposing a study, say to whom you'll speak, the kinds of questions you'll ask, and what you'll look for at a site.

Say how you'll evaluate your work: Describe the methods you will use to ensure your solution meets the criteria the RFP gives (or, for an unsolicited proposal, the criteria you have determined for the client). *Be sure to show that you'll apply the client's criteria and no others.* Again, you wish to demonstrate your solution is designed for this particular client.

Step 5: Write a Management Plan That Says Who and When

A management plan demonstrates not only that you have a solution but that it is workable in terms of time and personnel. Include the following:

The names and qualifications of who will carry out the work: Your reader must know what makes you (or your group) uniquely suited to solve the problem. Expand, therefore, the brief statement in your introduction about your qualifications. State the facts honestly and fairly, avoiding either hypcrbole ur undue modesty. Make sure that whatever qualifications you mention are relevant to the task at hand. List academic, business, or professional credentials and experience. Provide references (with names and contact information), cite your previous relevant work, and offer to forward samples of past work (if that won't compromise a previous client's privacy).

A critical path: Your reader needs to know when you will do what you propose. Provide a list that shows each essential milestone in your solution and the date by which you will have it complete. Say who will perform each task. For example:

July 10: Remove present LAN (Thomas, Jones)
July 12: Redo wiring (Quest Electric)
July 13: Uncrate and install new computers (Thomas, Jones)
July 14: Install software (Jones)
July 15: Test system (Jones)

Step 6: Prepare the Budget Plan

Obviously, you have a better chance if your solution costs less than the competition's. However, proposals don't always go to the lowest bidder. Your budget should include these items:

- People
- Equipment
- Other (travel, supplies, etc.)
- Contingency (generally ten percent)

The budget shows how you've determined the amount of money you're requesting and that you haven't just pulled an unreasonable number out of the air.

Step 7: Create an Appendix

Not every proposal needs an appendix. To decide if yours does, answer this question: *Is there important information that would distract most of my readers if I left it in the body of my proposal?* Only an expert can appreciate the fine points of how you'll do something; others might see only jargon.

As a tool to persuade, an appendix also acts as a calling card that shows decision makers your qualifications (even if they have to give it to an advisor to verify). But again, not every proposal needs one.

Step 8: Write the Executive Summary

Even though the executive summary appears near the start of your proposal, write it after you've completed work on everything else. That ensures it reflects what you've actually produced, rather than what you thought you would. Keep the summary brief; while there's no absolute right number of words, a single page or less works best. (The exception would be for a very long proposal.) Cover these issues:

- The problem
- Your solution
- The cost
- The benefits of approving this proposal
- The client's next step

The last item puts looks directly at the readers, asking them to decide whether your proposal warrants further discussion.

WORKING SMARTER

Using Your Word Processor to Write a Summary

Step 1: Create a New Document

Open both your proposal document and a new blank document (call it "Summary.doc" or something similar). Be sure you can go back and forth between them conveniently.

Step 2: Review What You've Written

Read through the proposal one more time; then enter the answers to these questions in the summary document:

- Who is your audience?
- What do they need to know?
- What technical details are unnecessary or need "translating"?

These items won't appear in the summary, but they help you refocus on whom you're writing for.

Step 3: Use the Headings

Copy all your informative headings from the proposal to the summary document.

Step 4: Summarize Paragraph by Paragraph

For each paragraph under a heading in the proposal, write one sentence in the summary document that states its main idea. To do this, look at the first and last sentences of the paragraph since these often contain the main idea. Include a detail or an example where your report supplies one.

Step 5: Connect Your Ideas

Define the relationships among ideas in your summary by putting a transitional word between each pair of sentences. This will test whether your summary is coherent (that is, about the same subject).

Transitional words include *first, second, however, consequently, moreover, furthermore, in addition*, and, of course, a great many others. Think of them as signals—links and arrows—that will point your reader in the right direction. (See Chapter 2 for more details.)

Step 6: Reduce the Length of Your Summary

Is your summary too long? For example, is it more than ten percent of the original? Summarize your summary if necessary. The final version should be less than one page.

Step 7: Field Test

Try out what you have so far on a typical member of your audience.

Step 8: Prepare the Final Version

Revise as necessary, field test again, and edit. Then copy the summary into the proposal.

Step 9: Write the Covering Letter

The covering letter (or letter of transmittal) is a separate document. It is the first thing your reader will see, so it has to make the strongest possible impression. Its purpose is to introduce the reader to the document you're sending.

People who read the covering letter might not read the full proposal but route it to someone else. To convince them to do so, prepare it carefully.

As with a summary, write a covering letter only after you've completed the proposal. Follow the standard letter format (see Chapter 6 on correspondence). Use a three-part structure:

- Provide the context to introduce the subject and purpose of the document. For example: "As we agreed, here is the my proposal for improving golf services at the Pleasant Ridge Golf Course."
- Provide a brief statement of one or two key points in the document such as the problem or your recommendations. For example: "The driving range at the golf course does not meet expectations because . . . "
- Provide a plan of action (the reader's next step) and a courteous closing: "Please call me if you have any questions about this proposal . . ."

Step 10: The Table of Contents

If the proposal has more than three or four sections, prepare a table of contents to make it easier for the reader to locate ideas. The reader should be able to glance at the contents and know where things are and how you've organized the document.

Step 11: Create the Title Page

After the covering letter, your title page is what a reader sees. That means it's part of the important first impression, read at the time when readers decide if what follows is likely to be worth their attention.

The title page needs four main items:

- The name of organization to whom the proposal is going
- The title of the proposal (and if you are responding to a RFP, the client's reference number)
- The date the proposal is due
- The name of the organization or person submitting the proposal

Everything on the title page focuses first on the client—the name of the organization, the proposal's reference number, and the due date. That sends an implicit message that your first concern is with the client, and not with yourself. Figure 8.2 (page 178) shows an example of a title page.

> The Municipality of Happy Vale
> 666 Blissful Road
> Happy Vale, British Columbia V5V 5V5
>
>
> Improving Profit at Pleasant Ridge Golf Course
> A Proposal
> Reference #2000-24
>
>
> September 21, 2000
>
> Submitted by: Horvath and Associates
> 1234 Platitude Way
> Daviesville, Ontario
> M5M 5M5
>
> Phone: (777) 555-1515
> Fax: (777) 555-5151
> horvath@isp.com

Figure 8.2
Proposal title page

Step 12: Design the Document:

Prepare the final document using the ideas discussed in Chapter 5.

Step 13: Review and Revise

Use the checklists in the next section to test the proposal's effectiveness. The best judge of a proposal's effectiveness is, of course, the person who will make the ultimate decision. You cannot, unfortunately, try out your proposal there, so you must have someone else respond to the document.

Have a colleague play the role of your touchstone reader, that is, the person who will decide whether or not to accept your proposal. Provide your colleague with as much background as you can about this person. Ask for a critical reading, one that will raise reasonable objections or questions. Revise the proposal so that you deal with all legitimate criticisms.

The amount of rewriting and testing you do, of course, depends on how much time you can invest in the proposal. But substantial rewriting and testing are crucial if you are to locate and fix problems before your readers find them.

Step 14: Copy-Edit

When you're satisfied with your proposal's content, structure, and design, you're ready to produce the version the client sees. Here, copy-editing is especially important: You are trying to establish your credibility as someone who not only is technically competent to solve the problem but will painstakingly look after every detail.

In particular, double-check how you've spelled names; your word processor will only flag them as possible errors. Have a colleague look over the document. Refer to Appendix I for details on fixing common writing mistakes.

Step 15: Deliver the Proposal

Finally, send out the document, making sure it's on time. Many organizations—especially government ones—simply cannot consider late proposals.

CHAPTER SUMMARY

A proposal is a document that must persuade its reader to give you resources in exchange for which you will solve a problem. Proposals focus on a specific difficulty the reader wants resolved, that is, a situation where there is a clear discrepancy between *what is* and *what should be*. You must not only demonstrate that a problem exists: You must also show that you have the expertise to solve it.

A proposal can respond to any of the myriad difficulties an organization may face. Proposals can come unsolicited or as a reply to a formal request. Organizations frequently don't fully articulate the problem they want solved, so you must research and present a statement that shows in concrete terms the current and desired state of affairs. You must also show that a solution is not only possible but cost-effective.

A proposal will be read by decision-makers and sometimes by their advisors. It is critical for you to know as much as you can about the audience for whom you're writing—its needs, its expertise, and its biases. The better you understand your readers, the better you can shape your messages to persuade them.

The key components of a proposal are:

- A description of the problem and its severity
- A technical plan that details what you or your colleagues will do
- A management plan that shows what will be done when and by whom
- A budget
- Supplementary materials such as appendices, summary, title page, and covering letter

Like other professional documents, a proposal must be thoroughly tested to ensure it is both complete and persuasive. Either you or a colleague must play the role of the eventual decision-maker, anticipating and responding to any weakness that would damage your chances of success.

CHECKLISTS

Does the problem statement:

Include a three-sentence summary of the problem

Give at least three specific and concrete examples of the problem

Say for whom and when there is a problem

Outline the severity of this problem, including some kind of measurement like dollars or time lost

Show both what is and what should be

Show that solving the problem will produce a genuine benefit

Does the technical plan:

Describe the methodology you will follow to investigate or solve the problem (for example, interviews, literature review, site visits, constructing or modifying something)

Say which specific questions you have framed and of whom you will ask them

Indicate where you may find solutions to questions and problems

List what have you already looked at on site and what you still have to look for

Describe the site

Anticipate and counter potential problems or objections to your plan

Offer other possible solutions with reasons why they are not as good as what you propose

Show how you will test your results or otherwise ensure quality control

Does the management statement describe:

What tasks will be done

When they will be started and completed

Who will perform each task

What qualifications these people will have

Does the budget include costs for:

Materials or special equipment

Time

Travel

Contingencies

Does the summary:

Run less than 10 percent of the proposal's length

State the problem in one or two sentences

State the proposed solution in about three sentences

Say how much the project will cost

List the benefits of approving this proposal

Does the covering letter:

Provide a context to introduce the subject and purpose of the document

Summarize one or two key points in the document

Include a plan of action (the reader's next step) and a courteous closing

Follow the standard business letter format

Is the final draft:

Thoroughly copy-edited

Complete

Your additional comments:

EXERCISES

Working in groups of three or four, write notes towards a proposal—not a full version—for each exercise below. Include the following:

a. A statement that shows that you've grasped the essence of the problem, stating it as succinctly as you can.
b. Your qualifications
c. Your deliverables
d. A statement of what should be versus what is
e. A technical plan saying what you'll do, why it's best, and how you'll carry out your tasks
f. A management plan stating what will be done when and by whom
g. A budget outlining the costs to produce your deliverables
h. An appendix listing topics too technical or too distracting to include in the body of the proposal
i. A covering letter to your primary reader

Use your group's collective experience to provide the necessary information. You may have to invent some things but make sure they're plausible.

Exercise 1

Your municipal government has placed the following advertisement in the local newspaper:

Isn't it time to clean up?

Groups or non-profit organizations considering cleaning up an area in their neighborhoods should propose their projects to the Mayor's Office for Environmental Action. The Community Clean-Up Fund makes up to $2500 available for projects which 1) achieve visible environmental benefits and also 2) encourage environmentally responsible behavior.

While most successful grants will be to clean-up garbage and recyclables on public lands or waterways, the Office for Environmental Action will consider other kinds of proposals that meet the above criteria.

The Office for Environmental Action includes the mayor (or his delegate), a representative from the municipality's Planning Office, and Councilor Laura Winer.

Exercise 2

The family of a recently deceased alumnus wants to honour his memory by providing $100,000 for a project that will benefit campus life. A committee is formed which issues the following statement:

> The Committee to Honour the Memory of the late Quigley L. Festoon will provide up to $100,000 for a project that will enhance the quality of student life on this campus. The Committee invites proposals from interested student groups. The Committee wants to know that:
>
> a) a real problem exists that affects many students
>
> b) you know how to solve it
>
> A three-person panel will judge proposals: the Dean of Engineering, the president of the Student Association, and a member of the late Quigley L. Festoon's family.

Exercise 3

You are a graduate of a business-writing course who believes that most students need to workshop their reports, that is, test ideas before formally presenting them for grades. You are proposing a business-writer's hotline that will vet work-in-progress and answer questions—everything from structure and logic to the details of grammar and mechanics.

It won't be, you make clear, any kind of shady operation to write essays for students looking to plagiarize. You also wish to stress that although the hotline would start with School of Business students, it could in time become a money-making venture serving the whole of the university and even the city's small-business sector.

Write your proposal for the Dean of the Business School.

CHAPTER

9

Reports

What This Chapter Covers

Ideas

Why Reports Are Important
Types of Common Reports
Description or Analysis?
A Report's Audience
Finding Your Report's Topic
Describing the Problem
Saying What Should Be Versus What Is
The Three-Part Structure
The Report Format

Actions

Step 1: Gather Your Data
Step 2: Prepare a Preliminary Draft
Step 3: Field Test for Logic and Argument
Step 4: Field Test for Structure
Step 5: Prepare the Summary
Step 6: Prepare the Appendix
Step 7: Prepare the Covering Letter
Step 8: Design the Document
Step 9: Prepare the Title Page
Step 10: Prepare the Final Draft
Step 11: Prepare the Table of Contents
Step 12: Submit the Report

Chapter Summary

Checklists

Exercises

| **Learning Objectives** | **At the end of this chapter, you will be able to explain:** |

- The importance of reports
- Types of common reports
- Ways in which reports describe and analyze
- Reasons for analyzing your audience
- Development and organization of your report in terms of a problem, its severity, and its solution
- Possible formats and components of a report

At the end of this chapter you will be able to write a report by:

- Gathering data
- Preparing a preliminary version of your report
- Field-testing for logic and structure and then revising accordingly
- Preparing the summary, appendix, covering letter, title page, and table of contents
- Designing the document
- Editing the final draft
- Field testing the final version and revising accordingly

Why Reports Are Important

Reports are at the centre of professional writing because they are the chief way organizations say what they are and what they want to become. A report can investigate, analyze, inform, or recommend—or it can do all of these things. In short, a report can describe anything an organization does.

Reports come in a range of sizes and formats, from the one-person, one-paragraph memo to work hundreds of pages long, done by many authors. What a report says, of course, is its most important feature; however, how it presents its content is also critical. A report must demonstrate the writer's credibility on every page. If that credibility is missing, then the content might be ignored, regardless of its value. Writers of reports, therefore, have to think about presentation as well as substance.

Electronic technology has revolutionized report writing. New tools help writers brainstorm and plan. Others help them gather and verify information. Still others make it possible for reports to appear as if professionally published. And, of course, word processing has changed forever how writers compose and revise.

That same electronic technology has also made the process of writing reports far more efficient, both for writers working alone and for those working with a group. This chapter focuses on techniques for developing a report's content; in passing, it also discusses electronic production. The chapters in Part I of this text discuss in detail some important issues for writing reports—for example, organization, graphics, and document design. We will deal with those issues here only when they have a special bearing on report writing.

A Note on Sample Reports: Looking at reports other people have prepared can be very helpful. However, given that there is no single standard for report content or format, it would be misleading to include just one or two in this text as models. It's also impractical to include a sufficiently large number to convey the range of possibilities. You're invited, therefore, to visit the *Ideas Into Action* Web site at **<www.pearsoned.ca/keller/>**. There you'll find a variety of reports from business, government, and industry, as well as some done by students as part of their coursework.

Types of Common Reports

Although reports can do many things, they generally fall into one of several major categories:

Periodic: A periodic report keeps an organization up-to-date on the activities of its various units. Typically, decision makers request such reports in order to monitor the current performance of an organization relative to its goals. For example:

- A quarterly financial report tells how much money comes in, how much goes out, and how much is left over.
- A monthly marketing report describes what was sold to whom and what can be sold in the future.
- An annual report provides shareholders with an overall sense of an organization's strengths and weaknesses over a single year.

Investigative: An investigative report explores a particular circumstance in order to discover and explain what is not well understood. For example:

- A government agency finds out why children under its protection are not being properly cared for.
- A brokerage learns how a junior trader overextended the company through currency speculation.
- A shareholders' committee learns if company executives unduly benefit from unspecified perquisites.

Feasibility: A feasibility report looks at the risks and benefits of undertaking various actions. For example:

- An engineering firm determines if a bridge can be built over a particular point on a fast-moving river.
- A community organization explores the possibility of a home-visiting program for the elderly.
- A corporation examines the implications of taking over a competitor.

Progress: A progress report details how a project is going—what has been done, what remains to do, and what problems must be overcome. For example:

- Research grant recipients say if they have maintained the schedule that they had promised.
- A programmer tells a product manager about how much and what type of computer code has been written during the past month.
- A construction company informs its client how much of a building has been finished.

Site: A site report tells its readers what someone saw when visiting a particular location or examining a particular situation. For example:

- A structural engineer evaluates the soundness of an older building.
- A medical team describes conditions in an emergency room.
- A computer consultant evaluates a new graphics program for a venture-capital company.

Policy: A policy report examines current procedures and may recommend new ones for the operation of an organization or one of its units. For example:

- A national restaurant chain wishes to comply with government demands for affirmative action.
- A corporation's printing department wants to improve service.
- A university redefines the ways faculty receives tenure and promotion.

One-Off: A one-off report responds to a situation that an organization has never before encountered and isn't likely to encounter again. Because there can be few guidelines for such reports, each must be approached differently. For example:

- A stereo manufacturer learns that one of its models regularly fails.
- A government must compensate a person falsely convicted of a crime.
- A volunteer organization discovers that its vice-president has absconded with funds.

In summary, then, there is no single kind of report; rather, the types are as varied as the problems in organizations.

Description Or Analysis?

Whatever the type of report, it will describe or analyze. In theory, these are separate activities, but in practice, reports are seldom one or the other. While "describing" implies a neutral language and an objective stance, no writer is ever without bias or blind spots. In choosing what to present, observers interpret situations, selecting what appears to them as significant. Nonetheless, we say a report is descriptive when it presents data but doesn't claim to draw conclusions or recommend specific actions.

An analytical report, on the other hand, doesn't merely present data but also thinks critically about it. Analytical reports typically concern themselves with larger contexts, trying to help readers transform mere data into structured and meaningful information. Such information is critical because it allows an organization to act, to remedy what needs remedying. The centre of an analytical report, therefore, is what actions it recommends and why. For example:

- An analytical report about the degradation of salmon habitat wouldn't just describe the amount of pollution in local streams or the number of fish that return to spawn. It would also consider (among other things) what destroys habitat, the policies that lead to such destruction, and the costs of improving rivers and streams. Such a report might recommend specific measures—perhaps restricting development or limiting commercial fisheries. Or it might recommend simply that current practices be continued or only slightly modified.

- An analytical report about a new graphics program would describe its features, comparing them to existing products. But a venture capitalist who might invest in the fledgling company developing the program needs an analysis of other factors, like the size of the potential market, the company's ability to maintain and extend the program, and competition from technically inferior but already established products. The decision to invest or not—the action—depends on the persuasiveness of the analysis.
- An analytical report written for a provincial highway ministry about cyclists' head injuries would describe their frequency, severity, causes, and costs. It would also consider preventative measures like road design, cyclist training, and laws requiring riders to wear helmets and equip their vehicles with lights. The writer would weigh the benefits of any recommended measures against their costs, so that the reader could make an informed choice about new laws or safety programs.

As these examples suggest, there is nothing automatic about the recommendations an analysis might produce. Whether anyone acts on a recommendation depends greatly on who reads the report; that in turn means that writers must simultaneously think of both a report's subject and its readership. Let's consider report audiences more fully.

A Report's Audience

Given the variety of possible reports, there is also a great variety of possible readers. When reports suggest action (how to make things as they *should* be), the primary audience is whoever has the authority to decide what future actions an organization will take. There may be other readers (the public, technical advisors, and so forth), but the primary reader must be someone in authority.

Sometimes, a primary reader is just one person—say, a sales manager tracking the performance of her staff or a client learning when his building will be ready for occupancy. An audience can be also be a small group, like a company's board of directors or a volunteer association's executive committee. Or an audience can encompass many people, like municipal voters or a company's shareholders. In all cases, writers must shape their messages according to who can act.

Knowing an audience requires knowing why they are reading a report in the first place. Here are some reasons and some sample questions an audience might want answered:

They want information: How much did you sell last month? Does Product A have more features than Product B? How many viable salmon streams are left in the Sooke watershed?

They want to know something difficult to find out: How did the Vice-President abscond with the money? How was a junior currency trader able to overextend the firm? Who knew that the plan to sell widgets was impossible and when did they know it?

They want an analysis of a complex situation: What are the risks of building this kind of bridge at that place in the river? What is fair compensation for an innocent person who spent ten years in prison? What are the implications of hiring staff purely by race or gender?

They want specific recommendations: How much should we invest? How do we ensure that a defective product is never again shipped? If we decide to set up a community eldercare program, what should we do first?

In addition to knowing why your audience is reading, you also have to articulate to yourself what your audience already knows about the topic. Writing for a sales manager, for instance, does not require descriptions of the company's products. Writing for prospective investors, however, requires exactly that.

Similarly, you have to know your audience's level of technical sophistication. If you use the word *polymer*, for instance, what must you add? Learning how much of a shared context you can assume is an empirical process—that is, you find out by asking. We'll look at how to do that in the Actions section of this chapter.

Finding Your Report's Topic

Much of the time, your topic will find you—that is, someone will assign it. For example, with routine periodic or progress reports, your superior will tell you to describe what happened or what you did during a given period. But topics for more complex reports, as we've seen in the chapter on proposals, need to be carefully articulated and defined. (Indeed, much of what you put into a proposal— the discussion of the problem especially—can be imported into a report.)

The difference between a proposal and a report, of course, is that in a report you are not bidding on the opportunity to do something; you are doing it. Nonetheless, the first task in both proposals and reports is the same: *You need to demonstrate that a problem exists*. You then need to show that it's severe enough to warrant action and that the benefits of solving the problem will outweigh the costs. Because report readers are interested in acting, they first need to know what problem you're reporting on. Only then can they understand your recommendations.

Describing the Problem

Regardless of the specific type of report, describing the problem is central. To repeat what we said in the chapter on proposals, do not offer generic discussions;

make sure that you draw all your examples from specific circumstances. Otherwise, your report will be a series of unsubstantiated claims.

Offer at least three concrete examples of the problem that unequivocally illustrate for whom it is a problem and its severity. Use some kind of measurement such as objects, customers, or money. For example:

- Salmon returning to spawn have decreased by 38% in the last three years. That means future commercial fisheries will be reduced.
- We have 125 fewer customers than two months ago in our Premium Delivery program. We will have to lay off two employees.
- Costs in the shipping department have risen from $150,000 to $378,000. Profits for this year will drop, as will share prices.

Your goal is to persuade readers that you understand the specifics of the situation and are not offering vague comments.

Saying What Should Be Versus What Is

Having established *what is*, turn your attention to *what ought to be*. Again, provide three concrete examples of what the organization would be like were the problem solved. And again, be specific about who benefits. For example:

- Protecting and restoring habitat will mean an expansion of the commercial fishery and the continued viability of twelve coastal communities.
- Adding new customers in the next month will mean that the organization can retain all of the present staff, thereby improving morale and saving future training costs.
- Reducing costs in the shipping department will add about $200,000 to the bottom line.

Once more, your goal is to persuade readers that yours is a solution tailored for their situation and no other.

The Three-Part Structure

Of course, most reports go beyond merely describing a problem:

- They analyze it, discussing root causes.
- They consider possible solutions, weighing the strengths and weaknesses of each one.
- They recommend specific actions.

These three major functions lend themselves nicely to a three-part report structure: *a problem, its possible causes and solutions,* and *recommendations*.

Along the way, a report can do others things (for example, provide technical descriptions, budgets, or illustrations). But a three-part structure allows both you and your reader to keep clear what you're writing about at any particular point in the report.

For example, if your topic is "The Degraded Wildlife Habitat of the Sooke Watershed," a catalogue of viable and threatened salmon streams could form part of the problem description. Various kinds of irresponsible behavior and their remedies could be part of "Possible Causes and Solutions." And what your primary reader should do to improve habitat belongs in your "Recommendations" section.

This is not to insist that everything in your report will fit neatly into one of these three major divisions. Nor is it to say that your report should always consist of only three formal parts. A part can be divided into sections so that readers can grasp its content in smaller chunks. But regard the three-part structure as an organizing tool, a way of thinking about and presenting your material. You want both yourself and your reader always to be able to say this: *I understand this point and why it comes where it does.*

Report Format

There is no single correct report format. Many organizations (especially governments and large corporations) have their own guidelines. If you're writing for them, you should obviously do as they say.

What should you do when you have no prescribed format? The general principle is to follow the logic of your report; that is, build it around a problem and its solution. In addition, you include other components. Here they are in the order in which they appear in most reports:

- Covering letter
- Title page
- Summary
- Table of contents
- List of figures
- Problem statement
- Analysis and possible solutions
- Recommendations
- References

We cover these components in the Actions section that follows.

WORKING SMARTER

Creating a Table of Contents

As we've seen in Chapter 5, styles allow you to quickly give your document a consistent appearance. They also let you quickly build an index or table of contents, which you need for long documents.

The details of how to build a table of contents vary with word processors, but the basic logic is the same:

1. Apply the same style to all headings at the same level of importance. For example, your main headings would use the Heading 1 style and the level underneath it would use Heading 2. Your style choices for headings must be consistent.
2. Place the cursor where you want the table of contents to appear.
3. Invoke the Table of Contents feature.

For long documents built from separate files, you first have to create a master document that includes or points to the smaller files. For example, you may have created a report with a file for each chapter. You need to indicate that the chapters are part of a single document and what their order will be. You can also create a list of figures in much the same way.

ACTIONS

In this section, we'll go through the steps for preparing a report. You should already have a topic picked out and have determined that you can complete the necessary research.

Step 1: Gather Your Data

Gathering data is your first task once you've selected a topic. Here are some basic data-gathering techniques:

Interview people on site as required. As we saw when we discussed proposals, you have to talk to the people most concerned with the problem. In a report, you build on those conversations. As you write, you will likely find that you need more information and must go back to your interviewees, as well as speak to new ones. The more your report draws on first-hand observations, the more concrete and persuasive it can be.

The term *on site* should be broadly interpreted. A site isn't limited to a physical location like a road or a building. A site can be virtual (like a Web page), a product (like a graphics application) or an abstraction (like a policy statement). In general, *site* refers to any relevant thing or place that you need to observe first-hand.

Gather on-site documentation, including graphics. At a site, you not only speak to people, but you gather documents to take away. When you visit a site, you have your best chance to collect relevant policy statements, previous reports, photographs, and so on. It's better to gather too much than too little; you can discard what you don't need more easily than making a second visit for what's missing.

Gather documentation (including graphics) from libraries, the Internet, or other sources. In some instances, you will need material that a site might not have. You may need to look at books, trade journals, government documents, or the materials from similar organizations. People on site can often suggest what to look for.

Keep careful records of sources and exactly what they say. Writing reports demands scrupulous citation of outside sources. Your credibility depends in large measure both on showing that you can support your arguments and on enabling readers to verify your sources.

Record keeping is also important when you interview people and later quote them in a report. If necessary, verify the accuracy of such quotes by double-checking with the interviewee before you get too far along in your writing.

Use your word processor's outline mode to transcribe ideas. An electronic outliner is useful for more than setting down and restructuring your research notes. You can also use it throughout the whole writing process to reorganize material. The program lets you play "what if?": *What if Part A came after Part B? What if I moved Part C to the Appendix? What if Part D were cut entirely?* An outliner allows you to painlessly try out different ways of organizing what you want to say.

Before writing, ask yourself if you have all the information you need. You can never be absolutely sure that you've gathered all the necessary information, and glaring gaps in your preliminary research can lead you in disastrous directions. But you have to balance the need to meet a deadline with the need to have research materials. Only you can decide when to start writing and when to do more gathering.

WORKING SMARTER

Macros

A macro is a long series of keystrokes that you invoke by pressing a few keys or even just one. For example, if you frequently find yourself writing "If I can add any further information, please call me at 555-5555," you can create a macro that will type it for you when you enter the macro's name or press an assigned function key. Macros are also very useful for words that your fingers never quite get the hang of. For example, if you usually misspell *individual*, a macro would correctly type it for you every time.

Macros creators come in two main types—separate applications or features built in programs such as word processors. Neither kind is particularly difficult to use. The separate ones work with any program you have and can do much more complicated tasks than just retyping a string of letters. However, they do cost extra, usually in the $50–$100 range. A macro feature in a word processor is obviously cheaper and often more convenient. See your word processor's documentation for details.

Step 2: Prepare a Preliminary Draft

Your analysis and recommendations are at the centre of your report. When you begin transcribing and structuring your research notes, start with those parts that most directly apply to your analysis and recommendations. Cover the essential issues of your report and put them in roughly the same order that they will appear in the final version.

When you prepare this early draft, don't worry about copy-editing and elegant language; leave that for later. Instead, concentrate on the broader issues of argument and organization. For example, in preparing your preliminary draft, do the following:

Specify your audience. Ask yourself these questions (but don't include the answers in your report):
- Who will accept or reject recommendations?
- What do they know now?
- What do they need to know?
- What is the level of their technical sophistication?
- What are their biases?

    Write down the name of the person you think has the most influence in accepting your recommendations. Use this person as a reference point, that is, someone you can visualize either nodding in agreement or frowning. Keep this touchstone reader in mind throughout.

Open with a promise to the reader. In a sentence of two, say what your report will cover.

Draft the problem statement. Include at least three concrete examples of the problem, its severity, and for whom it is a problem.

Prepare the necessary and appropriate process and physical descriptions. See Chapter 10 on descriptions for more specific advice. For example:
- If you are writing about an order-taking process, describe the sequence of events from when the customer calls to when the product ships.
- If you are writing about a mechanical device like a toaster, describe how its various parts fit together.
- If you are writing about a home-care plan for the elderly, describe the care systems now in place, how they interact, and what functions they either provide or fail to provide.

Integrate the necessary graphics into your draft. Complement your text with pictures, rather than simply embellish it. For example:
- If you want to show what a construction site looks like, insert a photograph.
- If you want to show how a device works, insert a diagram.
- If you want to show the relative contributions of various departments to a company's profit, insert a pie chart.

Chapter 4 on graphics gives more details.

Move to an appendix any material that would distract readers or otherwise deflect their attention from the problem with which you're dealing. For example, a highly technical discussion on salmon breeding would obscure the problem of degraded habitat, as well as your solutions and recommendations. You can discuss salmon breeding in an appendix. (You can have more than one appendix, each covering a different issue.)

Present possible solutions to the problem. Demonstrate to the reader that your analysis is comprehensive and fair by discussing the pros and cons of each potential solution. Chapter 2 on organization discusses the different ways to sequence material for the best persuasive effect.

Present the best solution, along with your reasons. This is clearly an essential step. Make sure your reader sees the logic behind your choice.

In a separate section, recommend the actions that your primary reader should take. Without repeating the whole of your analysis, briefly say why the reader should act on each recommendation. (A short paragraph for each one will usually do.) Use a numbered list to rank your recommendations by their priority or urgency. That way, although your readers may not be able (or willing) to implement everything you think needs doing, they can see at a glance which actions you think that they should do first, second, and so forth.

Step 3: Field Test for Logic and Argument

As this book stresses throughout, professional writing requires you to test your work with people similar to your eventual audience. You then revise based on the responses of your testers. Professional writing is, therefore, unlike creative writing, where the writer alone decides what stays and what goes.

The ideal tester would be the eventual reader, of course, but that's both generally impossible and unwise. You want to present a finished and polished product, not a work-in-progress. At this stage, you are only trying out ideas.

Look for colleagues or friends with enough background to play the role of your touchstone reader, that is, people who will think very much like the decision maker in your audience. Assure them that you want their honest opinions and that your feelings aren't an issue.

If you can't find someone suitable, you yourself will have to play the role of the eventual reader. That calls for maintaining a psychological distance from your work, which is difficult to do. But without objective critical thinking in advance, your client will be the only one other than you to vet your ideas. That's risky.

Your testers' responses are not orders that you must obey but rather red flags that you should think about. You don't have to agree with a comment, but you do have to consider it.

Ask your testers about the same issues you considered when you worked on your preliminary draft in Step 2. Ensure that they can give appropriate responses before you work on the next draft. If they can't, you've found places to revise; that's cause for celebration, not despair. Here are some things to check for:

1. Can your testers rephrase the problem? Ask them to try.
2. Do testers need details that are more concrete? Ask them where and what.
3. Are all necessary terms defined? Ask testers to point out places where they need more help.
4. Do testers need more and/or clearer graphics? Ask where and why.
5. Are there highly technical sections that distract them and so should be moved to an appendix? Which sections and why?
6. Have you clearly explained how you evaluated possible solutions? Ask readers to explain your logic back to you.
7. Do testers understand why your best solution is, in fact, the best? Ask them to restate your argument, along with your most convincing evidence.
8. Do testers see what recommendations you make, the reasons why, and their priority?

Step 4: Field Test for Structure

Step 3 should help you discover the soundness of your ideas. Once you've incorporated the necessary revisions into your draft, you're ready to consider the clarity of your presentation, that is, how easily readers will follow you. Your goal in the next draft is to improve the order and the clarity of your ideas.

Chapter 2 discusses organization in more depth, but here are some specific issues to cover when you test the structure and clarity of your report:

- Why does the first paragraph come first? Why does the second paragraph come second? (And so on.) If you're unsure, reorganize the structure, supplying a justification to yourself why you're using this specific order. (As we suggested, your word processor's outliner is very helpful when you restructure.) Do the same for the main sections of your report.
- Is there a link (that is, a transition) between every pair of paragraphs in your report? Is it clear why one paragraph leads to the next? Point out the transitions. If they're missing, add them.
- Is there a link between every pair of sections in your report? Is it clear why one section leads to the next? Point out the transitions. If they're missing, add them.
- Can you paraphrase your own sentences, at least the key ones? That is, can you put them in different words? If you yourself can't paraphrase, readers will doubtlessly have problems understanding. Ask yourself *who does what* in each sentence and recast as necessary. (See Chapter 3 on Plain English for more details.)
- Are your graphics sufficiently clear? Does the text that accompanies them explain their significance? Are callouts clear, that is, does the text that tells the reader what graphic to look at? Are graphics labelled and numbered? (See Chapter 4 on graphics for more details.)
- Are your headings and subheadings informative? Does each give the reader a context for what follows?

Step 5: Prepare the Summary

Write a summary as a separate document. (It is also sometimes called an executive summary or abstract). Here are the steps for writing a summary:

A. **Describe your audience.** Who is your audience? What do they know now? What do they need to know?

B. **Reorient yourself.** Read your problem statement and recommendations. Then write a sentence in which you state in general terms what your report is about.

C. **Focus yourself.** Write down your informative section headings.

D. **Begin summarizing.** For each section, write one sentence that states its main idea. Look at the first and last paragraphs since these often contain the main idea. What technical details are unnecessary or need "translating"? Omit them from the summary.

E. **Connect your summary sentences.** Look for the relationships among sentences in your summary by putting a transitional word between each pair. This will test whether your summary is coherent, that is, about the same subject. Think of transitions as links and arrows that point readers in the right direction.

F. **Check the length.** Is your summary too long for what your audience needs? For example, is it more than 10 percent of the original? Summarize your summary if necessary.

G. **Field test:** Try out what you have so far on a typical member of your audience. Revise as necessary, field test again, and edit.

Step 6: Prepare the Appendix

As we've said, an appendix holds material that would distract the reader from the main ideas in your report. For example, if you were writing about what type of computer equipment you'd recommend, the body of your report should include only the information necessary for the people who will decide to purchase it. Put the full specifications and fine points—CPU speed, backside cache, and other such arcane topics—in an appendix, so that they are available for the technical experts to study.

Testing is again the best way to find out if you've put the right items in the appendix. Ask your testers to tell you. There's nothing automatic about deciding what goes into an appendix. Try out your material to learn where it best serves readers.

Step 7: Prepare the Covering Letter

Write a covering letter (sometimes called a letter of transmittal) as a separate document. Follow the guidelines in Chapter 6 on correspondence.

Step 8: Design the Document

Make the document easy to follow and attractive. In some cases (with government, for example), you may have to follow specific guidelines for presenting your report. Those guidelines always take precedence over your own preferences.

However, even the most stringent guidelines will not spell out every detail, so you will still have latitude to choose the most effective way to present your ideas. The care you take in the design of your document signals the reader that you have thought out every detail—in your argument as well as your manuscript. Chapter 5 on document design gives you specific advice.

Step 9: Prepare the Title Page

After the covering letter, your title page is the first thing a reader sees. A carefully prepared title page helps persuade readers that what follows is worth their attention.

Not every report requires a title page. (Your client, of course, may have a mandatory format.) In general, use a title page when a report is neither a memo nor regular correspondence. The title page needs four main items:

- The title of the report (and the client's reference number, if applicable)
- The name of organization or person to whom the report is going
- The date the report is submitted
- The name of the organization or person who prepared the report

A report's title, like its various headings and subheadings, should tell readers something of what they're about to read. Here are some examples:

- Canadian Arctic Research Consortium: Major Activities June-September 1999.
- Calming Traffic on the Metropolitan Expressway: No Single Solution
- Habitat 2000: The Feasibility of Building Low-Cost Housing without Federal Government Support
- Quarry Gold Mining: Annual Report 1999
- Review of 1999 Forest Practices, Province of Newfoundland
- Second Report of Progress under the Canada-Ontario Agreement Respecting the Great Lakes Basin Ecosystem
- Queen Charlotte Islands Community Forest Feasibility Study

The chapter on document design goes into detail on such issues as fonts, centring, and white space.

Figure 9.1 shows a sample title page.

```
┌─────────────────────────────────────────┐
│                                          │
│              Improving Profit            │
│                    at                    │
│          Pleasant Ridge Golf Course      │
│                                          │
│              Contract #2000-24           │
│                                          │
│                                          │
│                                          │
│               Prepared For:              │
│          The Municipality of Happy Vale  │
│               666 Blissful Road          │
│        Happy Vale, British Columbia V5V 5V5 │
│                                          │
│                                          │
│                                          │
│               Prepared By:               │
│           Horvath and Associates         │
│             1234 Platitude Way           │
│             Daviesville, Ontario         │
│                  M5M 5M5                 │
│                                          │
│                                          │
│             September 21, 2000           │
│                                          │
└─────────────────────────────────────────┘
```

Figure 9.1
A sample title page

Step 10: Prepare the Final Draft

Preparing the final draft is not a single step but a cycle of revising, testing, and revising until the report sustains your credibility. Specifically, here is what you need to edit for in your final draft:

- Plain English
- Informative headings and subheadings
- Format (if there is a particular one you must follow)
- Graphics (numbers, labels, callouts)
- Title page
- Completeness (that is, all required front and back matter)
- Correctness (grammar, punctuation, spelling)
- Pagination (lower-case Roman numerals for front matter—title page, summary, etc.—and Arabic numbers elsewhere)

Note: You can use a header on each page to list the page number and briefly identify you or the report—for example, "Happy Valley Golf Club p.1."

Step 11: Prepare the Table of Contents

Reports longer than five or six pages should have a table of contents so that readers can find sections quickly. You prepare your table of contents, of course, only when the rest of the report has been finished and the pagination set.

Use headings in the table of contents identical to those you use in the body of your report. Include the appropriate page numbers. If there are more than a few graphics, create a separate list of figures.

This is also a good time to double-check if your headings and subheadings genuinely inform. Suppose you were writing about the problem of increasing head injuries among cyclists: Rather than simply writing "Introduction," you could write "Cyclist Head Injuries Are Increasing." Rather than simply "Conclusion," you could write "Education, Helmets, and Bike Lanes: Three Ways to Reduce Head Injuries." Informative headings should show both what is to come and how it connects to the rest of your document.

WORKING SMARTER

Creating an Index

The longer your report, the more likely your reader will appreciate an index. Creating an index with your word processor can save you literally hours of work. Details vary from program to program, but the basic method is the same:

1. Mark words and phrases to use as entries (that is, the headings of an index) and subentries (the words that will appear under a particular heading).
2. Place the cursor where you want the index to appear.
3. Invoke the Indexing feature.

The program will generate an index of entries, subentries, and the appropriate pages.

Step 12: Submit the Report

Finally, send out the document, making sure it's on time. If disaster strikes and if you absolutely can't meet your deadline, inform your client as soon as possible.

CHAPTER SUMMARY

Reports are the most significant way by which organizations say who they are and what they want to become. Reports can investigate, analyze, inform, or recommend—and can do so in any combination. The content of your report is its most important attribute, of course, but how you present that content greatly affects its success with readers.

Reports describe, but they often also analyze; that is, they don't merely present data but discuss it critically. The recommendations that follow an analysis advise readers what actions to take.

As with other kinds of professional writing, understanding your audience is essential. You need to know its level of expertise and the range of its expectations. Only then can you shape your message effectively.

Reports should focus on solving problems, making clear their severity and effects. This approach leads to a straightforward three-part organization: problem statement, possible solutions, and recommendations.

Writing a report is a process in which you first gather data, then draft and gradually refine your ideas. In addition to your main content, you also must prepare auxiliary materials, such as the summary, appendix, and covering letter. Computers can make this process more efficient.

Because reports can be complex, they need to be carefully tested with a touchstone reader, that is, someone who will act the role of the person for whom you're writing.

CHECKLISTS

RESEARCH

Interview people on site as required.

Gather on-site documentation, including graphics.

Gather documentation (including graphics) from libraries, the Internet, or other reference sources.

Keep careful records of where you heard or read something; quote your sources exactly.

Use an electronic outliner to structure (and restructure) your research notes.

Decide whether you have collected enough information to start writing.

Your additional comments:

THE PRELIMINARY DRAFT

To prepare content:

Draft a three-sentence summary of the problem.

Give at least three specific and concrete examples of the problem.

Say for whom the problem is a problem and under what specific circumstances.

Say how severe this problem is, using some kind of measurement like dollars or time lost.

Show both what *should be* and *what is* and the distance between them.

Show that solving the problem will produce a genuine benefit.

Describe the methodology you used to investigate or solve the problem (for example, interviews, literature review, site visits, constructing or modifying something).

Say which specific questions you have asked and of whom you have asked them.

Describe the site.

Include the necessary physical, process, and system descriptions.

Offer possible solutions to the problem, assessing their strengths and weaknesses.

Put forward your own solution with its justification.

Anticipate and counter potential objections to your solutions.

Make recommendations, listing them in the order the reader should act upon them.

To help the reader:

List the characteristics of your intended audience, specifically the touchstone reader.

Formulate a clear promise to the reader, briefly outlining the contents of the report.

Define all necessary terms.

Integrate the necessary graphics so that they convey information, not embellish the report.

Move overly technical or otherwise distracting material to an appendix.

Signal to the reader the possible solutions to the problem.

Signal other possible solutions with reasons why they are not as good as what you recommend.

Signal the best solution with reasons.

Signal recommendations and their priority.

Field test preliminary draft for organization.

Your additional comments:

THE MIDDLE DRAFT

To test for clarity, check that:

You can give reasons why the first paragraph comes first, why the second comes second, and so on.

You can show a link between every two paragraphs of your report.

You can show a link between every two sections of your report.

You can paraphrase your sentences—at least the key ones.

Headings and subheadings are informative.

Graphics are sufficiently clear.

Your additional comments:

THE FINAL DRAFTS

To prepare the summary:

State the problem in less than three sentences.

State the proposed solution in about three sentences.

Edit to less than 10 percent of the original.

To prepare the covering letter:

Provide a context to introduce the subject and purpose of the document.

Provide a brief statement of one or two key points in the document.

Provide a plan of action (the reader's next step) and a courteous closing.

Follow the standard business letter format.

To complete the final draft:

☐ Edit for Plain English.

☐ Label and caption all graphics.

☐ Ensure format is exactly according to requirements.

☐ Spell check, especially names.

☐ Correct all grammar, punctuation, and typing errors.

☐ Prepare the title page.

☐ Paginate.

☐ Prepare the table of contents.

☐ Assemble all parts of the report (including front and back matter, table of contents, list of figures, references, etc.).

Your additional comments:

EXERCISES

Assume that you have been asked by your superior to write a report to encourage employees to leave their cars at home and use either public transit or bicycles. Use your school or workplace as the organization in question. The following exercises take you through the steps for preparing your report. Work in groups of three to four people to do the first three exercises. Do the rest individually.

Exercise 1

Your first step is to learn about your audience and the problem:

a. What do you know about your primary reader's ideas or biases? What specific information does he or she want? For what purpose? What writing strategies would work best for this particular individual? Who will be the secondary reader (for example, a technical advisor)? What do you know about her or him and what strategies should you use?

b. Make a list of people (using their job titles) within and outside the organization whom you should interview. List three questions that you would ask each one.

c. Search the World Wide Web to find three examples of similar programs for encouraging employees to take public transit.

d. Do a library or Web search for three relevant articles from trade or professional journals.

Exercise 2

a. Describe the organization's environment and culture. Draft a questionnaire that you would administer to get answers to the following:

   1. About how many people come to work by car? By other means? Use a pie chart to illustrate percentages.
   2. What reasons do the people give if they use cars? Public transit? Bicycles?
   3. What parking facilities are available? What facilities are available for cyclists?
   4. How close does public transit come to the site?

b. Outline how you would administer the questionnaire. How would you avoid bias? How would you ensure that your results were reliable?

Exercise 3

Using reasonable numbers and assumptions, formulate a problem statement, being specific about how severe the problem is and for whom it is a problem. State the benefits of solving the problem.

Exercise 4

Outline three or four ways to solve the problem of encouraging employees to leave their cars at home. List the benefits and costs for each. Limit your statement to three paragraphs.

Exercise 5

Recommend what actions the company should take, justifying each one briefly. List your recommendations by priority.

Exercise 6

Produce an outline for your report in which you include the following:

a. A report title that reflects the problem with which you are dealing
b. Informative headings for each main section
c. Informative subheadings for each subsection

Make these headings and subheadings help readers see what is to follow and how it connects to the rest of your document.

Exercise 7

Draft a covering letter to your primary reader to accompany your report. Include the following:

a. A context that introduces the document the letter accompanies
b. A brief statement of one or two key points in the document
c. A plan of action (that is, the reader's next step) and a courteous closing

See Chapter 6 for details on how to write a covering letter.

CHAPTER

10

Writing Descriptions

What This Chapter Covers

Ideas

Describing the World
Physical Descriptions
      Mechanical Objects
      Natural Objects
      Other Phenomena
Process Descriptions
      Natural or Planned
      Planned Processes
      Natural Processes
      Processes with Decisions
      Mixed Descriptions
Audiences
Decomposing and Presenting
      Decomposing a Physical Object
      Decomposing a Process
      Presenting Descriptions
      Incorporating Graphics

Actions

Writing Physical Descriptions
Writing Process Descriptions

Chapter Summary

Checklists

Exercises

**Learning
Objectives**

At the end of this chapter, you will be able to explain:

- What kinds of things need to be described
- Why a description needs to be matched to the audience who will read it
- How physical descriptions show an object as it exists at a particular moment
- How process descriptions show a series of events over time
- How process descriptions can include decision points, making some actions contingent on others
- Why you must analyze your audience
- How you decompose and present objects and processes
- Why graphics must have the appropriate level of detail

At the end of this chapter you will be able to write both physical and process descriptions by:

- Describing an object's general features or a process's major steps
- Describing your audience
- Decomposing an object or process
- Preparing graphics and accompanying text
- Determining the most appropriate presentation for your audience
- Giving an overview, a description of the individual components or steps, and a second overview
- Editing, field-testing, and revising

I-D-E-A-S

Describing the World

Description is the stock and trade of the professional writer. Documents of all kinds require the reader know how an object or a process looks, how it works, or how it's a part of something larger.

What can be described? Virtually anything—a TV set, a lion, a policy statement. Descriptions of manufactured objects like TV sets are particularly common in technical writing, but, in fact, writers are often asked to describe a wide range of other things. For example:

- A municipality holding a referendum to build a new swimming pool must first provide voters with a description of both the current and proposed facilities.
- A company wishing to sell a communications system requires a description of the system's various components and how they work together.
- A tourist bureau needs descriptions of its area's attractions and activities.

Since there is also a wide range of possible readers, a writer could produce a number of different descriptions for each item. Descriptions of the same lion, for example, would differ for a Grade One student, a veterinarian, or a big-game hunter. Knowing who will read a description, therefore, is every bit as important as knowing the object that gets described.

Descriptions frequently require pictures as well as words. Consider, for instance, how much easier it is to describe a spiral staircase if you supplement the description with a picture. Chapter 4 discusses graphics in detail, but we'll also make passing references to them here.

Physical Descriptions

There are two main kinds of description—**physical** and **process**. They can easily overlap, as we shall see later.

A physical description gives a mental picture of what an object looks like—its dimensions, its parts, its materials, and so forth. For example, here are some of the parts of a couple of familiar objects:

- **A ballpoint pen:** barrel, ink reservoir, ballpoint tip, etc.
- **A car:** body, engine, transmission, etc.
- **A parliamentary government:** the head of state, the Prime Minister, the Cabinet, the House of Commons, etc.

Physical descriptions can also be general or specific. That is, they can either describe an entire class of objects (like cellular telephones or dogs) or they can describe specific instances of those classes (like the Phonomatic Model 6227A or Spot).

In what follows, we'll look at some examples of physical descriptions. None is particularly technical, so you don't need any special expertise.

Mechanical Objects

A mechanical description is a special case of physical description; it focuses on an object (like a lamp or a clock) that has been manufactured to perform a specific function. Let's start with a typical mechanical description. Here is one about rivets (that is, metal fasteners), written for engineers and technicians who need to assemble lab equipment:

> Rivets are used to permanently join sheet-metal or sheet-plastic parts together. They are frequently used when some degree of flexibility is desired in a joint, as when joining the ends of a belt to give a continuous loop. The most common rivet shapes are shown in Figure 10.1. Rivets are made of soft copper, aluminum, or steel. To join two pieces, a hole, slightly larger than the body of the rivet, is drilled or punched in each piece. A rivet is inserted through the holes, and a head is formed on the plain end of the rivet using a hammer or, preferably, a riveting machine. The hammering action swells the body of the rivet to fill the hole.
>
> "Pop" rivets, [also] illustrated in Figure 10.1, are useful in the lab. These can be installed without access to the back side of the joint.
>
> John H. Moore, Christopher C. Davis, and Michael A. Coplan, *Building Scientific Apparatus*, (Reading, Mass.: Addison-Wesley Publishing, 1983.)

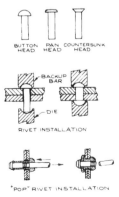

Figure 10.1
Rivets

Source: John H. Moore, Christopher C. Davis, and Michael A. Coplan, Building Scientific Apparatus, *(Reading, Mass.: Addison-Wesley Publishing, 1983.)*

Although the description is primarily physical, it includes something of the process of how parts are joined. The writers also assume that certain technical terms need no further explanation such as "sheet-metal" and "sheet-plastic". But since this description is for lab workers, it leaves out many details that are even more technical. A materials engineer, for example, might want to know the strength of each rivet. That isn't necessary for the intended audience.

A specific description of a rivet would also include the features of a particular sample, such its dimensions, material, and cost.

Natural Objects

Physical descriptions aren't limited to manufactured objects. Cecil Adams writes a popular science column that appears in many newspapers. Here is his description of the aurora borealis, written for a general audience:

> The aurora are the result of collisions between atoms in the upper atmosphere and fast-moving protons and electrons that come from—or are energized by—the sun. They are generally not visible at latitudes below 60 degrees, although intense solar flare activity can and does make them visible at lower latitudes on occasion. (Chicago, by way of reference point, is about 42 degrees north.) There's no way to predict these solar flare-ups, and they follow no seasonal routine; however, when they are intense enough to cause auroral activity around your areas, your friendly TV weatherman will usually say so.

> Cecil Adams, *The Straight Dope* (New York: Ballantine Books, 1984), 163.

Adams assumes that his readers, although not scientists by any means, will understand terms like "protons" and "electrons" from the context in which they appear. If he had paused to deliver a detailed explanation of those words, he would have risked obscuring the main thrust of his description. The type of detail he provides is appropriate to a casual newspaper reader; he does not intend it for either scientists or kindergartners.

Other Phenomena

Physical descriptions are not necessarily about only mechanical objects or natural events like the aurora. For example, Stanley Coren, a psychologist and dog trainer, offers this description of canine tail-position:

> Tail position is an important indicator of social standing and mental state. There will be some variations, of course, depending upon the natural tail position of the dog: a West Highland white terrier will carry its carrot-shaped tail higher than a golden retriever its flowing, feathery tail, and a greyhound's relaxed tail position is lower yet.

Almost horizontal, pointing away from the dog but not stiff: This is a sign of attention. It roughly translates as "Something interesting many be happening."

Straight out horizontally, pointing away from the dog: This is part of an initial challenge when meeting a stranger or intruder. It roughly translates as "Let's establish who's boss here."

Tail up, between the horizontal and vertical position: This is the sign of a dominant dog, or one who is asserting dominance, and translates as "I'm boss here."

Stanley Coren, *The Intelligence of Dogs* (New York: The Free Press, 1994), 103-4.

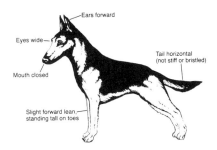

Figure 10.2
Canine body language

Source: Stanley Coren, The Intelligence of Dogs *(New York: The Free Press, 1994)*

Coren gives a clear mental picture of a behavior trait typical of all members of a class. At the same time, he clarifies his general description by references to specific breeds (West Highland white terriers, golden retrievers, and greyhounds). Coren also is writing for a popular audience (not professional breeders or veterinarians, for instance). He therefore makes his language highly accessible and even colloquial ("I'm boss here") without compromising the rigour of his description. He also complements his description nicely with his graphic, which is shown in Figure 10.2.

These three examples—garbage disposers, the aurora, and tail position—indicate the range of physical descriptions, which can go from quite technical to quite popular. There is no one right or wrong kind of description; there are instead those that are more appropriate or less appropriate for their readers. We'll discuss readers later in this chapter.

Process Descriptions

A physical description captures an object as it exists at one particular moment. A process description, in contrast, looks at events over time, giving a mental picture of their sequence. A process description is always organized chronologically, that is, with some event happening, then another, and then another after that. However, the sequence isn't necessarily linear, in which Step 3 always follows Step 2, which itself always follows Step 1. Many processes have points at which a decision is made that affects subsequent steps (for example, a doctor's examination of a patient eliminates the possibility of a certain disease, so the doctor doesn't order laboratory tests for it).

A process description is akin to a set of instructions in that both take the reader through a sequence of steps. However, the goal in a process description is to have readers understand a task, not perform it. Some readers, for example, might need to know how logging roads should be built but do not themselves want to build them. Other readers may not want to visit Nepal but do want to learn how climbers scale Mount Everest. And still other readers taking their cars for repair might want to know how a car stops but not how to do a brake job.

Natural or Planned

The events in a process description can occur naturally or by deliberate human planning. Here are some instances of each kind:

Natural:
- A leaf changing colour
- A fetus evolving
- A volcano erupting

Planned:
- Delivering mail
- Making ice cream
- Testing blood

Let's look at some examples of both.

Planned Processes

As an example of a planned process, here is Steven Pinker's description of an experiment that determines the extent to which five-month old babies can do mental arithmetic:

> In Wynn's experiment, the babies were shown a rubber Mickey Mouse doll on a stage until their little eyes wandered. Then a screen came up, and a prancing hand visibly reached out from behind the screen and placed a second Mickey Mouse behind the screen. When the screen was removed, if there were two Mickey Mouses visible (something the babies had never actually seen), the babies looked for a few moments. But if there was only one doll, the babies were captivated— even though this was exactly the scene that had bored them before the screen was

put in place. Wynn also tested a second group of babies, and this time, after the screen came up to obscure a pair of dolls, a hand visibly reached behind the screen and removed one of them. If the screen fell to reveal a single Mickey, the babies looked briefly; if it revealed the old scene with two Mickeys, the babies had more trouble tearing themselves away. The babies must have been keeping track of how many dolls were behind the screen, updating their counts as the dolls were added or subtracted. If the number inexplicably departed from what they expected, they scrutinized the scene, as if searching for some explanation.

Steven Pinker, *The Language Instinct* (New York: William Morrow, 1994), 69.

Pinker intends this description for general readers; a professional audience would want further details such as the number of babies in the experiment or the length of time the babies looked at the Mickey Mouse dolls. Since Pinker is a linguist who is arguing for *Homo sapiens*' inborn ability to process language, he wants to show only that babies have surprising intellectual powers. So although the experiment was itself rigorously done (it appeared in a peer-reviewed and respected journal), Pinker omits details about its scientific validity. Moreover, he explains the two separate stages of the experiment together in terms suitable for a general reader of a language text, rather than for a cognitive scientist.

Natural Processes

Here is a second process description, this one by Des Kennedy showing how a vampire bat feeds:

Not the huge and fearsomely fanged bloodsucker of horror movie fame, it's a small creature whose attack is both subtle and insidious. The vampire approaches its sleeping prey by night; domestic livestock and even humans are likely targets. Stealth is its weapon; often the bat will alight softly nearby and crawl onto the victim's body, looking like a large spider. Softly it moves and chooses a piece of exposed skin: the neck or leg of a steer, often the big toe of humans. From a tiny incision made with its scalpel-sharp teeth, the bat laps up blood. The attack is so softly and cunningly done that the victim often remains peacefully asleep. An anti-coagulant in the bat's saliva keeps the blood from clotting, and so the bat gorges itself. One observer described how a vampire licked blood steadily from a domestic goat for ten minutes, finally becoming so bloated with blood it couldn't fly.

Des Kennedy, *Living Things We Love To Hate* (Vancouver, White Cap Books, 1992), 8.

Kennedy is a skilled popular writer, who conjures up the old horror-movie stereotype to make his writing vivid. Although he is describing a process, he mixes in the physical—the bat looks like "a large spider" and its teeth are "scalpel-sharp." Kennedy also uses narrative: his is a story of stealth, not of an evildoer but of a hungry mammal, which concludes with a creature so full of its victim's blood that it can't fly. For all this, the description is rigorously chronological: The bat approaches its prey, bites, and laps blood. Kennedy could have presented his description more technically, such as by using a numbered list. That would, of course, weaken the dramatic effect he wanted to create.

Processes with Decisions

The flow of events in these examples has been strictly linear—that is, Event 1 was followed by Event 2 and so on. But consider the way a typical magazine publishes an article (or "piece" in the parlance of publishing). At specific junctures, people make decisions that affect the flow of the entire process:

Step 1: The editorial board meets the first Monday of every month and chooses topics for the issue four months in the future. The board assigns each topic it chooses to an editor.

Step 2: Within 48 hours of the editorial meeting, the assignment editor chooses and contacts a writer from among staff and freelancers.

Step 3: The editor and writer agree on the topic, the approach, the number of words, the fee, and the dates by which the writer must submit preliminary and final drafts.

Step 4: By the first due date, the writer researches, writes, and submits the preliminary draft to the editor.

Step 5: The editor decides if the article is generally acceptable.
  - If so, the editor edits the piece, returning it to the author for minor revisions and clarifications.
  - If not, the editor returns the piece to the writer for major revisions or kills the piece entirely (that is, no longer considers publishing it).

Step 6: The writer completes revisions and resubmits the piece.

Step 7: The editor decides if the revised version is acceptable.
  - If so, the editor forwards the article to the senior editor for approval.
  - If not, editor asks for further rewrites or kills the piece.

Step 8: The senior editor decides if the piece is acceptable.
  - If so, the senior editor forwards the article to production.
  - If not, the senior editor returns it to the editor for further revision or kills the piece.

This description differs from the first two because at various points editors decide to ask for revisions or abandon the piece altogether. If a piece is killed, the subsequent steps in the process still exist even though they are not carried out in this particular instance. In the examples of the baby experiment or the vampire bat, you could represent the processes linearly:

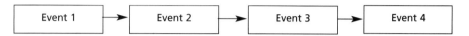

Figure 10.3
A linear representation of a process

However, to show a process like the publication of a magazine article, you need a flow chart. The one in Figure 10.4 shows some of the middle steps of that process.

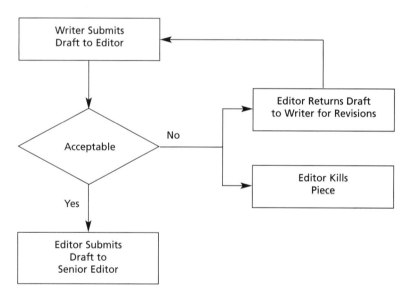

Figure 10.4
A flow chart representation of a process

A flow chart, as the chapter on graphics discusses, works best for presenting processes where some actions are contingent on others being done. A flow chart must show all the important steps in the process, whether or not they occur in a particular instance.

That is not to say that a flow chart must show *every* possible step; you still must decide on the appropriate level of detail. For example, an editor will make many small decisions before deciding which revisions to ask of the writer or whether to kill the piece. If your intention were to show only the main actions of the process, you wouldn't include smaller editorial decisions like which words to capitalize or where to insert commas. Like all descriptions, how much to show of these decisions depends entirely on what your audience needs.

Mixed Descriptions

As we've seen, a description does not have to be purely physical or process. Indeed, many things cannot be described solely as either a physical object or as a process. A car, for instance, is a collection of mechanical parts, but it is also a collection of processes (gas being ignited in the engine, pedals being depressed to activate brakes, etc). Lions are a collection of lion parts but also are a collection of processes that hunt, kill, and devour prey. You must choose which components or processes to include based on what your audience needs to understand. And that (as always) requires knowing your readers. Let's consider that.

Audiences

Given the physical solidity of an object—say, a 1999 Mercedes—at first glance, there may appear only one way to describe it. But knowing who will read your description is as important as knowing the object itself. To illustrate, think of what you might include in your Mercedes description for the following readers:

- An insurance agent
- A buyer in a showroom
- An automotive engineer

For the insurance agent, you'd need little more than the make, model, and serial number. The buyer in the showroom, however, would want to know about features (automatic transmission, CD player, anti-lock braking systems). And the engineer would want more yet (the kind of fuel injection, the materials used for the brakes, etc.).

The questions you ask about audiences for descriptions are the usual ones for professional writers:

- What do readers know now?
- What do they need to know?
- How will the audience use the description?
- How technically sophisticated are the readers?

You must know these answers as well as you know the object or process you'll describe.

Decomposing and Presenting

Regardless of the type of description, you'll perform two basic writing tasks: decomposing and presenting. Decomposing refers to breaking down an object into its constituent parts. Presenting refers to choosing the most effective way to display the decomposed object to your readers.

Decomposing a Physical Object

To decompose a physical object, think of yourself holding a screwdriver. Picture an object and imagine taking it apart, starting with the most accessible component. In some cases, it will be possible for you to literally decompose a physical object, rather than doing it just mentally.

If you were decomposing a computer (literally or mentally), for example, you would undo the screws that secure the case and remove the outer shell. Then you would take the various cards out of their slots and remove the power supply, the hard drive, and so on.

You can use imaginary screwdrivers on natural objects as well. A human being, for example, can be "taken apart" into a respiratory system, a digestive system, a circulatory system, and so forth. (That's what a description in an anatomy textbook might do.) You can also decompose abstract objects like social systems: A school be broken down into its students, faculty, administrators, and support staff.

Decomposing a Process

To decompose a process, think of yourself holding a stopwatch, rather than a screwdriver. Observe and record a related set of events that take place over time. With a process description, you record the different tasks, their sequence, and who or what does each one.

For example, if you were decomposing the mail system, you might do it this way:

1. Person A picks up letters and packages from mailbox and drives them to a central site.
2. Person B sorts letters and packages by the first part of the postal code.
3. Person C sorts letters and packages by the second part of the postal code.
4. Person D loads letters and packages onto trucks.
5. Person E drives letters and packages to local distribution centre.
6. Person F picks up letters and packages from distribution centre and delivers them door to door.

To decompose the human digestive process, you might record the food entering the mouth, being chewed, swallowed, broken down by various enzymes, and so forth.

These two sequences are primarily linear: Person A picks up letters, brings them to the postal substation, etc. Others are primarily causal: Fuel and air are mixed and ignited in your furnace to create heat. Still others are cyclical: Leaves emerge in spring, mature in summer, turn red in fall, die in winter, and are replaced by the new leaves of a new spring.

As you decompose physical objects or processes, you quickly face the issue of granularity, that is, what will constitute the smallest unit of your description. Theoretically, you can decompose a car down to its subatomic structure or decompose the process of leaves changing their colours down to a nanosecond. Of course, that much information would obscure any possible pattern or order. Your readers wouldn't see a forest but merely a great many trees. That leads us to the question of how to present parts once we've decomposed an object or process.

Presenting Descriptions

A description is not just accurate or inaccurate; it's also appropriately or inappropriately presented to its particular audience. Not every presentation works for every reader.

For example, if as a child you took apart the kitchen clock, you may remember the sinking feeling when your mother came into the room to find a partially reassembled clock and several leftover pieces. Later, staring at the walls of your bedroom, you probably realized that you needed to work on how you presented decomposed parts to her in the future.

Writing descriptions requires you to reassemble things mentally for your audience, but that doesn't necessarily mean including every part. Your main objective is having readers see a pattern, an internal logic, in what you describe. That may require that you leave out parts. For readers to understand how a clock works, for example, they don't need to know how the manufacturer's logo is affixed to the clock face.

You are not deliberately being inaccurate when you leave out parts; instead, you are choosing the most useful possible pattern. Having "nothing left over" means choosing and arranging only those components that match the mental picture that your audience needs. Your goal, therefore, is to produce not a simple listing of parts but a meaningful arrangement.

Let's look at some common ways of presenting a description:

- **Spatial:** Outside to inside, top to bottom, left to right, north to south . . .
- **Size:** Biggest to smallest, smallest to biggest . . .
- **Hierarchical:** Highest to lowest, most important to least important . . .
- **Functional:** A does X, B does Y, C does Z . . .
- **Chronological:** Event A, Event B, Event C . . .
- **Causal:** A causes B, B causes C, C causes . . .
- **Cyclical:** A, B, C, A, B, C . . .

You are most likely to use the first four—spatial, size, hierarchical, and functional—for a physical description; the last three—chronological, causal, and cyclical—you'd be most likely to use in process descriptions.

You must also signal how you're presenting your description with words like *first, second, third,* or *on the right, next to it, above it,* and so on. Think of signalling as the glue that holds together the pieces you're presenting.

For example, here are various ways you might signal different kinds of descriptions of a school:

- **Spatial:** The auditorium is immediately *north* of Mrs. Ingram's classroom, which is *north* of Mr. Innis's.
- **Size:** The gym is the *largest* room in the school and auditorium is the *next largest.*
- **Hierarchical:** The school priorities are *first and foremost* the curriculum, *then* socialization, and *then* physical fitness.
- **Functional:** Students *learn*, faculty *teach*, and administrators *administrate*.
- **Chronological:** The children *first* open their books, *second*, read the story, and *third*, write a summary.
- **Causal:** Johnny said something mean to Tommy, which *caused* Tommy to say something worse to Johnny, which *in turn caused* Johnny to hit Tommy with his lunch box.

Incorporating Graphics

In Chapter 4, we discuss graphics in general, but there are a few issues to keep in mind when you incorporate graphics into descriptions.

A graphic should complement the text, not substitute for it. For example, suppose you were describing a pencil and used the rather simple-minded diagram below. In addition to giving basic information, the text should lead the reader's eye to different sections of the graphic:

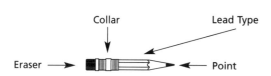

Figure 10.5
A simple diagram

A pencil is made up of five main parts, as we can see in Figure 10.5: the shaft, the eraser, the collar, the point, and the lead.

The largest part is the shaft, which consists of a lead enclosed in wood. Leads come in many colours and weights; the shaft is generally painted the colour of the lead (except in the case of black leads) and the weight of the lead is stamped on the shaft.

At one end of the shaft is the eraser (usually rubber), which is held in place by the metal collar. At the other end of the shaft is the point, which the user creates with a pencil sharpener.

The level of detail of the graphic should also match the level of detail of the text. For example, if you were describing an automobile's engine system, Figure 10.6 shows an appropriate amount information, including the engine system's relationship to the rest of the car.

As always, the test of a graphic is how much it helps your readers; and, as always, you have to test and find out.

Figure 10.6
A diagram with appropriate detail

Source: AUTOSHOP-Online <www.autoshop-online.com/auto101/eng.html>

Writing Physical Descriptions

Step 1: Describe the Object's Major Features

- What is the object? Name it (for specific descriptions, include the make and model).
- Is the object general or specific? That is, are its attributes typical of all such objects or are some its attributes found only in one particular model or instance of a general class?
- What is it used for?
- Who typically uses it?
- How does it work?
- Of what materials is it made?
- What are its dimensions (height, width, depth), weight, and shape? For more abstract objects (like human systems) say what concepts or people are involved or interact with them.
- Is the object part of something larger?

  Not every question may be relevant, but consider them all.

Step 2: Describe the Audience

- Name an actual member of your audience. This will be your touchstone reader, that is, the person whom you will imagine smiling or frowning as he or she reads your description. If you can't name one, think of a composite touchstone reader.
- Is your touchstone reader a specialist? A general reader?
- Why is your touchstone reader reading? For work? For pleasure? To decide something?
- What is your reader's technical sophistication? Expert? Intermediate? Novice?
- What does your reader now know about the object? Be specific.
- What does your reader need to know? Be specific.

Step 3: Decompose the Object

If you are describing a mechanical object that can literally be taken apart without destroying it, do so carefully. Place the pieces on a workbench or other flat surface. Lay out the parts in the order in which you remove them. Work from the outside in or follow whatever order gives you the best access. Keep careful records of the pieces and the order in which you removed them.

If you are decomposing the object mentally, think of yourself with a screwdriver and disassemble the object. Draw simple diagrams to represent each piece. Again, work from the outside in or use whatever order is most logical.

Decide on the appropriate level of granularity—how small the smallest unit will be. Go back to the Step 2, and ask yourself this: *What level of detail does my touchstone reader need?* Whether you continue decomposing depends entirely on your answer.

One way to think about the granularity is to ask which parts contribute to the same function. For example, a car's brake system is made up of a master cylinder, brake pads, brake shoes, brake fluid, and so forth. If your readers need to know only the general operation of a car, you could present the braking system as a unit. However, if they need to know how the braking system itself works, you would have to describe each component.

Step 4: Prepare a Graphic

Locate an existing graphic or create one to supplement the text. Draft the text that leads the reader's eye through the graphic. Choose one whose level of detail suits your readers' needs. That is, don't overwhelm the reader with unnecessary information but make sure the graphic displays every component you describe in the text.

Step 5: Plan the Presentation

Determine the best order for presenting the components of the object, based on the way your readers need to see it. For example:

- Top to bottom
- Inside out or outside in
- Left to right or right to left
- Most important to least important

Step 6: Orient the Reader

Move from planning to writing. Prepare your preliminary draft, starting with a brief overview of the object (about one paragraph). Using your notes from Step 1, do the following:

- Name the object.
- Say what it does and who usually uses it.
- If relevant, say how it works and how it is part of something larger.
- If relevant, list its dimensions, weight, and shape.
- Include any other relevant attributes.

Note: Descriptions always use the declarative voice, as in "The operator presses Button A." Instructions, in contrast, always use the imperative voice, as in "Press Button A."

Step 7: Identify the Parts

Present each component in the order you determined in Step 5. For each:

- Identify the component. Direct your reader to the appropriate section of the graphic. Use callouts (such as "See Figure 2").
- Locate the component on the graphic as appropriate.
- For the first component, signal how you're organizing the description with the appropriate word or phrase (for example, "on the bottom," or "at the left").
- For subsequent components, signal the relationship to the other components that immediately precede and follow.
- Say what each component is used for.
- List physical characteristics as appropriate (for example, material, dimensions, weight, and shape).

Step 8: Help Readers Regain Their Bearings

Conclude your description by giving readers a second overview. Discuss these points:

- How the parts work together to perform the main function
- Why readers should know about the object
- What variations on the object readers may encounter

Step 9: Edit

Edit for visual and logical clarity. Use bullet lists and nest them as appropriate. For example:

- Component 1
  - Component 1A
  - Component 1B
- Component 2
- Component 3

See the chapters on Plain English and document design for further details.

Step 10: Test the Description

If possible, try out the description with sample members of your intended audience. If no one is available, ask a colleague or friend to play the role of your touchstone reader. Focus your testers on these issues:

- Does the opening provide the necessary overview of what's being described?
- Is the method of organization obvious to the reader?
- Are any parts missing?
- Is the text clear? What sentences are ambiguous?
- How well does the graphic complement the text?
- Does the ending give the tester the necessary concluding overview?

Step 11: Revise as Necessary

Using the information you've gathered from your testers, revise and retest your description.

Writing Process Descriptions

Step 1: Describe the Process's Major Steps

- What is the process? Name it.
- Who uses or controls it?
- What does it accomplish?
- Are there inputs and outputs?
- What are its significant steps? List them.
- Is the process linear? Causal? Cyclical?
- Are there any decision points? If so, identify the paths forward and back from them.

Step 2: Describe the Audience

- Name an actual member of your audience. This will be your touchstone reader, that is, the person whom you will imagine smiling or frowning as he or she reads your description. If you can't name one, think of a composite touchstone reader.
- Is your touchstone reader a specialist? A general reader?
- Why is your touchstone reader reading? For work? For pleasure? To decide something?
- What is your reader's technical sophistication? Expert? Intermediate? Novice?
- What does your reader now know about the object? Be specific.
- What does your reader need to know? Be specific.

Step 3: Decompose the Process

Imagine yourself holding a stopwatch and observing the process. Make notes from your answers to the following questions:

- What occurs first, second, third, and so on?
- What happens in each of these steps?
- Who or what performs or controls each step?
- Is the step a decision point? If so, describe what happens from this point either forward or back to the main flow of the process.

In many instances, the steps you end up with can be further decomposed. As with physical descriptions, whether you continue depends entirely on what you are trying to accomplish. The degree of granularity must fit the task. Go back to Step 2, and ask yourself this: *What level of detail does my touchstone reader need?* Whether you continue decomposing depends entirely on your answer.

One way to think about the granularity is to ask which parts contribute to the same function. For example, a car's braking process includes the driver depressing the brake pedal, fluid moving through the brake lines, and pistons pressing brake pads against a drum or disk at each wheel. If your readers need to know only the general operation of a car, you could present the braking process a unit. However, if they need to know how the braking process itself works, you would have to describe each step.

Step 4: Prepare a Graphic

Locate an existing flow chart or create one. Think of how you will use it to supplement the text. The text should lead the reader's eye through the flow chart.

Choose a flow chart whose level of detail suits your readers' needs. That is, don't overwhelm readers with unnecessary information but make sure the flow chart shows the same decision points and paths as your text describes.

Step 5: Orient the Reader

Move from planning to writing. Start your preliminary draft with a brief overview of the process (about one paragraph). Include:

- What the process does
- Who performs or controls it
- Why it's important
- Whether it's part of a larger process

Step 6: Identify Each Step

For each step in turn:

- Identify the step and locate it on your flow chart.
- Say what it does.
- Say who or what performs it.
- Say how long it takes.
- Provide a transition, that is, a statement that leads the reader to the next step.

Step 7: Help Readers Regain Their Bearings

Conclude your description by giving readers a second overview. Include:

- How the steps work together to perform the main function or purposes
- Who uses or controls it
- Why readers should know about the process
- Any variations on the process that readers may encounter

Step 8: Edit

Edit for visual and logical clarity. Use numbered lists and nest them as appropriate. For example:

- Step 1
  - Step 1A
  - Step 1B
- Step 2
- Step 3

See the chapters on Plain English and document design for further details.

Step 9: Test the Description

If possible, try out the description with sample members of your intended audience. If no one is available, ask a colleague or friend to play the role of your touchstone reader. Focus your testers on these issues:

- What assumptions does the description make about what is familiar to its intended readers and what they need to know?
- How valid are these assumptions?
- Are there missing or incomplete steps?
- Are there transitions between steps?
- Are all decision points identified?
- Are the possible paths resulting from all decisions shown?

Step 10: Revise as Necessary

Using the information you've gathered from your testers, revise and retest your description.

CHAPTER SUMMARY

Readers require descriptions for a wide range of objects and processes, and those descriptions must be appropriate to your readers' knowledge and interests.

A physical description shows what a natural or mechanical object looks like at one particular moment. A process description, on the other hand, shows a series of events over time and may also include decision points, that is, places in the process where some actions become contingent on others. A flow chart is the most useful graphic to capture such decision points.

Knowing who will read your description is as important as knowing the object or the process itself. When you understand your audience, you can decide how much detail they need and the most effective way to present it. Similarly, graphics should neither overwhelm readers with information nor omit items they require.

Writing descriptions is itself a process that demands planning so that you understand the object and your audience. Only then can you decompose the object or process (that is, break it into its constituent parts), plan your presentation, and choose your graphics. As with all professional documents, you must thoroughly field test your description and revise it accordingly.

CHECKLISTS

PHYSICAL DESCRIPTION

Have you described your audience in terms of:

The touchstone reader

Level of expertise

Level of technical sophistication

What the reader needs to know

Why the reader is reading

Have you described the object in terms of:

The object's name

General or specific instances

The object's function

The object's typical user

☐ Dimensions, weight, and shape

☐ The materials the object is made of

☐ The way the object works

☐ Being part of something larger

☐ Other important features

☐ The appropriate granularity

Does the preliminary draft:

☐ Start with an overview

☐ Identify and present each part in order

☐ Say what each part is used for

☐ Conclude with the overview

☐ Integrate a graphic

☐ Express itself clearly

☐ Pass tests with sample readers

Does the revised draft:

☐ Incorporate testers' feedback

☐ Use Plain English

☐ Lead reader through graphic

☐ Pass tests with sample readers

Your additional comments:

PROCESS DESCRIPTION

Have you described your audience in terms of:

☐ The touchstone reader

☐ Level of current expertise

☐ Level of technical sophistication

☐ What the reader needs to know

☐ Why the reader is reading

Have you described the process in terms of:
- The process's name
- Who uses or controls it
- What it accomplishes
- The process's inputs and outputs
- The main steps
- Flow (linear, causal, cyclical, etc.)
- Any decision points and the paths forward and back from them
- Being part of something larger
- Other important features
- The appropriate granularity

Does the preliminary draft:
- Start with an overview
- Identify and present each step in order
- Say what happens in each step
- Say who or what performs or controls the step
- Identify any decision points and describe path forward or back from them to the main flow of the process.
- Integrate a flow chart if one is needed

Does the revised draft:
- Incorporate testers feedback
- Use Plain English
- Lead readers through graphic
- Pass tests with sample readers

Your additional comments:

EXERCISES

For these exercises, don't worry about exact details; invent reasonable specifications if you can't find actual ones. Quick graphics would be helpful in all cases, but don't spend too much time on elaborate drawings.

Exercise 1

Work in groups of two or three to prepare a physical description of a computer lab with which you're familiar. Break it into its component parts as if you were dismantling the room with a screwdriver. Your audience is someone who is thinking of setting up a similar lab elsewhere and needs to know what should be in it and how it fits together. Decide on how detailed your descriptions should be for this audience.

Exercise 2

Work in groups of two or three to prepare a process description of the same computer lab as in Exercise 1. Think of the dynamics of the lab, that is, the movement of people from the time they enter the lab area, through finding a computer, printing a file, getting help, and so forth. Your audience is someone who is thinking of setting up a similar lab elsewhere and needs to know what should be in it and how it fits together. Decide on how detailed your descriptions should be for this audience.

Exercise 3

Working individually, write physical descriptions for three of the objects in the list below. Your readers are your classmates; describe them as an audience (for example, the level of their technical sophistication). If you're unfamiliar with these topics, substitute something similar.

a.   A bicycle rack that can be locked

b.   A pay telephone that accepts credit and calling cards

c.   A combination CD/AM/FM player

d.   A fast-food hamburger (specify from which restaurant chain)

e.   A scanner (or other piece of computer equipment)

f.   The student government at your school

g.   A typical army

h.   A room in your home

i.   A particular dog or cat you know (like Spot or Tiger)

j.   A refrigerator

Exercise 4

Working individually, write descriptions of the following processes. Your readers are your classmates; describe them as an audience (for example, the level of their technical sophistication). If you're unfamiliar with these topics, substitute something similar.

a. Making a pizza with cheese, pepperoni, and anchovies
b. Verifying that the bank has received payment for a loan
c. Keeping score in bowling
d. Using a cellular phone to tell a radio station about a traffic tie-up
e. Registering for a writing course at your school
f. Housebreaking a puppy
g. Tuning a car engine
h. Logging on to the Internet via a dial-up connection
i. Driving a car with a standard transmission
j. Generating a list of Web sites that have information about Sir John A. MacDonald

CHAPTER

11

Writing for General Readers

What This Chapter Covers

Ideas

Why Technical Writing Can't Be Technical
What General Readers Need
What General Readers Want
Starting With What Readers Know
Symbols and Comparisons
> One-Dimensional Comparison: Using Metaphor and Simile
> Multi-dimensional Comparison: Using Analogy
> Comparisons by Professionals
> Einstein's Relativity
> Good and Bad Comparisons
Telling Stories and Making Promises
> The Story of Ike and Mike
> Making Promises and Sending Signals

Actions

Step 1: Generate Common and Uncommon Comparisons
Step 2: Work Out the Possibilities
Step 3: Give Your Mind a Chance
Step 4: Eliminate Weak Comparisons
Step 5: Consider the Audience
Step 6: Find the Common Ground, Not the Commonplace
Step 7: Eliminate the Too-Clever Comparison
Step 8: Consider Multiple Comparisons
Step 9: Test and Revise

Chapter Summary

Checklists

Exercises

Ideas into action

Learning Objectives

At the end of this chapter, you will be able to explain:

- That much technical writing is written for general readers who want to understand a topic without becoming experts
- Why you should tell people what they don't know in terms of what they do know
- How technical writers—like poets—use metaphor and analogy
- How a comparison fails when it draws attention to itself, claims too much, or is wrong for a particular audience
- Why good technical writers tell stories and make promises

At the end of this chapter, you will be able to write for general audiences by:

- Generating comparisons
- Working out the similarities and differences between your topic and what you're comparing it with
- Eliminating weak comparisons
- Analyzing your audience
- Field testing and revising

I D E A S

Why Technical Writing Can't Be Technical

When people think of technical writing, they often think of dense, jargon-filled prose that only an expert could understand. However, much technical writing is for readers who don't understand a topic and don't have specialized knowledge on which to build. Technical writing, therefore, must be accessible to its readers, regardless of their backgrounds.

Experts do, of course, read about technical topics, but they do so to further their already advanced understanding. General readers, on the other hand, want to learn about a topic without becoming experts themselves. Writers forget that distinction at their peril.

What General Readers Need

Suppose you were a novice buying your first computer. You would likely look for guidance—perhaps reading a few magazines, talking to friends, listening to sales people. And when you finally brought your machine home, you would put the manuals next to it and keep on friendly terms with the Help key.

The best help, not surprisingly, is clear and straightforward. The language must be plain and the explanations—as Einstein remarked in another context—as simple as possible but no simpler. If the help is not helpful, your frustration would simmer and eventually boil over. A vital part of your work as a professional writer is saving readers from simmering and boiling.

Writing for a general audience requires many of the same skills as writing for specialists, such as clear organization, Plain English, graphics that complement text, and knowledge of audience. Part I of this book discusses those issues fully, so we'll mention them only in passing here. Our focus will on the specific needs of general readers.

What General Readers Want

General readers want to understand a topic but only to a point. That is, they neither expect nor wish to become experts. They are quite happy knowing, for example, what happens on each of the four strokes of an internal combustion engine without also knowing the molecular reactions between fuel and air. They are happy knowing how refrigerators chill food without also knowing the pressure necessary to liquefy Freon. They're happy knowing which home security systems work without also knowing the physics of infrared motion-sensors.

For greater detail, they would look to more technical works, ones that demand a significantly higher level of prerequisite knowledge. Such demands are very much relaxed in writing for non-specialists. However, that makes the writer's job more difficult: the material must be accurate and clear regardless of the audience's level of sophistication. Explaining things simply turns out be anything but simple.

Starting With What Readers Know

A basic idea should inform all your writing: *Tell people what they don't know in terms of what they do know.* That is, when you explain something, your first task is knowing to whom you're speaking; you then look for some common ground between what they already know and what you want them to know.

Let's look at a straightforward example. A brief definition should immediately follow the first use of a technical term. Once your readers know that definition, you can use the technical term freely in other places. In other words, you build on that newly acquired knowledge—*what they know*—to go on to other things—*what they don't know.*

Symbols and Comparisons

That principle turns out to have wider application. When we speak to others, everything we say depends on our listeners' knowing the meanings of our words. Suppose I wanted to communicate *chalk* to you: I could show you a piece, let you touch it, and perhaps if you were willing, let you taste it. But such dependence on your senses would be inefficient, not to say unhygienic.

Instead, I depend on your knowing a coding system—sounds and letters—so that I can write or say the word *chalk* and conjure up its image in your mind. Again, I'm telling you what you don't know—something about chalk—in terms of what you do know—a coding system of sounds and letters. If I used the word for *chalk* in a language you didn't understand, my attempt to communicate would obviously fail.

In short, I am symbolically using *Thing A* to lead you to *Thing B*. Sometimes symbols are arbitrarily chosen or imported from another language. Sometimes they purport to imitate the world (like *ding-dong*). But much of the time, symbols are built on comparisons.

Right now, for example, you may feel that I am drowning you in a *sea* of words and that you can't keep your head above *water* (and, in fact, I may be all *wet* too). But what you're doing when you think like that is comparing *Thing A* (my words) to *Thing B* (a lot of water). The most effective technical writing also depends on comparisons, in ways similar to poetry. Please don't stop reading.

One-Dimensional Comparison: Using Metaphor and Simile

Poets use metaphor extensively, that is, figurative language in which one thing is called another, *implicitly* comparing the two (as in the water example above). Poets also use simile, which *explicitly* compares two different things, often linking them with the words "like" or "as." "My love is like a red, red rose," wrote Robbie Burns. In this simile, he didn't mean that the object of his affection was a tall, skinny green girl with a bright red mass on her head, perhaps surrounded by buzzing flies. With apologies to Burns, he probably thought something like this:

> There's this girl I want to tell you about, and she's really beautiful, and I love her a lot. You've never her seen her, but I want to tell you how I feel. You do know how beautiful a rose is, especially, let's see, a red one. And red is the colour of blood and so passion. She's no wimp, this girl—I'll need two reds, then, not just one. So I'm going to tell you what you don't know—*what my love is like*—in terms of what you do know—*a red, red rose.*

Well, that's probably not exactly what Burns thought. But what he was doing was what we do every time we speak, although he did it in a particularly memorable way. His love was no more a rose than the word *chalk* is a piece of chalk. But both rose and *chalk* lead you to know something you didn't know before.

When we learn, therefore, that gas molecules behave like billiard balls, our physics teacher is doing what poets do. When we learn that eighteenth-century thinkers saw God as a watchmaker, our philosophy teacher is doing what poets do. And when we learn that computer memory is like human memory, our computer-science teacher is also doing what poets do, that is, using simile.

Multi-dimensional Comparison: Using Analogy

Comparing one thing to one other is helpful, and so is simultaneously comparing several dimensions of one thing to several dimensions of another. That kind of comparison is called an analogy. (It's not always better, as we'll see.) Here's an example: In Shakespeare's *Henry IV, Part I*, two rebels compare the recently deposed king Richard and the current king, Bolingbroke (the deposer) to *roses* and *weeds*.

Shakespeare uses roses somewhat differently than Burns, although both writers knew that people value roses highly. But Shakespeare also knew that his audience saw the world as a set of hierarchies that placed some objects higher—and so literally closer to God—than others. In the plant world, roses are higher than weeds, at least, so his audience was likely to think.

Shakespeare differs from Burns because Shakespeare's comparison works across more than one dimension. The logic goes this way:

Richard and roses are at the top of their respective hierarchies, humans and plants.

Bolingbroke and weeds are at the very bottom of the same hierarchies.

The relationship between Richard and Bolingbroke is the same as the relationship between roses and weeds.

Richard, therefore, is to Bolingbroke as a rose is to a weed.

Expressing this formally, the analogy says that A:B::C:D, or A is to B as C is to D.

Other plants also are ranked, so other pairs of humans could be similarly compared. In fact, because all objects in the universe are ranked, a pair from one domain can be compared to a pair in another. So the rebels might have also used lions and hyenas, the sun and a meteor, gold and lead. The individual elements are not equal to each other, but their relationships are parallel.

Shakespeare's audience knew those hierarchies as well as people today know that radio waves are both invisible and real. He could exploit that knowledge and tell his audience what they didn't know—the relationship between Richard and Bolingbroke—in terms of what they did know—the relationship between roses and weeds. But, as we'll see next, you don't have to be a poet or a playwright to use metaphor, simile, and analogy.

Comparisons by Professionals

Comparing goes on all the time in technical writing, and here are a few first-rate examples:

- Neely Turner (quoted by Rachel Carson) compares people who control insects with DDT and other chemicals to Old West vigilante justice:

  The regulatory entomologists . . . function as prosecutor, judge and jury, tax assessor and collector and sheriff to enforce their own orders.

  Rachel L. Carson, *Silent Spring* (Boston: Houghton Mifflin, 1962).

- Lewis Thomas conjures up the horrors of war as he explains the body's response to bacteria:

  Our arsenals for fighting off bacteria are so powerful, and involve so many different defense mechanisms, that we are more in danger from them than from the invaders. We live in the midst of explosive devices; we are mined.

  Lewis Thomas, *Lives of a cell* (London: Viking Penguin Inc. and Garnerstone Press, 1974).

- Francis Crick makes us think of writers typing away when he talks about amino acids:

  > A protein is like a paragraph written in a twenty-letter language, the exact nature of the protein being determined by the exact order of the letters. With one trivial exception, the script never varies. Animals, plants, microorganisms, and viruses all use the same set of twenty letters although, as far as we can tell, other similar letters could easily have been employed, just as other symbols could have been used to construct our own alphabet.

  > Francis Crick. *Life Itself: Its Origins and Nature* (New York: Simon and Shuster, 1981).

These comparisons explain complex ideas. But let's consider an idea even more complex: the theory of relativity. Our guide will be Albert Einstein.

Einstein's Relativity

Many people can repeat Einstein's famous equation that $E=mc^2$. To appreciate the full details of this relationship among energy, mass, and the speed of light, however, you need far more than basic algebra. Einstein usually wrote for mathematically sophisticated physicists, but at other times, he wanted to reach audiences that didn't have that expertise. On those occasions he used this comparison:

> Suppose that a man stands on the observation deck of a moving train and drops a small rock. From where this man stands, the rock's trajectory as it drops to the ground is a straight line. Now suppose another man watches the first from the side of the railroad track as the train goes by. From where this second man stands, the rock's trajectory isn't a straight line but a curve. Two men observe apparently the same phenomenon at apparently the same instant, yet their observations are quite different. Who is right and who is wrong?

> [This is a simplification of a passage from Einstein's *Relativity: The Special and the General Theory* translated by Robert W. Lawson (New York: Crown Publishers Inc., 1961) and quoted in William Zinsser's *Writing To Learn* (New York: HarperCollins, 1989).]

The answer, of course, is that each man is right from his own perspective. And that's one of the basic tenets of relativity. To fully grasp the implications of this story takes a great deal more than imagining a rock dropping from a train. But here Einstein wasn't teaching the subtleties of relativity but telling his readers what they didn't know in terms of what they did or at least could readily imagine.

Good and Bad Comparisons

Like everything else, some comparisons are better than others. For writers, a comparison is good to the degree it helps readers understand. But here are three main ways a comparison can be bad:

Misreading the audience: One can make a very good analogy on logical grounds that would still fail to help its audience understand. Suppose I said that steering a boat is like steering a car, although I knew you couldn't drive a car. Regardless of how logically apt my comparison would be, it would fail to help you.

Comparisons can also fail when an audience understands them but is put off. For example, a *Monty Python* sketch features a bemused monarch gradually realizing that people are comparing him to all sorts of disgusting objects.

Drawing attention to itself: A second type of poor comparison is one that draws attention to itself rather than to what's being explained. For example, John Donne compares the love he and his wife share to a drafting compass (both lovers and compass are joined at the highest level but separated at the lowest). Some of Donne's readers remember the ingenuity of the comparison more than the love. Of course, intrusiveness is a matter of taste, and not everyone objects. So in the Actions section later in this chapter, we'll talk about testing comparisons to see how readers react.

Claiming too much: A comparison can also be bad when it claims more than it can deliver. For example, both the Mafia and the Canadian Medical Association have codes of conduct, try to influence persons in authority, and discipline their members. But unless you wish to imply that doctors are criminals who really should be in jail, the comparison fails. Another example might be the old one that compares a country to the human body—the king, for example, is the head, the army is the arms, and so forth. But modern audiences see the world very differently from earlier ones and likely would reject the comparison as logically suspect.

Comparing one thing to another is an important tool when you write for a general audience, but, of course, it's not the only one. Let's consider two others.

Telling Stories and Making Promises

Telling stories and making promises work particularly well with general audiences. When you tell a story, you can teach (like Aesop and his fables) and you can entertain ("Once upon a time . . ."). When you make and keep promises about how you're explaining things ("Let's see what happened to Goldilocks when the three bears returned"), you help readers follow along. And when you combine storytelling and promise making, you really increase your chances of success.

The Story of Ike and Mike

A story, of course, can play fast and loose with fact and still be true, or at least, true enough. That works well with general readers, who want to understand a topic but only up to a point. Suppose you wish to explain to Grade 8 students Heisenberg's uncertainty principle, which says that one cannot simultaneously know the exact position of an object and its exact speed. Here is how one student in a technical-writing course did it:

> Two friends, Mike and Ike, are playing a rather vicious version of hide-and-seek. They're in a small room, and Mike is blindfolded. He holds a number of rocks in his hand and his object is to hit Ike with them twice in a row. Every time he throws a rock and hits Ike, Ike screams in pain. That sound should tell Mike where Ike is. But Ike—no fool—immediately runs away. Mike can hear Ike running, but no matter how hard Mike tries, he can't hit Ike a second time. That shows you can't know the location of an object and its speed at the same instant.

Physicists, of course, will be more than a bit uncertain with this account of uncertainty. Nonetheless, the story succeeded because the Grade 8 audience understood enough (not all, by any means) about the uncertainty principle to satisfy them. (The technical writer gave the story to Grade 8 students to test.)

Stories often incorporate comparisons to great effect (people who want to spray insecticide are like old West vigilantes, two men watch as one drops a rock from a moving train). So the line between storytelling and technical writing isn't as clear as it sometimes seems.

Making Promises and Sending Signals

Chapter 2 talks about ways to signal readers how you're structuring your work. Many of those signalling techniques—headings and transitional devices, for example—apply here. But they do need a bit of changing.

When you write a technical article or a report, you and your readers share a ready-made context: Chemists know, for example, what they're likely to find in a chemistry journal and the conventions for presenting experimental results. The same holds for any other specialty. General audiences, however, aren't likely to know a specific set of conventions and will need more explicit signalling. For that, the notion of making promises helps.

An editor once told a famous writer that his latest work started by saying, "Once upon a time, there were three bears," but then went on to talk about Hansel and Gretel. The writer, of course, wasn't really writing about a little girl or bears, but the point holds: Writers must begin with a promise and then signal how everything in the story keeps that promise.

Think of a popular article that begins, "Using a riding mower safely means you don't have to be a circus daredevil." It promises to tell you how to use the mower without risking life and limb. That promise raises expectations in readers; they'll hear about removing objects on the lawn, keeping children or pets away, storing fuel, and so on. If the article discusses the virtues of mulching, it breaks its promise—mulching is a story for another day.

Raising and meeting expectations is part of every kind of writing, but it's especially important when you write for ordinary readers. They start, after all, without much to build on. Anything that further confuses them will cost you their attention, perhaps forever.

Professional writers and poets do not use metaphor, analogy, and stories to hide their meaning, any more than you would hide the meaning of something you wanted to say. Good writers take advantage of what they know about their audience and use "poetic" techniques to make their meaning clearer to that audience. Let's now turn to putting these ideas into action.

ACTIONS

In what follows, we examine techniques for finding and using comparisons. Give your imagination free rein (at least for a while) and temporarily suspend that part of your mind that censors itself. Many of your comparisons will likely prove ridiculous or at least inappropriate. But you first have to generate a number of them before you can winnow out the bad ones.

Step 1: Generate Common and Uncommon Comparisons

Visualize what you want to explain. Then think of a something quite different that it calls to your mind. Do not reject anything, but jot down comparisons as they occur. If you're stuck, ask to what your topic is usually compared and then ask to what it's never compared. Work quickly, so that you don't have a chance to think too much too soon.

For example, suppose you are trying to explain football to a friend who seldom watches it and then is always bored. You especially want to explain the passion football evokes in many people and some of the game's intricacies. Here's a list of things to which you might compare football:

- Armies fighting a war
- Politicians fighting an election

- Debaters debating
- Pigs wallowing
- Crocodiles attacking
- Tanks colliding
- Gladiators battling
- Movie stars competing
- Lions chasing antelopes
- Ballerinas leaping

WORKING SMARTER

Freewriting

If you're having trouble letting your mind generate possible comparisons, try freewriting. Freewriting is a technique first widely publicized by Peter Elbow, a writing teacher and researcher. The idea is to help you get going on a topic by writing non-stop, putting down whatever comes into your mind. If you truly can't think of anything to say, start by typing "I can't think of anything to say." After typing for three to five minutes, look at the result and choose about three things that surprise you. Use them as the basis for another go-round.

Stephen Marcus, a pioneer in using computers to teach writing, has developed this electronic variation of freewriting:

1. Blank the screen on the monitor.
2. Type for three to five minutes.
3. Turn the screen back on.
4. Highlight the interesting and the surprising.
5. Copy the highlighted material to a new document.
6. Repeat as needed.

You can do the same kind of exercise with lists.

Step 2: Work Out the Possibilities

Briefly explain the similarities and differences between your topic and each item on your list. Don't make final judgments but examine your comparisons and perhaps generate others. Try for about ten items. With that done, put your list away for a while.

Here are some possibilities for a football list (to which you're invited to add):

- Football and war both involve two sides, a contest, physical violence, and strategy. However, the goal in football isn't to kill your opponents or take over their lands.
- Football and politics both have opposing sides, supporters, and winners. However, politics are not (usually) physical and voters determine the outcome, rather than the number of touchdowns and field goals.
- Football and debating are types of combat with winners and losers. But debaters try to win by intellectual, not physical, force. Also debates are subjectively judged, while the scoring in football is objective.
- Football players and pigs are both extremely physical, emit grunting noises, and get covered in mud. But football is a contest that requires skill and tactics; pigs basically eat and wallow.
- Football players and crocodiles attack adversaries and use guile. But football players don't kill and seldom bite each other. And crocodiles would look silly in helmets.
- Football players and tanks both are big and protected by armour. However, football players aren't mechanical devices but humans who think.
- Football players and Roman gladiators fight each other for other people's entertainment and wear special equipment. However, gladiators generally fought one-on-one (not as part of a team) and often to the death.
- Football players and movie stars both compete for fame, glory, endorsements, and wealth; but movies are not formal contests and most stars are not large physical specimens.
- Football players chase other football players and lions chase antelopes. However (as in the comparison with crocodiles) football players don't kill and rarely bite each other.
- Football players leap over opponents and ballerinas leap over each other; both are graceful. Ballet, however, is not a contest nor do people deliberately knock each other over.

Step 3: Give Your Mind a Chance

Let some time pass (at least an hour, but a day is better) before continuing so that your mind has some time to percolate, as it were. Most people have experienced working late on a problem, then going to bed and waking up with the solution that had eluded them. That's because even when we're not consciously thinking of a problem, our minds continue to work on it. Letting time pass can generate new and often better possibilities.

Step 4: Eliminate Weak Comparisons

Begin to filter your list. Selecting the best comparisons depends on two factors: How well and how appropriately the comparisons explain. Reinstate your more rational self and eliminate comparisons that don't really explain your topic.

Make sure your comparisons don't claim too much or promise more explanatory power than they can deliver. Other people may well, of course, dismiss your reasoning and your choices. Different comparisons will work for different readers; the real test will come when you try them out with a sample audience.

Here is the filtering process applied to the football list:

- "Football as politics" does suggest opponents in a contest. But a political winner is the one who is more popular with the voters, not the team that scores more points on the field. Moreover, politics sometimes includes more than two opponents in the same election.
- "Football as debaters" is like the comparison with politics; it too doesn't go much farther than a contest and neglects that a third party, rather than an absolute score of the participants, determines the winner.
- "Football as movie stars" stretches the comparison to the breaking point. Stars do want to be Number One at the box office, but they don't square off against each other in a particular place at a particular time.

Step 5: Consider the Audience

Having eliminated comparisons that appear unworkable, now imagine your audience. If you can, name one or two typical members and keep them in mind throughout. What do they know? What can you tap into? What are their prejudices? What do they like? Do they have a sense of humor?

For instance, if the friend to whom you're explaining football knows about war or ballet, you can explore those two comparisons further. You can't be completely sure about your audience's knowledge, but you do want to avoid any comparisons that might be like our example of telling someone who doesn't drive that steering a boat is like steering a car. Neither do you wish to insult or otherwise turn away your readers. You'll hardly win converts to football, for example, by telling your readers that players are pigs.

Step 6: Find the Common Ground, Not the Commonplace

Your list most likely will include a number of comparisons that others have used. That in itself is not a bad thing because some comparisons—"Life is a journey," for example—have great resonance. However, others will be worn out commonplaces, as overused as the hackney horse that anyone could hire. A hockey penalty box, for example, may hold bad guys, but it seems like every sports announcer alive calls it a "sin bin." Similarly, you might really feel "as fresh as a daisy" on a fine, spring morning, but you'll sound as limp as yesterday's noodle. Clichés signal that you're out of ideas.

Step 7: Eliminate the Too-Clever Comparison

At the other extreme from the cliché is the too *uncommon* comparison, the one so clever that it calls attention to itself rather than your topic. Look at your list and ask yourself if any item does this.

For example, "football as ballet" may be true insofar as some players do leap gracefully. But it gets quickly ridiculous, conjuring up images of large men in football gear and tutus, prancing on their toes.

Step 8: Consider Multiple Comparisons

Can you use more than one item on your list?

Searching for the perfect comparison—the one that maps every function in one realm onto every function in another—wastes a lot of time. It's better to look for comparisons that do their explanatory jobs well enough, even though not perfectly.

Imperfect comparisons can help in another way: You may be able to use more than one for different parts of your topic. For example, football may be like war in its violence and tactics; but a charging lineman blindsiding a quarterback is something like a predator pouncing on unwary prey.

However, multiple comparisons risk muddling ideas. Football players may use military tactics, but they aren't animals following their natural desires for dinner. No hard and fast rules apply here; it's your readers who will decide whether your comparisons are helpfully mixed or hopelessly muddled—so ask them. Let's move on to testing.

Step 9: Test and Revise

Professionals write for specific audiences, not themselves. Poets and novelists have final say about the appropriateness of their comparisons, but professional writers must try out their comparisons by testing with a real audience.

As we discuss many other times in this book, find someone who is typical of your intended audience. Ask them if your comparison:

- Depended on knowledge they didn't have
- Claimed too much
- Helped them understand what you were explaining
- Distracted them or called attention to itself
- Was a worn-out cliché
- Was unintentionally funny or offensive
- Enabled them to explain the topic to another person

As always, assure your testers that you're looking for frank responses. Then revise accordingly and retest.

CHAPTER SUMMARY

As a professional writer, you will often write for general readers who wish to know about a topic without becoming experts. Your main strategy for this audience will be to tell them what they don't know in terms of what they do. Much good technical writing uses metaphors and analogies to accomplish that.

Using comparisons requires that you know your audience well so that you can choose the ones that will help most. You also have to ensure that your language does not draw attention to itself or claim too much explanatory power. You can also increase your document's effectiveness for general readers by making promises and telling stories that dramatize and enliven your subject.

To use metaphor and analogy, start by generating comparisons and working out the similarities and differences between what you're explaining and what you're comparing it to. Computers can help you brainstorm possibilities. Once you have eliminated the weak comparisons, test the remaining possibilities with yourself and with touchstone readers.

CHECKLISTS

Describe your audience in the following terms:

Names of one or two typical members who will act as touchstone readers

Reading level

Previous knowledge about the topic

Reason for reading (for example, pure entertainment, general knowledge, preparation for more advanced study)

Biases, prejudices, sensitivities

For comparisons:

Generate eight to ten possibilities

Don't censor your thoughts as they occur

Give your mind enough time by putting aside your work

Sketch out the basic possibilities for your comparisons

Eliminate comparisons that claim too much

Eliminate comparisons that would offend or otherwise turn away your audience

Eliminate comparisons that are clichés

Eliminate comparisons that call attention to themselves

Consider using multiple comparisons

Test reactions from members of target audience

Revise accordingly

Other Issues:

Make and keep promises.

Follow organization principles (see Chapter 2).

Keep language plain (see Chapter 3).

Have informative headers.

Have helpful and sufficient graphics.

Your additional comments:

EXERCISES

The first seven exercises take you through the steps for writing comparisons while the last exercise gives you some practice in writing promises for your readers.

Exercise 1

Work in groups of three or four and suggest comparisons that are often used for these items:

    a.   Computers

    b.   Relationships between men and women

    c.   Politics

    d.   Information

Write a sentence or two to explain each one. For example: "Computer memory stores data just as humans keep information in their brains."

Exercise 2

Working in groups of three or four, generate a list of metaphors for:

    a.   Life

    b.   The university or college you attend

    c.   Food in your least favourite restaurant

    d.   The natural world

    e.   Your best friend

    f.   Your worst enemy

Visualize each of these items and then think of a different thing or activity that the item calls to mind. Jot down the comparisons quickly without dwelling on any one in particular. Don't censor yourself but give free rein to your imagination. Then briefly explain the similarities and differences between your topic and each item you jotted down.

Exercise 3

Extend your metaphors to see how well each one explains your topic. Push them to the point where they break, that is, lose their explanatory power.

Exercise 4

Working individually and using the comparisons in Exercise 3, imagine different audiences. For example:

    a.   Your classmates

    b.   Your grandparents

c.   Grade 8 students

d.   Kindergarten students

e.   A police officer who has just stopped you for speeding

Name one or two typical members and keep them in mind throughout. What do they know? What can you tap into? What are their prejudices? What do they like? Do they have a sense of humor? Write a sentence or two explaining how appropriate each comparison would be.

Exercise 5

Working with your list of comparisons, eliminate the clichés and overly clever examples.

Exercise 6

Combine two of your comparisons for the same topic. Does that increase their individual effectiveness? Or will the combination likely confuse your readers? Write a brief note explaining why you would or would not use them together.

Exercise 7

Working with other members of your class, take turns playing the role of touchstone reader, that is, someone who is typical of your intended audience. Ask them if any of your comparisons:

a.   Depended on knowledge they didn't have

b.   Claimed too much

c.   Helped them understand what you were explaining

d.   Distracted them or called attention to itself

e.   Was a worn-out cliché

f.   Was unintentionally funny or offensive

g.   Enabled them to explain the topic to another person

Exercise 8

Again, working individually, write "promises," that is, opening sentences for articles that explain how the following things work:

a.   Nuclear power plants

b.   Airplanes

c.   Democracy

d.   Water evaporation

e.   Evolution

PART

3

What the New
Professional
Writers
Produce

12 | Writing for the World Wide Web

13 | Writing Media Releases

14 | Speaking to Groups

CHAPTER

12

Writing for the World Wide Web

What This Chapter Covers

Ideas

Why the Web Matters
Why Text Is the Main Way of Communicating
Fickle at the Speed of Light
Helping Readers See How Ideas Fit Together
Planning Your Site
Integrating Navigation Devices
Web Layout and Appearance

Actions

Step 1: Plan Your Site
Step 2: Describe the Audience
Step 3: Prototype and Test
Step 4: Create a Site Template
Step 5: Build Content
Step 6: Insert Links
Step 7: Adjust the Layout
Step 8: Alpha Test
Step 9: Beta Test
Sample Questions for Usability Testing

Chapter Summary

Checklists

Exercises

Learning Objectives

At the end of this chapter, you will be able to explain:

- Why professional writers must be able to create Web pages
- How Web readers differ from print readers
- Why you must plan the common features of your Web site
- Why you must break content into separate pages
- What questions you must ask about your Web audience
- Why you must prototype your site and create a template for it
- The basic principles of Web navigation
- The types of links
- The use of frames
- How to help readers connect ideas
- The principles of Web layout and appearance
- The importance of white space on the screen
- Choosing and using colour

At the end of this chapter, you will be able to produce Web pages by:

- Planning your site
- Describing your audience
- Prototyping and doing preliminary testing
- Creating a site template
- Writing content and inserting navigation devices
- Field testing

IDEAS

Why the Web Matters

Seldom has there been a better match between a medium and the people it serves. In an age when information is both everywhere and ever changing, the World Wide Web instantly brings together writers and readers. For professionals, the Web—a vast collection of linked documents—is quickly becoming as indispensable as the telephone.

Although the much-vaunted fortunes to be made on the Web will be limited to a very few, companies of all kinds already use the Web to tell the world about themselves and what they do. The Web has also become an important tool for communicating *within* organizations. Further, information increasingly flows in two directions, as readers of Web pages respond immediately to what they see. The potential is there for a truly rich conversation.

The opportunity for writers, therefore, is greater than ever—provided they have the necessary skills. Simple text editors for HTML (Hypertext Markup Language, the Web's *lingua franca*) have been largely replaced by far more powerful authoring tools, and writers now can concentrate on the job of creating information. To that end, they use not only words but also graphics, video, and sound. This chapter discusses the issues in creating Web sites, not the details of HTML.

Why Text Is the Main Way of Communicating

Pro golfers have a saying: "Drive for fun, putt for money." Web authors need something similar: "Graphics for fun, words for money."

Despite the undeniable value of graphics, words still carry most of the Web's content. Surfers can set their browsers to not display images and still read and navigate well-designed pages. But they cannot continue without text. Worry too much about making your site "visually exciting"—like the notorious example of having a duck walk across the page—and you risk forgetting how ordinary text keeps readers reading.

Fickle at the Speed of Light

All writers, of course, should know who their readers are, what those readers know, and what they need to know. Web authors have to consider one more issue: The Web isn't print, and Web readers don't read like print readers.

Web readers are fickle—and fickle at the speed of light. They leave a page as soon it no longer interests them. They are also unlikely to scroll much beyond what is immediately visible when a page loads. Think of how you yourself surf: You probably glance at a site's first page, looking for the Web equivalent of a newspaper headline that interests you. If you find one, you read on a bit, just until you lose interest in the content, get confused, or just plain bored. Then, click, you're gone.

Web readers are fickle because there's so much that competes for their time— millions of sites, thousands of newsgroups, and hundreds of e-mail messages. The same ceaseless tide of information that makes the Web so powerful also makes readers edgy, impatient, and ready to move on to that mythical better page that's always just a click away. In fact, Web readers scan more than they read.

Even worse for writers is that reading on the Web isn't physically comfortable. For example:

- Web readers can't curl up in front of a roaring fire with a good page. Instead, they often hunch over keyboards for hours, straining their eyes and hurting their necks.
- Web readers can't read screens as quickly as they can read hard copy, and that makes their time at the monitor seem even longer.
- Web readers quite literally look at text through a window, that is, only a relatively small screen area. They can easily lose track of how individual ideas connect. Following a site's structural logic is more difficult yet when they have to either link too often or scroll too much.

The unhappy combination of lots of choice, physical discomfort, and cognitive confusion produces an audience with a low tolerance for writing that wastes time.

Regardless of how good their content, Web writers must know *how* their readers read if they hope to shape *what* their readers read. Assuming you have something to write about, how do you say it so Web readers keep reading? One way is to ensure that readers understand your content without undue difficulty; that's what we'll consider next.

Helping Readers See How Ideas Fit Together

Web sites are often designed like inverted trees, with the main page at the top and all the pages or branches beneath, as shown in Figure 12.1. That's better than no design at all and certainly useful when you're planning your site. However, it's probably not how visitors will experience it.

A good Web site isn't linear, like a book that starts at Chapter 1. Instead, it's a network where hierarchies of topics shift as readers shift their interests. What is in the middle of the tree becomes the top of the tree when the reader decides that subject is the most important at that instant.

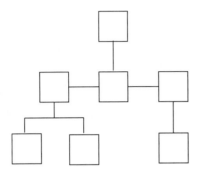

Figure 12.1
Web-site tree structure

For example, a reader may want to know all about a company's product, then want to hear about its stock shares, and later want to find out who in the company can answer technical questions. It's the Web writer's job to accommodate that wide range of choice.

In contrast to sites organized like a tree, some sites seem to have no organization at all. Useful information may be buried so deeply that no one but the author can find it. In these cases, readers can't make informed choices about what they'll find. And if they can't find what they want, they leave.

You need, therefore, to help readers keep their bearings, to show them where they can go next. Navigation techniques—buttons, text links, menus, etc.—carry much of the load, but so must text and layout. However, before you can decide what kind of navigation, text, and layout to use, you first have to plan your site.

Planning Your Site

Just as with planning a print document, planning a Web site requires you to know your purpose and your audience. You need to answer two questions in particular:

- Why will people visit your site?
- How can information be so compellingly presented that they will stay?

Without answering the first question, you cannot judge what content to include or how to structure it. Without answering the second, you cannot judge how to present this content in a way that exploits the Web's power and makes your site more than just a book that somehow found its way onto the Internet.

For example, suppose Amalgamated Consolidated Incorporated (ACI) asks you to do their Web site. Will you discuss its products? Its employees? Its financial performance? If so, which aspects of its products, employees, or performance? What other topics are possible? And once you have decided what to include, how will you use the Web to communicate? With text? With multimedia? With opportunities for readers to ask questions? How will you integrate these elements?

Buckminster Fuller once described how he chose projects to work on: He asked what is there in the world that needed doing that he knew something about and that no one else was doing. To recast Fuller's comments in terms of Web-site planning, you need to ask what information would benefit visitors to your site, how to collect that information, and how to present it in a way that exists nowhere else either on the Web or in print.

Breaking a Site Into Pages

Once you have thought about what information will be on your site, you'll likely have a lot to say. But you can't say it all at once. Instead, you have to break your ideas into medium-size units.

A Web page is such a unit; it falls nicely between a site and a paragraph, both logical divisions that express a single topic. Page divisions give readers a place to pause, to rest, and to assimilate what they've read.

How long should a page be? There's no magic set number of sentences. Rather, it's a question of readability, of how much visitors to the site can keep straight. Readers need to rest periodically, especially at a computer screen. The best way to know if a page is too long is to test how much it forces readers to scroll. Long pages make it all too easy for readers to lose their place. Testing is a critical issue, and we'll come back to it later.

Early on in your planning stage, therefore, you have to break your larger topic—for example, Amalgamated Consolidated Incorporated—into medium-size chunks and tentatively assign each its own page. The division, of course, will be subject to testing and revision.

Planning for Your Web Audience

For what readers are you creating a site? You would ask a similar question, of course, for any writing you do. But because the Web makes it particularly easy for readers to leave, the issue of audience requires special attention. Here are two questions:

• What information do my readers want when they come to my site?
• What do they plan to do with that information?

For example, are visitors to the Amalgamated Consolidated Incorporated site looking for answers to specific questions about products (what the company makes, how these products work, who can fix them)? Are they looking for information that changes rapidly (prices, new models)? Are they looking for general information about the company (how long it has existed, its performance on the stock market)? Are they looking for phone numbers (to purchase a product, to complain)? In other words, you must determine how people will *use* your site, not just how they will *read* it.

Prototyping Strategies

Once you have decided for whom you're creating your site and what you'll put on it for them, you should prototype your site. You should do a quick mock-up of the common elements on every page. For example, every page on the site should have the same logo, the same links to the main sections, and the same contact information.

You can simply sketch a sample page on paper. However, the best way to create such a prototype—and indeed, most of your site—is to use a Web authoring program that (as much as possible) keeps you from having to know HTML. Learning HTML is unnecessary for all but the most complex and interactive sites. The designers of HTML, in fact, never intended people to learn it but instead correctly assumed that Web authoring programs would take care of the messy details, just as a word processors shield their users from the minutiae of formatting codes.

There are many Web authoring programs on the market, ranging from simple to complex and costing from nothing to several hundred dollars. In fact, the latest versions of the major word processors let you save documents as Web pages. The results may not be good enough for complex sites, but they are adequate for many others.

Once you have created a prototype, test it out with a few people (potential typical users are best, but colleagues will do). Your goal is to find out early on if your initial assumptions about users and content are correct.

Creating a Template

Once your prototype has passed muster, you need to build a template for your site. That is, you create a file that will be the model for all pages. For example, every page should include:

- The organization's logo
- Links to main pages
- Space reserved for main text
- Contact information
- The date of the last update

A template will save you much repetitive work (for example, setting up the basic layout, inserting a logo, and choosing colours). You can still make adjustments to individual pages as required.

WORKING SMARTER

Saving Your Template

Save your template as a file that cannot be overwritten, only copied and saved under another name. That protects you from inadvertently altering your template. Such files are called read-only or stationery depending on the platform. Refer to your operating system's manual for details.

Keeping Your Layout Consistent

A template's most important function is to ensure a site has a consistent look and feel; this consistency enables readers to predict where they'll find content. Unless colours, fonts, and navigation links look the same throughout a site, readers will have to reorient themselves, constantly learning how each new page works. It's difficult enough for readers to do that with two pages; when a site has many, the burden increases dramatically.

Integrating Navigation Devices

The Web's great virtue is letting readers follow their interests, picking the routes through information that *they* decide upon. When Web surfers want to get somewhere, they don't want to hunt, backtrack, or "mouse" around the page any more than necessary. Navigation devices that make it easy to get around a site are therefore crucial. Here are some general principles:

Accommodate the reader, not yourself. All professional writing is about accommodating the reader, and that's especially important for helping readers navigate Web sites. They need information to help them predict what they will find when they click. For example, text should supplement graphics. It's hard to tell, for instance, where you'd go if you clicked on the thunderbolt in Figure 12.2. Adding a text link as in Figure 12.3 lets readers know what they'll find when they click:

Storm Information

Figure 12.2
An unhelpful graphic

Figure 12.3
Text complementing graphic

The text link, moreover, permits people who have graphics disabled (usually because of a slow network connection) to navigate. Readers want more than one way to get to other pages.

Be consistent. Consistency makes readers comfortable. Therefore, place navigation devices in the same place every time. The first page creates your reader's expectation; subsequent pages have to fulfill it. Mainstream navigational techniques (text links, menus, etc.) build on what readers are already familiar with. Use them rather than creating your own techniques, unless you have a compelling reason not to.

Don't insist on one path. The spirit of the Web is that readers control where they go and when they go. Even with a purely linear site, let them choose which pages to visit, showing them what comes next without also insisting that they go there. For example, use *Next* and *Previous* links but also offer a menu of all relevant links.

Next		Previous
	Section 1	
	Section 2	
	Section 3	
	Section 4	

Test navigation with real users. Don't depend on your own familiarity with navigational devices to gauge how others will perceive them. Instead, get a wide range of opinions about what is or is not working. Test your assumptions.

Specific Kinds of Links

The navigational devices discussed in the following sections aren't arranged in a hierarchy from better to worse. They are simply more suited or less suited to the information's content and context.

Text Links

Text links—that is, words that take you to a new page when you click them—were once all that was possible on the Web. They have retained their importance because they remain reliable and bandwidth-efficient. Text links can stand alone or be part of a menu of two or more items. As we've seen, they are also essential to supplement graphic links since not all readers will be willing (or able) to display graphics. Text links can be part of horizontal or vertical menus. For example:

> You can get the latest information at our Web site:
> [News]-[Weather]-[Sports]
>
> You can get the latest information at our Web site:
> [News]
> [Weather]
> [Sports]

Text links are valuable because they:

- Are the easiest type of link to create and edit
- Are essential for readers who have disabled images or use text-only browsers
- Require very little bandwidth
- Can be styled (with bold, italic, larger, smaller, or coloured type)

Their main drawback is that they don't create much visual interest.

Embedded Text Links

An embedded text link is a grammatical part of the sentence in which it appears, as opposed to being simply a menu item. That makes it easier for the reader to predict what page will be displayed. For example:

> You can read the latest news, weather, and sports 24 hours a day.
> The most fuel-efficient cars the government tested were the Honda Civic and the Toyota Tercel.
> As of June 19, Chemistry 101 and English 356 are both full.

Embedded text links are powerful because they:

- Provide readers with an immediate context, giving them a good idea of what they'll find if they click
- Are easy to create and edit
- Require very little bandwidth

However, sentences in which an embedded link appears require careful drafting to avoid awkwardness.

Graphic Links

A graphic link, as the term suggests, consists of a graphic rather than text. Although they can be visually interesting, they can also demand—and waste—a lot of bandwidth.

Graphic links generally are GIF or, less frequently, JPEG files (the two most widely supported graphic standards on the Web). You therefore require special software to create such images or convert them from other formats.

A graphic link can be an icon, an image, or specially designed text, as Figure 12.4 illustrates.

Icon   Image   Styled Text   Navigation Bar

Figure 12.4
Sample graphic links

Graphic links have the following advantages:

- They can present information without text if they are well-known symbols.
- They are visually interesting.
- Any text they contain will appear exactly as you want regardless of what fonts the reader has installed.

On the other hand, they need skill to create, can use substantial bandwidth, and depend on users' having their browsers set to display graphics.

Rollover Graphics

A rollover graphic changes colour when the reader moves the mouse over it, holds down the mouse button, or clicks.

Changing colour in this way provides visual feedback to readers about their actions. However, rollovers have these drawbacks:

- They require sophisticated tools to create.
- They use medium bandwidth.
- They depend on graphics being enabled in the reader's browser.

Image Maps

An image map is a graphic in which various sections are hot, that is, linked to different URLs. Clicking on different hot spots takes readers to different pages. Image maps are excellent for geographical maps, floor plans, or diagrams where you want to provide extra information about an object's individual components. For example, Figure 12.5 shows an image map of a building's interior. When readers click on one of the areas labeled A to K, the browser links to more detailed information about that part of the building.

Image maps are highly interactive and allow readers to visualize spatial relationships. They require medium bandwidth, depending on the graphic. They also require specialized graphic tools to create.

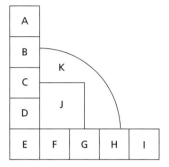

Figure 12.5
An image map

Pull-Down Menus

Pull-down menus display of a series of links that drop down when the reader simultaneously "mouses" over the menu and holds down the mouse button. For example, holding down the mouse button over the closed menu in Figure 12.6 produces the full menu in Figure 12.7.

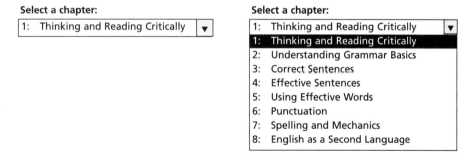

Figure 12.6
A closed pull-down menu

Figure 12.7
An open pull-down menu

Pull-down menus offer these advantages:

- They make good use of screen space and reduce screen clutter.
- They are bandwidth-efficient.
- They are standard navigation tools in modern operating systems, making them familiar to most users.

On the negative side:

- Readers must have a browser that supports JavaScript.
- Readers must have JavaScript enabled.
- The designer must know how to code JavaScript and forms.

Site Maps

A site map is a list of links (usually text-only) that appear on a separate page. They are arranged according to what typical readers are most likely to look for. Figure 12.8 shows an example.

**AMALGAMATED CONSOLIDATED
INCORPORATED SITE MAP**

PRODUCTS
    WidgetMaster 2000
    Flossimatic 300
    GizmoMagic 9000

TECHNICAL SUPPORT
    Phone
    Faxback
    Web Based

COMPANY NEWS
    New Products
    Jobs with ACI

Figure 12.8
A site map

Site maps give readers a helpful overview of the entire site, especially if the site is complex and its structure difficult to conceptualize. They also help readers gauge how much of a site they've seen. However, site maps take time and effort to create and update.

Using Frames for Navigation

Frames are areas in a browser's window that can display content different than the content elsewhere in the window. That permits keeping some information—typically navigation links—visible at all times. Figure 12.9 shows an example of a page with two frames; the main text for the page is on the right and navigational links to other pages are on the left.

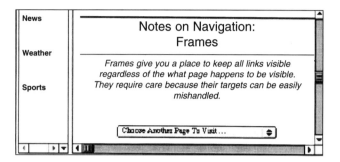

Figure 12.9
A web page with two frames

With frames, navigation information is always available. However, frames do require writers to carefully set their targets (that is, where the browser will display information). And some readers object to frames because frames can get nested within other frames, making the page confusing and hard to read.

Connecting Ideas Backwards and Forwards

The Web encourages readers to move from any page to any other page rather than follow a single, linear path. That's a double-edged sword: Readers can follow their interests but also can jump to the middle of a discussion, rather than its start. You can help them by beginning each page with a brief recap of what they should know before reading the page. The recap should link back to the pages with the earlier part of the discussion.

For example, suppose you're writing a page that is part of a site about how to buy a used car. Suppose further that the first page matches types of cars with types of consumers; the second page lists desirable models; and the third page talks about making sure that a specific car on the lot is worth buying. That third page could start like this:

> Once you have decided <u>what kind of car you need</u> and <u>which models among them are desirable</u>, you can begin shopping, ready to see if something on the dealer's lot is worth buying.

The sentence looks both back and ahead. The underlined words link back to the pages that should be read first. The rest of the sentence prepares the reader for what follows on the current page. This technique allows readers to access previous important information while not slowing down those readers who have already visited (or don't care about) the other pages.

Web Layout and Appearance

To repeat, the Web is not print. When you design a print page, it stays the way it looked the last time you saw it. When you design a Web page, the reader controls the screen. For example:

- Web readers can change the dimensions of your page, its colours, its typefaces, and its font sizes.
- Web readers may see your work on small monitors with low resolution that can't show more than 256 colours. Moreover, what fits well on one screen may not all fit on another, forcing readers to scroll horizontally in order to see everything.
- Web readers may have older browsers—or even new ones—that significantly change what looked good on yours.

Since Web designers often work with high-end equipment, they can easily neglect what their work will look like on less powerful computers. Here are some ways to deal with these issues.

Design for Relative—Not Absolute—Control

Assume your audience has mid-range equipment—15-inch screens, 256 colours, and a 33-kilobaud modem. Although entry-level computers now offer much more, literally millions still browse the Web with lesser technology. Make your page accessible to as many people as possible unless you absolutely know your audience and what computers they use, as when designing for an intranet within an organization, for example.

Don't assume that all your readers have the latest browser. Browsers may be free for the downloading, but that doesn't mean they get downloaded. You can inform visitors that your site has special requirements but be prepared to lose potential readers who just won't bother. The best way to get your audience to upgrade their browsers is with compelling content—that is, something so good that they will download new software just to experience it. But first make sure that the new browser solves a genuine design problem, rather than merely being there for its own sake.

Create windows no wider than 580 pixels, that is, about the width of a 15-inch monitor. Make them even narrower if you wish readers to see their desktops behind the browser window. You absolutely, positively don't want readers to scroll horizontally.

Layout Grids

A layout grid ensures page elements maintain their positions relative to each other, and tables are the preferred way to create layout grids.

The more complex your table—for example, tables nested within each other or varying row or column spans—the more precisely you can place page elements. However, the more complex the table, the larger the file size for your page and the longer it takes the browser to render it.

- Express both table and column width in percentages, not in pixels; for example, set the left column to 25% and the right column to 75% of the table. That way, it will always be rendered proportionally.
- Set the border of your tables to 0; that will hide the grid lines when the browser displays the page.
- Set column and row spans to vary the configuration of your grid; that is, you don't have to have the same number of columns throughout a table. Changing the number of columns and rows is particularly useful when you mix text and graphics, as illustrated in Figure 12.10.
- Set cell spacing (the space around the cell) and cell padding (the space inside the cell) to further control appearance. Typical values range from zero to four pixels.
- Set alignment within a cell to left, right, or centre for text. For readability, on a two-column grid, right align the left column and left align the right column as in Figure 12.11.

Again, more complex tables are slower for browsers to display.

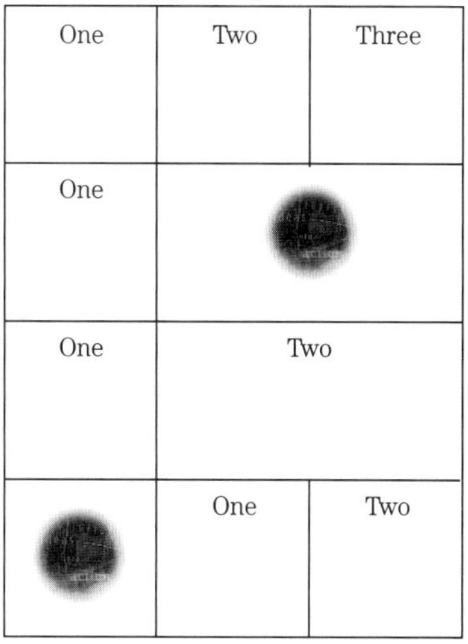

Figure 12.10
Tables as layout grids

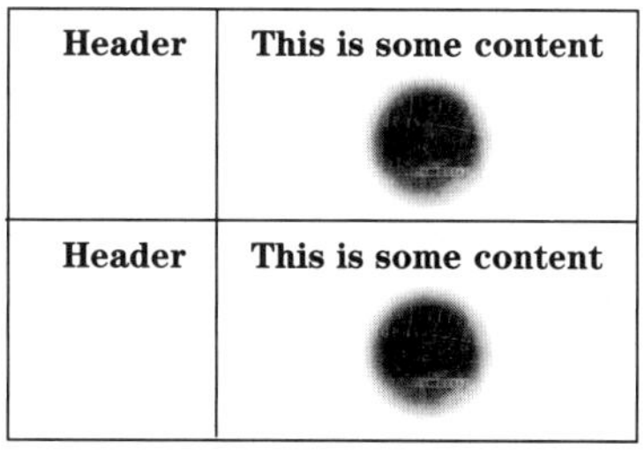

Figure 12.11
Aligning content

Using Frames as Layout Grids

Like tables, frames ensure page elements maintain their positions relative to each other. Use frames when you want some specific content such as the navigation links always to be visible.

- Set the widths of frames as percentages of the browser window so that the browser will render them proportionately.
- Set frames to Auto scroll; that forces the browser to insert scroll bars if all the content isn't visible. If everything is visible, the browser won't insert the scroll bars.

Using Layers as Layout Grids

Layers are rectangular objects in which you can place other objects (including other layers). They allow you the most control placing your page elements. However:

- Use layers only if you know that your audience uses Version 4 (or higher) browsers.
- You will need an authoring tool that lets you position layers.
- Layers can display differently on different computers, even though, in theory, layers offer single-pixel precision in positioning page elements.

White Space: When Nothing Is Something

White space is any portion of your page that's not content. (It doesn't have to white, just blank.) Despite its seeming status as "nothing," white space is an important part of your Web page.

As with print, white space gives each element breathing room, reducing the difficulty readers have making sense of your content. White space enables a page's visual arrangement to be analogous to its logic, that is, to mirror what is more important or less important. Readers see at a glance the relationships among ideas.

For example, white space around headings and subheadings shows the reader where one element leaves off and the other begins, as Figure 12.12 demonstrates. The white space—above, below, and at the sides—provides the visual clues for how you've structured your material.

Web designers have two main ways to insert white space above and below objects:

\<P\> inserts a blank line.
\<BR\> starts a new line.

Widgets in History

People of many nations have used
widgets for centuries. King Regbert of
Luxania would often call his court
together on important occasions and
make two points:

- Widgets provide an important source
  of vitamins and minerals.
- Widgets make swell pets.

Widget Design

Creating a good widget is never easy, as
thousands of would-be widget makers
have learned. Typically, they forget
three things:

1. Widgets get hot and burn fingers.
2. Widgets need drainage holes or they
   back up.
3. Widgets *are* biodegradable.

Figure 12.12
Using white space to show relationships among ideas

Creating White Space With Lists

Lists instantly convey the relationships among items. Browsers automatically align
list items, regardless of how the reader changes font or window size. Because lists
carry their own white space, they clearly demarcate units of information. For
example:

> Here is what you should bring to Camp Nature Hugs:
> - Towels
> - Sleeping bag
> - Toiletries
> - Rubber boots

The bullets and white space combine to make each item easy to see. That's
particularly helpful on the Web where people generally scan rather than read,
often on low-resolution monitors.

A bullet list indicates that no item takes precedence over another. In the above
list, for example, towels are just as important as rubber boots. Numbered lists, on
the other hand, imply hierarchy or sequence, as in these two examples:

Recommendations to Reduce Cars Speeding on Spruce Street
1. Put in speed bumps.
2. Widen sidewalks and reduce lane width.
3. Introduce photo radar.
4. Arm the neighbors.

Starting Your Car on a Cold Day
1. Make sure the transmission is in Park.
2. Depress the gas pedal to the floor and hold it there.
3. Insert the ignition key.
4. Turn the ignition key and hold it until engine starts. If the car doesn't start within 15 seconds, wait 15 seconds and try twice more.
5. If the car still doesn't start, call the auto club.

Nested lists set off ideas according to their importance or sequence. For example:

1. **Widgets in History**
   People of many nations have used widgets for centuries. King Regbert of Luxania would often call his court together on important occasions and make two points:
   1.1 Widgets provide an important source of vitamins and minerals.
   1.2 Widgets make swell pets. They are especially fond of children, although accidents do happen.

2. **Widget Design**
   Creating a good widget is never easy, as thousands of would-be widget-makers have learned. Typically, they forget three things:
   2.1 Widgets get hot and burn fingers.
   2.2 Widgets need drainage holes or they back up.
   2.3 Widgets are biodegradable.

Creating White Space With Vertical Alignment

You can create white space by aligning text and graphics. Figure 12.13 shows an example with three different alignments.

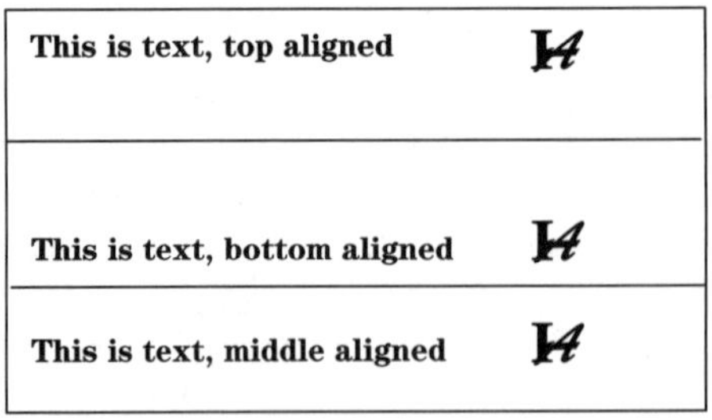

Figure 12.13
Creating white space with vertical alignment

Creating White Space With Horizontal Alignment

You can also set the amount of horizontal white space that appears between text and graphic, as illustrated in Figure 12.14.

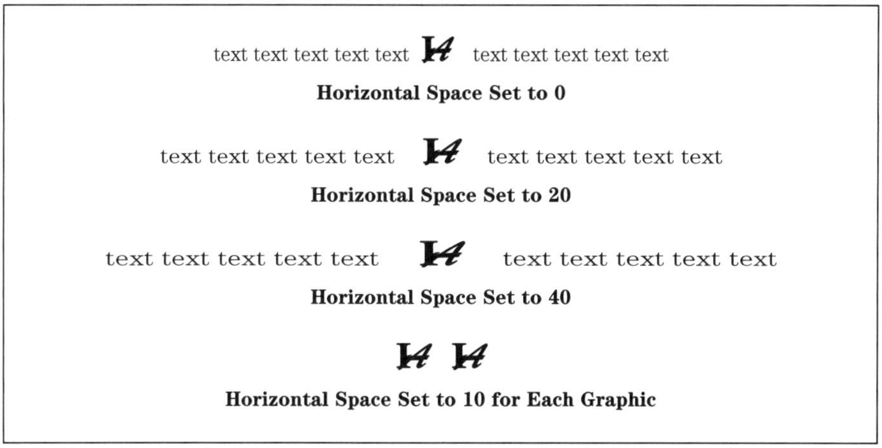

text text text text text 🎹 text text text text text
Horizontal Space Set to 0

text text text text text 🎹 text text text text text
Horizontal Space Set to 20

text text text text text 🎹 text text text text text
Horizontal Space Set to 40

🎹 🎹
Horizontal Space Set to 10 for Each Graphic

Figure 12.14
Creating white space with horizontal alignment

In addition, you can set horizontal space between graphics. The two graphics at the bottom of Figure 12.14 each has its horizontal space set to 10 pixels, making a total of 20 pixels between them.

Creating White Space With Paragraph Length

As we've seen in the chapter on document design, a paragraph should be both a logical and visual unit. That is, not only should a paragraph be about one topic, it should also help readers assimilate information. When readers come to the end of a paragraph, they can pause and reflect on what they've just read. Or they can simply rest.

While this is true for print as well as the Web, long unbroken expanses of text on the screen are especially hard to read. White space around paragraphs signals the start and end of units of information. Given that reading on a screen isn't easy at the best of times, this is an important way of helping readers.

Choosing Fonts for Your Web Site

You can't be sure what fonts users will have on their computers, with two exceptions: Times Roman and Arial ship with Windows and the similar fonts Times and Helvetica ship with the Macintosh operating systems. Here's what they look like:

> Times/Times New Roman
> **Helvetica/Arial**

Times is a serif typeface, that is, one with short lines that extend from the letter. Helvetica is a sans serif typeface, that is, one without extenders.

Generally, serif typefaces are used for body text since studies show they increase readability. San serif typefaces are used for headers because they stand out. A common rule of thumb is to limit yourself to one serif and one sans serif typeface in your document. Adding more than two typefaces to a page can create visual noise and disorient readers. You can, however, vary the size, style, and colour of your two basic typefaces.

Font Families

Times and Helvetica are always safe choices, but at times, you may want something else. In such instances, you can specify a font family, that is, a list of roughly similar fonts. The browser will look for all the fonts installed on the reader's computer; when it finds one on that list, it uses it. If it doesn't find one, it substitutes the browser's default font.

Suppose, for example, you wanted to use Palatino rather than Times. You could specify a font family with Palatino as its first member and similar-looking fonts (such as Bookman or Times) as its other members. When the browser loads your page, it will check if the reader 's computer has Palatino installed; if so, it will use that. If Palatino isn't there, however, the browser goes down its list until it finds one of your choices installed. If it finds nothing, it again uses the default. Using font families, therefore, gives you a greater—again, not absolute—control over how your type will eventually look.

Styled Text

As with print, you can emphasize words on the screen by styling text. For example, you can use bold or italics, or change the size or colour. Too much variety, however, generates noise, not interest.

Unlike print, italics should be used sparingly since words in italics are harder to read on the screen, especially in smaller font sizes and on lower-resolution monitors. Also, text size on the Web is most often expressed in relative rather than absolute terms. That is, you don't specify 12 or 14 points; instead, you size in relative values, going from 1 to 7, with 3 as the usual default. Figure 12.15 shows examples of these relative sizes.

Version 4 and higher browsers will display fonts in point size. However, once again, many readers won't have the latest versions. If you absolutely can't generate the font, effect, or size you want, your only option is to create a graphic of the text

Size 1
Size 2
Size 3 (Default)
Size 4
Size 5
Size 6
Size 7

Figure 12.15
Web font sizes

exactly as you want it. Of course, a graphic requires more time to download than ordinary text.

Dividing the Page With Horizontal Rules

A horizontal rule divides a page, signalling that two elements are separate, for example, sections of a report or graphics and text. Figure 12.16 shows two such divisions.

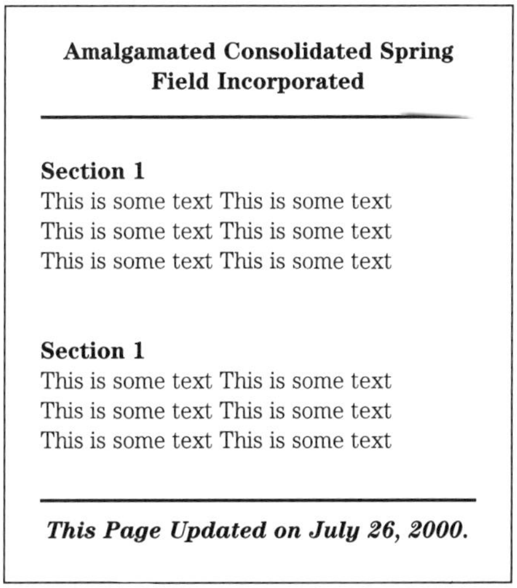

**Amalgamated Consolidated Spring
Field Incorporated**

Section 1
This is some text This is some text
This is some text This is some text
This is some text This is some text

Section 1
This is some text This is some text
This is some text This is some text
This is some text This is some text

This Page Updated on July 26, 2000.

Figure 12.16
Dividing the page with horizontal rules

A horizontal rule can extend across as a set number of pixels or span a specified percentage of a page or table cell, as shown in Figure 12.17.

100%

75%

50%

Figure 12.17
Varying widths for horizontal rules

These rules span 100, 75, and 50 percent respectively of the page or table cell they're in.

Colour Choice

Colour is a matter of taste, and your readers may not share yours. To repeat, your first responsibility as a professional writer is to accommodate your reader, not yourself. Pages where colour intrudes defeat that purpose.

As with other elements of your design, your choice of colours should serve a function such as emphasizing certain elements, evoking associations or feelings, or increasing legibility. Your choice of colours can be as important as your choice of words or images in keeping your readers reading. The *Ideas Into Action* Web site includes screen shots of ways you can use colour. Here are some of its more important uses:

- Making text more legible
- Calling attention to important elements
- Creating an emotional atmosphere
- Evoking cultural associations

The Colour Wheel

Although a full discussion of colour goes well beyond this text, you need to know something about the colour wheel, a basic tool for choosing colours. The *Ideas Into Action* Web site at **<www.pearsoned.ca/keller/>** shows a colour wheel along with examples of how you can use colour. You can also find colour wheels in books on design.

The colour wheel illustrates how red, yellow, and blue—the primary colours—relate to one another. By mixing these three colours, you can produce all the others. Using a colour wheel can help you choose better colour combinations. Here are three rules of thumb:

- Colours that are opposite each other on the colour wheel (complementary colours) create intense, almost vibrating images that can tire the eye.
- Colours next to each other on the colour wheel create agreeable effects.
- Colours two or three apart on the colour wheel set up strong contrast.

Backgrounds

Choosing a background colour for your Web page is less a matter of taste than of ensuring readers can read what's there. White produces a clean page, and readers are used to seeing white as a background in print material.

Other possibilities for backgrounds are very light pastels; they may not excite you, but most readers find them inoffensive. Strong colours—bright and deep reds, blues, or greens—may tire the eyes of your readers. And although black is used on many sites, studies show that many readers also find it harsh.

Web-Safe Colours

Relying on the colour wheel exclusively is problematic because it includes many more than the 256 colours that the vast majority of Web surfers can see on their screens. If the colour you chose isn't available, the browser will substitute others, sometimes radically changing your design. Unfortunately, only 216 colours look the same on all computer platforms. These colours are part of the Web-safe palette, and most Web authoring programs include it. Whatever colour choices you make, therefore, be sure they are part of the Web-safe palette.

Colours for Links

On the Web, the convention has grown up that blue or purple indicates unvisited links while red indicates visited ones. Although this is only a convention, it is powerful one. When you choose other colours for your links, you risk disorienting readers and losing their goodwill.

ACTIONS

The steps that follow take you through planning, designing, and testing your site. When you think about content, follow the guidelines for other documents discussed elsewhere in this book. However, keep in mind that the Web is not print, and the way you present information as a site differs from how you would present it as hard copy. The focus of what follows is what makes Web presentation different.

As with creating other kinds of documents, the steps are both sequential and iterative. Go through them in order but expect to return to them as your develop and refine your site.

Step 1: Plan Your Site

Begin by articulating an overview of your site and answering these questions:

- Why will someone Web visit my site?
- What information will they need?
- How will it be so compellingly presented that they will stay?

Construct an outline of the material you will include, breaking it into logical units, one for each Web page. Refer to this step frequently (especially after testing your site with sample users) to make changes as needed.

Step 2: Describe the Audience

Produce a profile of the users who will visit your site. The more detailed this profile, the more you will know about what your site should include. Here are some questions to answer about your audience:

- What are the names of some typical readers for your site? If you can't actually name a few touchstone readers, list some characteristics of people whom you would want to visit your site.
- What will readers expect when they come to your site?
- What do they plan to do with that information?

In light of this information, go back to Step 1 and refine your plans for the site's content.

Step 3: Prototype and Test

Do a quick mock-up of your site. Include the following:

- A list of main topics (with as many sub-topics as you can)
- A few representative graphics
- Information about persons or organizations your users might want to contact

Test your mock-up with some potential users; ask them what information you should add or remove from your site.

Return to Step 1 and Step 2 and refine your answers about content and audience.

Step 4: Create a Site Template

Use a table or frames as a layout grid and create a template to use throughout the site. Consider the following issues:

Layout
Choose locations on the template for:
• Site logo
• Page headers
• Navigation devices
• Body text
• Site information like author's name, copyright notice, and date of last revision

Colours
Choose colours for the background and text (both headings and content). Check for:
• Text legibility
• Emphasis on important details or new sections
• Emotional atmosphere
• Cultural associations
• Links
• Web-safe colours

Fonts
Choose fonts for headers and body text. Consider:
• Size
• Legibility
• Serif and sans serif
• Likely availability on the reader's browser

Save the template as a read-only or stationery file, that is, one that you can work on without altering the original.

Test with one or two users, making the necessary changes to your template.

Step 5: Build Content

Create or import your text and graphics. Keep each page to a single topic.

Step 6: Insert Links

Depending on your content, use the following navigational devices to link the parts of your site:

- Text links in menus
- Embedded text links
- Graphic links
- Pull-down menus
- Image maps
- Site maps

Link ideas backwards and forward. That is, anticipate both of the following:

- The previous information readers will need to understand the current page
- The further information readers will want to see on another page

Step 7: Fine-Tune the Layout

Insert white space, using the following techniques as appropriate:

- Paragraph and line breaks
- Lists
- Horizontal and vertical alignment
- Paragraph length
- Horizontal rules

Step 8: Alpha Test

Test your entire site yourself on your browser, checking that:

- Links work properly
- Graphics display properly
- Text is legible
- Necessary content is present
- Layout is uncluttered

Make the necessary revisions and repeat the alpha test.

Step 9: Beta Test

Beta test your site with touchstone readers, that is, typical users.

- Prepare a set of about five to seven questions that reflect your major concerns about the site at this stage of development.
- Use these questions to create a document that you will give your testers.
- Begin your document with two open-ended responses for your testers:

- • What I liked best about the site was . . .
- • What I needed more help with was . . .
- Leave space for any additional comments you hadn't anticipated.
- Leave room for entering the number of the version tested, the names of your testers, and the date the testing was carried out.
- Have your testers go through your work. Don't intervene unless you absolutely must.
- Observe your testers as they work through the site, recording any problems or comments.
- After the testers have gone through your site, ask them to fill out your form.
- Use the information you've collected as you prepare the next version of your project.

Sample Questions for Usability Testing

You should not, of course, overwhelm your testers with every possible question. That's why you should select about five to seven issues that concern you the most at each testing stage. Here are some issues you can modify according to your own needs:

Reader Navigation
- Point to a place where readers could get lost. Point to another where that's unlikely. Have you made all material accessible to readers? Is it always completely evident to readers how to move through your site? (This is critical.)
- Is there a link on every page that leads to a main menu or some other kind of site overview?
- Does everything work as advertised? What page does not behave as you intended? Account for all links and the pages they point to.
- When you use graphics and other multimedia, do they load quickly or do they need optimizing? Can someone with a 33.3k modem visit your site without undue delay?

Screen Design
- Point to a page where the screen is clean and readable. Point to another where it is cluttered. (Your goal for screen design is to help the reader locate necessary information.)
- Have you limited yourself to one serif font for text and one sans serif font for headings?
- Point to a screen with adequate white space. Point to another that needs more.
- Which paragraphs are broken up into readable units? Which aren't?

- Can you find a place where the reader's eye has to travel too far across the page? Which column widths are proportionate to window size? Which aren't?
- Can you find a place where the eye has to jump too frequently to the next line? In other words, are columns too narrow?
- Do the graphics communicate or merely decorate?

The Writing

- Is the content of the site logically presented? Can it stand up to the same scrutiny as any other document you'd write?
- Is the text a series of grand generalizations? Do assertions go unproven? Do you need to narrow your focus?
- Is your material accurate? Are secondary sources acknowledged?
- What wording doesn't adequately suggest where a link will take readers? Can readers always make reasonable guesses about the content they'll see when they click?
- Is the writing plain? Do readers know *who does what* in every sentence? Are there more than one main clause and one subordinate clause in each sentence? (See Chapter 3 on Plain English for details.)
- Are typos so numerous that your credibility is questioned?

CHAPTER SUMMARY

Professional writers are increasingly called upon to produce Web sites. To do that effectively, they have to understand that the Web is different than print and that its readers are much quicker to abandon a page. The very essence of hypertext, after all, is to let readers choose their own paths rather than follow an author's. This radically changes the relationship between reader and writer.

A range of techniques increases your chances of keeping readers at your site. To begin, you have to plan so that you provide the information your particular audience wants. Your site must also be easy to navigate, have a consistent appearance, and connect ideas backwards and forwards.

Web readers can change your page's colours, window size, and fonts, or their browser can render your pages differently from what you expected. You can still gain a measure of control over your page's appearance by using a table as a layout grid, inserting adequate white space, choosing fonts, and dividing the page with horizontal rules.

Writing Web pages is a process where you plan your site, analyze the audience, and create a template for further use. You then enter content, add links, and fine-tune appearance. Even more than with other documents, you must thoroughly field test your pages, checking not only their content but their behavior.

CHECKLISTS

PLANNING THE SITE

Determine the reasons readers will visit your site and the information they will need.

Prepare an outline of your site, one topic per Web page.

Determine what readers expect when they come to the site and what they will do with the information they find.

Field test a mock-up of site with list of topics and sample graphics.

Prepare site layout with logo, backgrounds, page and section headers, navigation devices, text, and site information.

Choose colours for legibility, emphasis, emotional and cultural associations, and links, using only Web-safe colours.

Choose font size and typeface (serif for text, sans serif for headings) based on availability on users' equipment.

Save site template as a read-only document.

Test site template with typical users and revise accordingly.

Integrate navigation devices (text menus, embedded links, graphic links, pull-down menus, image maps, site maps).

Use white space (paragraph and line breaks, lists, horizontal and vertical alignment, horizontal rules).

Link ideas backwards and forward.

USABILITY TESTING

Alpha test navigation, content, legibility, and layout.

Beta test using five to seven specific questions that particularly concern you and general questions on what user liked or disliked, plus additional comments and testing information.

Revise based on observations of testers and testers' written comments.

Your additional comments:

EXERCISES

David Katz of the Doggs'N'Katz Specialty Shoppe has hired your company to develop a Web site for his store. He doesn't need anything complex, but he does want his customers to find out about his products and prices. He also wants them to know about local pet news (such as dog shows, health warnings, and clubs) and general information (about breeds, national organizations, new products, etc.).

The Doggs'N'Katz Specialty Shoppe lives up to its name; it sells only products for dogs and cats (nothing for birds, goldfish, or gerbils) and no live animals. Mr. Katz tries to carry the largest selection of premium cat and dog foods anywhere, as well as a large selection of toys. He also offers a grooming service. The store is located in the WestBurban Mall (at the junction of the Goodyear and Firestone Expressways) and it's open the usual mall hours.

Work in groups to do the following exercises.

Exercise 1

Draw up a list of specific questions you would ask Mr. Katz if you could. As a group, quickly generate the answers so that you have some working assumptions when you plan the site.

Exercise 2

Articulate an overview of the site, focusing on its likely visitors and their needs. Start by defining a typical audience of dog and cat lovers. What will they expect when they visit? What will they do with the information they find? How can you present that information so that it will be especially compelling to this audience?

Exercise 3

Do a quick mock-up of the site including a list of pages you'll have and the topics they'll cover.

Exercise 4

Select one person in the group to sit at a computer and enter the group's ideas into a word processor. Using a table as a grid, lay out a template that shows the basic appearance of all the site's pages. Include a site logo, navigation devices, placement of body text, colours, and fonts. Don't forget to save the template for future reference.

Exercise 5

You won't have time to write content for the whole site but generate some for a few topics on the main page.

Exercise 6

Add dummy links to the main page—for this exercise, inventing locations that give a general sense of where the site can take visitors. Use at least one of the following kinds of links: text links in menus, embedded text links, graphic links, pull-down menus, and image maps.

Exercise 7

Work with another group and beta test your sites for each other.

CHAPTER

13

Writing Media Releases

What This Chapter Covers

Ideas

The World Out There
Editors: A Special Audience
       Editors Are Sophisticated Readers
       Editors Are Sophisticated Writers
       Editors Are Busy
When to Write a Media Release
The Elements of a Media Release

Actions

Step 1: Identify Your Audience
Step 2: Determine What You Need to Say
Step 3: Draft the Lead Paragraph
Step 4: Add Supporting Information
Step 5: Test and Revise
Step 6: Write the Headline
Step 7: Write the Subhead
Step 8: Format the Media Release
Step 9: Test and Revise Again
Step 10: Prepare Electronic Versions
Step 11: Compile a List of Recipients
Step 12: Clear the Release
Step 13: Send the Release

Chapter Summary

Checklists

Exercises

C H A P T E R — 13

Learning Objectives	**By the end of this chapter, you will be able to explain:** • Why media releases are important to an organization • Why you reach the general public only through editors who are themselves sophisticated, busy readers and writers • Why your media release must get to the right editors and not waste their time • When to issue a media release • What are the basic components of a media release **By the end of this chapter, you will be able to:** • Define your audience for a media release • State your main message in a sentence • Draft your lead paragraph • Add supporting information in the order of decreasing importance • Write your headline and subhead • Format the release • Field test and revise • Prepare electronic versions • Prepare a list of recipients • Clear the release with your organization • Distribute the media release

The World Out There

Organizations speak not only to their clients and to their employees but also to the rest of the world. When a company announces important new products, services, financial results, or personnel changes, it issues a **media release**, that is, a document sent to the media, who then choose to report its contents as they see fit. Professional writers need to know, therefore, how to increase the chances that journalists—both print and electronic—will report the information that an enterprise wants made widely known.

A favourable news report is better than advertising; it's both free and (in theory) objective. Not surprisingly, therefore, news outlets are continually asked to say good things about a company—for example, that its new widget is better than sliced bread and that everyone should buy it. Media releases compete with each other for an editor's attention because there is only so much time and space available. A media release's goal, therefore, is to convince an editor to run its contents or at least phone for more information. This chapter covers the techniques to make those actions more likely.

Editors: A Special Audience

Your audience for a media release is more complex than for other documents. Although you really want to reach the public, you have to go through an intermediary. For example, suppose your company wants to announce a new widget. There may be trade journals whose editors know as much about widgets as you do. However, there may also be other editors who don't know much more than the general public. You must therefore pitch your writing to them, keeping technical terms to a minimum and explaining those you can't avoid.

Regardless of the specific editors you're trying to reach, you can assume they all share these characteristics:

- They are sophisticated readers.
- They are sophisticated writers.
- They are busy.

Let's look at the implications of each of these points.

Editors Are Sophisticated Readers

People in the media make their living by finding out how the world works. They've heard it all before—or at least a great deal of it. They know promises get broken and people lie. They certainly know hype when they see it and that the "latest and greatest" anything usually turns out rather ordinary. As a result, they read skeptically, and you won't get far by trying to dazzle with them with empty talk. You should, of course, put the best possible face on what you say, but you must promise only what you can deliver.

Dishonesty is obviously bad for its own sake, but it's also bad for your career: editors remember their sources. You might be lucky and fool them once, but editors who get fooled twice don't keep their jobs for long. When you lie, your credibility is damaged—and often beyond repair. You will get the attention of editors only if what you have to say is important to their readers; editors naturally care more about their readers than about you or your business.

It may seem obvious, but you also need to know what you're talking about. As trained journalists, editors look for the classic five Ws: Who, What, Where, When, and Why. If you don't do your homework and find out, you will be found out.

Editors Are Sophisticated Writers

Editors are also sophisticated writers who themselves use language everyday. As a result, they pay almost as much attention to the quality of a media release—its clarity and care—as to its content. They will quickly spot sloppy writing and assume that you and your company are sloppy too. Once again, your credibility is easy to damage and hard to repair. Agonize over the details and send out nothing that hasn't been thoroughly checked.

Editors Are Busy

Editors for the major media—big city newspapers, national magazines, television networks—receive literally dozens of media releases every day. Some, in fact, get hundreds. Even small outlets like community newspapers and local radio stations receive a lot relative to their size. While they are happy to get ideas for stories, they want to know only about what will interest their readers and want to know about it quickly.

Writers of media releases should do two things, therefore:

Send media releases to the right people. If you're selling widgets, don't tell someone who writes about gizmos. Most media have beat lists, that is, the names of staffers and their specialties. Look for a beat list in a publication's masthead or at its Web site. If you can't find it, send a brief note—not the media release itself—to the editor-in-chief asking for the name of the right person. You will not win friends with busy people by wasting their time with things that don't concern them. Nor will you win friends by being ignorant about their time—for example, when their deadlines are and how much lead time they need. When in doubt, ask.

Be brief. That's good advice for all writing, but especially when writing for the media. A meandering media release that doesn't quickly announce its topic and make its point risks being ignored. Editors simply don't have much time. Journalists are trained to write in an inverted pyramid, that is, with key ideas coming first and details following in order of decreasing importance. They expect public relations professionals—and that's what you are when you issue a media release—to write that way too.

When to Write a Media Release

Typically, companies issue media releases when they:

- Announce or ship a new product
- Secure major new contracts or clients
- Enter into partnerships with other organizations
- Issue financial results (like earnings or dividends)
- Make important personnel changes

Of course, organizations and their reasons for issuing media releases can vary widely.

The Elements of a Media Release

Regardless of the occasion, media releases consist of the following elements:

- The organization's logo
- A headline, 10 words or less, that describes the content
- An indication of which editor should read the release
- A subhead, 20 words or less, that summarizes the content
- The city of origin and the date of the release
- A lead (that is, the first sentence of the first paragraph) that grabs the reader's attention
- A lead paragraph, 50 words or less, that conveys the most important information such as the company's name, the product, service, or information being promoted, its price, its function, and its potential users
- Additional paragraphs with supporting details in descending order of importance, such as how the announcement bears on the company's operations or mission, date of availability for new products or services, endorsements from clients, and further information about the company.

- A contact phone number or e-mail address for more information
- *–30–* (the typographer's symbol that marks the end of an article)

The length of the entire release should be a page or two but never more. (Print it double-sided so there's less paper to get lost.) If editors need more information, they'll call you. Your goal is to say everything crucial by the end of the lead paragraph.

Here is a sample media release with all of these elements:

Amalgamated Consolidated Incorporated

GauzeWorks upgraded to Version 2

Attention: Health Technology Editor

ACI's home medical emergency software adds new features, lowers price.

Arnprior, Ontario: April 27, 1999.

ACI today shipped Version 2 of GauzeWorks, software that helps families deal with medical emergencies, dropping the retail price to $49.95. Added to this version are more than fifty new topics, including puncture wounds and hangnails. Version 1 has been completely updated, including GauzeWorks exclusive Bleed-O-Meter™.

"Our family has really been helped by GauzeWorks," says Edward Lapdog, whose 42-year-old son David accidentally had a pineapple lodged in his ear. "GauzeWork's clear step-by-step procedure made the process of removing the pineapple a breeze," smiles Lapdog, adding, "David even got to eat most of the pineapple itself."

Anne Blott, ACI's president and founder, is delighted by the new version. "It will save lives, for sure," Blott remarked, "while providing a fun time for everyone." She is especially pleased with the updated Bleed-O-Meter™, which counts the amount of blood someone loses if wounded by a tuning fork. "It's terrifically handy," Blott noted.

The medical profession has lauded GauzeWorks. "When I'm playing golf, " says Dr. Lamont Pedicure of Ferwood Plains, PEI, "I know my patients are well taken care of with GauzeWorks. In fact, I never operate without referring to it myself."

GauzeWorks is available immediately from leading software retailers. Upgrades from Version 1 are $24.95 and can be ordered directly from http://gauzeworks.com.

ACI's head office is at 123 Trailer Park Way, Arnprior, Ontario. Phone: (666) 555-1213 Fax: (666) 555-1454.

CONTACT:
Julian Overshoes, Media Director
voice: (666) 555-1215
fax: (666) 555-1678
mikey@aci.com.

–30–

The first few lines say who should read the release (health-technology editors) and summarize the main point ("ACI's home medical emergency software adds new features, lowers price"). The opening paragraph specifies key facts about GauzeWorks like its price and new features. Editors can quickly decide whether the release is newsworthy. If they keep reading, subsequent paragraphs amplify what has been said by quoting satisfied customers, highlighting improvements (like the Bleed-O-Meter™), and saying where to get more information. The brevity of the release helps editors do their jobs but does so without sacrificing information.

A C T I O N S

Step 1: Identify Your Audience

- List the kind of readers you want to reach with your media release.
- List the publications that reach that audience.
- For each publication, list the editor responsible for your particular topic. (Check the publication's masthead. If you're still unsure, contact the editor-in-chief, say who you are and who you represent, and ask for a name. Don't ask for a fax number and e-mail address unless you can't find them elsewhere.)
- Read the publications and then list the level of technical expertise the editors probably have.

Step 2: Determine What You Need to Say

- In a sentence, state the main message of your media release.
- Compile material to support that main message: details, quotes, and so forth.

Step 3: Draft the Lead Paragraph

- In 50 words or less, state the main message, supplemented by key information like the name of the company, the product, what it does, who it's aimed at, and its cost.
- Make the first sentence grab the editor's attention but do not hype or overstate.

Step 4: Add Supporting Information

In subsequent paragraphs, add other information in order of decreasing importance. Keep paragraphs short—about three sentences. Limit the whole media release to a single page if possible or two at the most. Here are some suggestions about what to include in these paragraphs:

- What makes the media release newsworthy—new features, new people, and so on
- How what is being announced fits with the company's direction
- What people have to say about the news (Provide quotes—endorsements from clients, comments by company management, etc.)
- Useful further information about the company

Be scrupulously honest. Don't promise to change the world; instead, set out the facts as clearly as possible. Be positive and upbeat about the product, service, or announcement but don't oversell.

Step 5: Test and Revise

Check that:

- The lead paragraph conveys your main message
- The information in the subsequent paragraphs supports the lead paragraph and appears in decreasing order of importance

After you've reviewed, ask a colleague to do the same. Specifically, ask for input on factual errors, sentences that need to be clarified, and further points that should be made. Revise as necessary, keeping to 50 words for the lead paragraph and a total of one to two pages for the whole media release.

Step 6: Write the Headline

Describe the contents of the release in *10* words or less.

Step 7: Write the Subhead

Summarize the contents of the release in *20* words or less.

Step 8: Format the Release

Include these items in this order:

- The organization's logo
- A headline, 10 words or less, that describes the content
- An indication of which editor should read the release
- A subhead, 20 words or less, that summarizes the content
- The city of origin and the date of the release
- A lead paragraph, 50 words or less
- Additional paragraphs with supporting details, following the inverted pyramid principle
- A contact for more information
- –30–

Keep the page design simple, limiting yourself to one sans serif font for headlines, subheads, and contact information. Use a serif font for body text.

Step 9: Test and Revise Again

- Read the media release aloud, checking that it is conversational but not slangy. (See Chapter 3 on Plain English for guidelines.)
- Check for grammatical errors.
- Double-check all facts (addresses, prices, version numbers, copyrights and trademarks, etc.).
- Spell check.
- Give the material to one or two colleagues. Have them verify facts, spellings of names, and other critical information.
- Revise as necessary—your credibility is at stake.

Step 10: Prepare Electronic Versions

- Prepare a Web version of the release, put it on the company's site, and provide links to it.
- Prepare a plain-text version for e-mail. Do not send the release as an attachment since some editors might not be able to open it.

Step 11: Compile a List of Recipients

Check that each person who receives the media release has the responsibility for the topic.

Step 12: Clear the Release

Ask someone with authority in your organization to approve the release before you send it. If there is a technical component, ask the technical people to approve it as well. Secure permissions from anyone whom you've quoted.

Step 13: Send Your Media Release

Send out your release via e-mail, fax, regular mail, or courier. Contact the publication before you send out your release, asking which method they prefer. Don't bombard the editor with all versions.

CHAPTER SUMMARY

Organizations use media releases to announce new products, financial results, or important personnel changes. Editors are your primary audience because they decide if their readership sees what you've written. You must therefore convince editors—who are both sophisticated and busy—that you have something to say to their readers. Because editors receive so many media releases, you must follow the prescribed format and keep to the point.

Writing a media release requires that you carefully target the editors most likely to publish what you produce. You grab their attention and then concisely inform them of your key points, adding further information in order of decreasing importance. You not only field test and revise a release for accuracy and format; you must also clear the media release with your organization before distributing it.

CHECKLISTS

Preparing the media release:

- [ ] Audience identified
- [ ] Lead paragraph 50 words or less
- [ ] Lead paragraph makes key points such as the company's name, the product, what it does, who it's aimed at, and its cost
- [ ] Other information arranged in order of decreasing importance
- [ ] Total length less than two pages (ideally just a single page)
- [ ] Headline describes content of media release in 10 words or less
- [ ] Subhead summarizes the content in 20 words or less

Checking the media release:

- [ ] Format correct
- [ ] The company logo
- [ ] Headline
- [ ] Which beat editor or writer should read this release
- [ ] Subhead
- [ ] The city of origin and the date of the release
- [ ] Lead paragraph
- [ ] Other paragraphs
- [ ] Contact information, including company address, phone, fax, e-mail, Web site
- [ ] –30–
- [ ] Tested by writer and one or two colleagues for factual errors, clarity, and missing information
- [ ] Revised as necessary and tested again for grammatical errors, typos, and incorrectly spelled names

Sending the media release:

- [ ] Electronic versions prepared
- [ ] Necessary approvals granted
- [ ] Sent via the most appropriate medium (mail, courier, fax, or e-mail)

Your additional comments:

EXERCISES

Exercise 1

Think of a piece of software you use frequently. Assume a new version has been released with five features that you wish it really had. Write the lead paragraph for a press release about this hypothetical release.

Exercise 2

Using the Web or print versions of national magazines and newspapers, locate three editors responsible for each of the following areas:

a.   Automobiles

b.   Annual profit statements

c.   Environmental safety

d.   Computer spreadsheets

e.   CDs from popular rock groups

Exercise 3

Write a media release about one of the following topics, listing the kind of readers you want to reach and the publications that they're most likely to read:

a.   An upcoming event at your school (for example, a visiting speaker, a fund-raising drive, or a debate)

b.   The appointment of new president for a club or educational institution you go to

c.   The formation of a new campus group to raise environmental awareness

Your release should be between 200 and 300 words. Make sure you have included all the necessary elements in the correct order.

CHAPTER

14

Speaking to Groups

What This Chapter Covers

Ideas

Speaking in Public
Persuasion Face to Face
Who's Listening?
How Long Do I Have?
Making Your Promise and Keeping Focused
Organizing Your Talk with the Rule of Three
Thinking in Terms of Slides
Using Computers to Prepare and Present Your Talk
Specific Ways to Use Technology
The Basic Principles of Designing a Talk
Delivering Your Presentation

Actions

Step 1: Gather Your Material
Step 2: Analyze the Audience
Step 3: Articulate a Promise
Step 4: Articulate Three Main Points
Step 5: Prepare a Storyboard
Step 6: Design the Look of the Presentation
Step 7: Test and Revise Yourself
Step 8: Test and Revise with a Colleague
Step 9: Copy-Edit
Step 10: Rehearse
Step 11: Prepare Leave-Behinds
Step 12: Prepare Backup Versions
Step 13: Prepare the Question-and-Answer Session

Chapter Summary

Checklist

Exercises

Learning Objectives

By the end of this chapter, you will be able to explain:

- What advantages speaking has over writing
- Why you must know who will be listening to you and for how long
- Why you must make promises about and organize the presentation
- Why you need to think in terms of slides
- How technology can improve your presentation
- What basic principles and strategies you use for preparing a talk

By the end of this chapter, you will be able to prepare a presentation by:

- Gathering material
- Describing your audience
- Formulating a promise around which to organize your talk
- Preparing a storyboard of slides
- Designing a template for all slides
- Testing a preliminary version of your talk
- Rehearsing your presentation
- Field testing
- Copy-editing
- Preparing leave-behinds, backup versions, and question-and-answer responses

┤I┤D┤E┤A┤S├

Speaking in Public

Sooner or later, you'll have to get up to speak.

Surveys continually show that speaking in public rates as one of the worst fears people have. No one, after all, likes the prospect of looking foolish in front of an audience. But many jobs demand public speaking, whether it's an informal talk to a few colleagues or a full-blown presentation to many strangers.

For some people, speaking in public is exhilarating; for many others, it never becomes more than tolerable. If you are in this second group, you can measurably reduce your discomfort by knowing techniques for preparing and delivering presentations. This chapter deals with those techniques.

Persuasion Face to Face

Your relationship with an audience differs greatly when you speak to them rather than write to them. Most obviously, you're there in the flesh, a real person whose appearance, voice, and demeanour are on display. That, of course, can be a disadvantage, but with some practice you can present yourself as likable and trustworthy, someone with whom audiences sympathize and whom they want to do well.

If being physically on display makes demands, it also confers benefits. Most importantly, you have the chance to gauge your audience's reactions to you and your ideas. You can instantly see when they are with you—intellectually and emotionally—and when they're not. That affords you the opportunity to adjust your presentation: you can reiterate some points, skip over others, invite questions, and clarify your meaning. You have a great advantage over writers who can only imagine how their readers are responding.

To have your physical presence work to your advantage does not require you to be extraordinarily gifted or charismatic. It does require that you meticulously prepare your information, its format, and its delivery. Let's start by considering the information you have and the audience who will hear it.

Who's Listening?

The psychologist Jerome Bruner has argued that one can say something worthwhile about any subject to any audience. For example, you can quite accurately describe the solar system to both kindergarten and university students. *How* and *what* you tell a kindergarten class about the sun and planets, of course, will be very different from how and what you'd tell university students. Each group brings its own perspective, and you must shape your message accordingly. You neither talk down nor show off to either group. The same principles apply to speaking in public.

Let's assume that you have a body of information to convey. As with other types of presentations, your first question must be "Who will be listening?" If you can name real people, so much the better. If you can't, you'll have to make some informed guesses about their backgrounds and biases.

That allows you to ask "What does this audience need to know?" That is, why is this specific group going to listen to you and what information do they want? What information do they already have? Are they specialists in your topic? Absolute beginners? Which technical terms can you use without explanation? Which terms must you explain, find substitutes for, or drop altogether? Without a clear sense of who will be listening—and what they will be listening for—you can't make intelligent choices about what to include and how to express it.

For example, suppose you're giving a talk about your company's line of computers. If your audience consists of computer experts, you can talk about RAM and backside cache and DIMMs at will; you don't have to think of simple ways of explaining these terms—in fact, if you do, your audience will think it odd. If the audience were, on the other hand, non-technical people, not only would they fail to understand RAM and DIMMs and so forth, they might assume you are deliberately hiding behind obscure language.

Few audiences, however, are either all experts or all novices. Most audiences are decidedly mixed, making the job of speaking to them more difficult. But the more you know about the nature of your particular audience, the better chance you have to prepare for them.

How Long Do I Have?

It may seem astoundingly obvious, but you also need to know—and remember— how much time you'll have to speak. Your choice of material depends every bit as much on the time available as on who will hear it. A fifteen-minute talk is not simply half as long as a thirty-minute one; your emphasis and details must be quite different.

Most of us have heard speakers whose awareness of time was faulty. Some walk sheepishly away before their time is up, leaving the impression they had little to say. Others have to be stopped before they can conclude, leaving the impression that they can't themselves get a handle on their topic or understand the time constraints of their audience. Either way, they make an unfavourable impression.

Planning, therefore, begins with two basic questions: *Who is listening?* and *How much time do they have?*

Making Your Promise and Keeping Focused

Once you have a sense of your audience and the time available for your presentation, you can select and shape your materials. As with written presentations, you'll need to make a promise to your audience—a question you'll answer, a problem you'll solve, a theme you'll clarify. Therefore, you must determine what is at the core of the mass of information you have available.

Keeping that promise in front of your audience ensures they won't lose sight of your central theme. Regardless of what you're saying at any particular moment, they'll have the sense that all your ideas fit into something larger. You yourself will have a point of reference, against which you can measure the value any particular idea. In brief, both you and your audience will stay on track as you speak.

Organizing Your Talk with the Power of Three

You must keep your promise with examples, details, ideas, and so forth from your material. However, you'll need a way to organize this information so that your audience will see how its various parts connect. Other chapters in this book discuss the power of three, but here's a brief summary: Humans can't keep long lists of things in their heads, and this is especially true when they have to listen. By grouping ideas into three main units, you make it easier for them to remember.

That's because *three* is the smallest number that establishes a pattern. If something happens once, it's merely an accident; twice, it's merely a coincidence; three times, however, and it's Providence—that is, some larger force governs it. When you present information in threes, you're appropriating the pattern that three implies and so showing that you are in control of your material. That makes you more credible.

Look through your mass of material, therefore, and select the three key ideas that best keep your promise. Although the ideas can themselves be general ("Widgets are an important part of our business"), they must be supported by concrete details (for example, a chart showing how many widgets were sold or the amount spent on researching new ones).

Think in Terms of Slides

Once you have articulated your promise and three key items to support it, you can begin to think in terms of slides, that is, individual screens of information that you'll display as you speak. Each slide must be coherent, that is, about one topic. It should also be integrated into your whole presentation. For example, a slide might consist of a graph showing the exact number of widgets you sold last year; this graph would contribute to the larger topic of how widgets are profitable.

You should define a purpose for each slide, such as giving an overview of your main points, supplying an illustration or example, or providing contact information. You can think of your slides the way an animator thinks of a storyboard, that is, a set of drawings that shows the key events in a cartoon. For example, an animation storyboard might start with:

Slide 1: Bugs Bunny munches on a carrot as he walks through the woods.
Slide 2: Elmer Fudd is in the woods hunting.
Slide 3: Bugs sees Elmer, Elmer sees Bugs.

Similarly, each slide is a milestone in your talk. The number of milestones you need depends on the time you have available and the complexity of your material. As a general rule, however, the fewer slides, the better: A live audience has to move at your pace and can't stop to review material or linger over a single point. They can easily be overwhelmed by a whirlwind of images of the screen. Too few slides are less of a problem because you can fill in what's missing in the course of your talk.

As a rule of thumb, you'll need about five slides:

• Introduction or overview (for example, the problem to be solved or the question to be asked)
• Supporting point A (with concrete examples, details, etc.)
• Supporting point B (with concrete examples, details, etc.)
• Supporting point C (with concrete examples, details, etc.)
• Conclusion or recommendations

This is, to repeat, only a rule of thumb, not a law written in stone.

Using Computers to Prepare and Present Your Talk

Your preparation and presentation can be much improved by technology. The content of your talk must always be its most important feature, but how you present content is increasingly critical. You can no longer display a series of indifferently prepared, hand-written overhead transparencies and still be considered professional. Contemporary audiences expect polished visuals that complement what you say and render it more accessible. This is not to say audiences demand Hollywood production values, but they do expect clarity and seriousness.

A number of software tools produce attractive slides. They range in sophistication and cost from high-end, dedicated presentation programs to simple word processors. Using any of them will improve a presentation. Here's why:

- They help you organize your ideas before you create your slides.
- They allow you to import text and graphics from existing documents, reducing preparation time.
- They permit editing of your slides, from large-scale reorganization to correcting simple typos.
- They give your presentation a consistent look and feel, so your listeners don't need to continually reorient themselves.
- They run on different computer platforms, letting you create slides on one kind of machine and show them on another.
- They help you appear professional and well versed in current technology.

However, presentation software has its downside:

- It can be expensive.
- It takes time to learn.
- It makes it easy to overdo your presentation.

The last item is worth underscoring: Because these programs offer so many design possibilities—animation, blinking, transitions, sound, colour—they make it easy to go too far. The resulting effects can overwhelm content, inducing eyestrain and fatigue. Like many other design tools, slide effects have to be used as a means to good design, not as a replacement for it.

Specific Ways to Use Technology

It isn't possible to cover the details of every piece of available software. However, they share some common features to make the following tasks easier:

Organizing your thoughts: Presentation programs generally come with electronic outliners, as do word processors. Outliners help you break up a mass of information into individual slides. They allow you, for example, to brainstorm a list of topics, adding sub-topics and details as they occur to you. You can then experiment with the order, adding or deleting items as necessary. This is particularly useful when you have to change the information for different audiences or time allotments.

Using existing information: Like other electronic writing tools, presentation programs let you import information. For example, you may be asked summarize a report you've written. You can quickly import its headings, graphics, recommendations, or other elements. Even if you don't have a document of your own to import, you may have access to other electronic documents that you can use to speed your preparation.

Giving a consistent look to your presentation: Presentation programs generally include templates—that is, professionally designed samples in which a set of colours, typefaces, and graphics work well together. Choosing a template allows you to maintain a consistent appearance throughout, freeing your audience from learning a new set of visual signals with each new slide. You can also achieve much the same thing with the Style feature of your word processor: For example, you can decide that your main headings will be shadowed bold 24-point Helvetica small caps and apply this style to all text you want to use as a heading.

Editing your presentation: As we've mentioned, the outline feature allows you to easily reorganize, add, or delete information. But presentation software helps with the details as well. You can use it to fix misspellings, grammatical errors, and typos, all of which look dreadful and unprofessional projected on a large screen.

The Basic Principles of Designing a Talk

Despite their powerful features, presentation programs don't free you from knowing the basic principles for preparing a talk. Here are a few of the most important:

Limit the number of design elements. Your presentation should always be legible and clear, never distracting your audience or calling attention to itself. To that end, limit your design to two or three colours and one or two typefaces. Figure 14.1 shows a slide with so many different fonts and sizes that it's largely illegible. Figure 14.2 shows a simpler and better design.

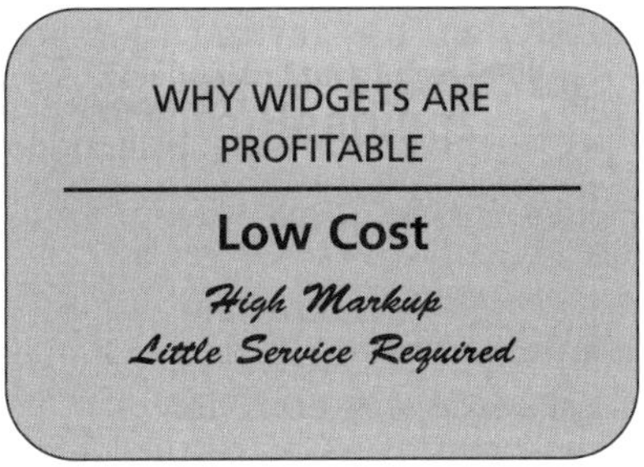

WHY WIDGETS ARE PROFITABLE

Low Cost
High Markup
Little Service Required

Figure 14.1
A poorly designed slide

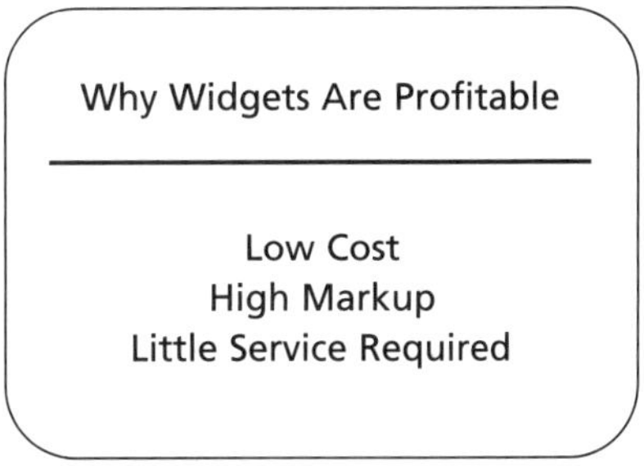

Why Widgets Are Profitable

Low Cost
High Markup
Little Service Required

Figure 14.2
A simply designed and legible slide

Use key phrases, not whole sentences. A slide's text should complement what you'll say, not substitute for it. Slides should help your audience follow the broad outlines of your ideas rather than reproduce every nuance. When you create slides that simply copy your printed text, your audience will read them and stop listening to you. Consider Figure 14.3, which shows a slide based on the previous section of this chapter.

Organizing Your Thoughts:
- Presentation programs generally come with electronic outliners, as do word processors.
- Outliners help you break up a mass of information into individual slides.
- They allow you, for example, to brainstorm a list of topics, adding subtopics and details as they occur to you.
- You can then experiment with the order, adding or deleting items as necessary.
- This is particularly useful when you must modify the same information for different audiences or time frames.

Using Existing Information:
- Like other electronic writing tools, presentation programs let you import information.
- For example, you may be asked to summarize a report you've written.
- You can quickly import its headings, graphics, recommendations, or ther elements.
- Even if you don't have a document of your own to import, you may have access to other electronic documents who contents you can use to speed your preparation.

Giving a Consistent Look to Your Presentation:
- Presentation programs generally include templates—that is, professionally designed samples in which a set of colours, typefaces, and graphics work well together.
- You can achieve much the same thing with the Style feature of your word processor. For example, you can designate the attributes of a heading style as 18-point Helvetica, small caps, shadow, bold, etc. and apply it to all the text you want to use as a heading.

Editing Your Presentation:
- As we've mentioned, the outline feature allows you to easily re-organize, add, or delete information.
- Presentation software helps with more "local" issues like spelling, grammar, and typos, all of which look dreadful and unprofessional projected on a large screen.

Figure 14.3
A slide with too much text

Faced with this slide, an audience would likely tune out anything the speaker says and just read. Even less effective would be for the speaker to read the slide to the audience. Why, after all, should they come to hear someone talk when the information can readily be sent to them as text?

Figure 14.4 shows a revised version of the slide. As you speak, you can amplify this edited version, supplying extra details. More importantly, the slide gives you the opportunity to show your expertise directly and conversationally, adding value to the information on the screen. You are not simply displaying information but also giving your audience a reason to be listening attentively.

Use builds and other effects. A build (also called a reveal) displays items on the screen at the rate you choose, rather than all at once. Normally, when you

Ideas into Action

Organizing Your Thoughts:
- Use outliners to prepare individual slides
- Brainstorm
- Experiment with order
- Modify same information for different occasions

Using Existing Information:
- Import headings, graphics, recommendations, or other elements
- Use your own documents or others

Giving a Consistent Look to Your Presentation:
- Consistent appearance needed
- Templates—design elements that work well together
- Style feature of word process works similarly

Editing Your Presentation:
- Errors look unprofessional projected on a large screen
- Re-organize, add, or delete information
- Spelling, grammar, and typos

Figure 14.4
Using phrases, not sentences

show a new slide, everything on it is immediately visible, permitting audiences to read ahead instead of listening. A build keeps you and your audience moving at the same pace by initially showing only the first item (for example, *Organizing Your Thoughts*); the second item (*Using Existing Information*) appears only when you click the mouse or press a key.

Other effects are more problematic. Motion can be invaluable with some content (for example, when you're showing how traffic flows) but quickly become distracting with topics that don't require it. Blinking text and rotating images can similarly distract. Even a sympathetic audience will have trouble concentrating when one part of your screen keeps insisting on attention. If you do use effects, therefore, use them sparingly and go to a new slide once you have made the point.

Prepare leave-behinds. Rather than forcing an audience to take notes and perhaps miss something important, prepare a one-page handout that you leave with your audience. Include your promise and your three key points, as well as contact information so that people can find you easily if they wish to learn more. Again, don't overwhelm them with details.

Prepare for the question-and-answer session. Without a question-and-answer session, a presentation is no more interactive than a book. Q&A

sessions let audiences ask for clarification or additional information. You can anticipate what topics your audience may ask about by thinking of what you had to cut from your talk. If what you have to say is contentious, someone in the audience will likely want to challenge it. Therefore, think like a lawyer preparing a client for cross-examination: Anticipate all likely questions, regardless of how much you would prefer not to deal with them.

Delivering Your Presentation

Preparing your talk, of course, is only part of the task; you also have to deliver it. Here are some ideas for doing that:

Get there early. Give yourself enough time to find and check the room where you'll speak. If you'll be away from your home base, look for your local host, or at least a technical person. Introduce yourself. If you have asked for special equipment, make sure that it's there. If you're bringing your own equipment, ask to do a test run. Resolve any glitches before you speak.

Have a backup strategy ready in case there is a problem. For instance, make a Web-based version of the slides you are planning to show with your presentation software. (You can generally count on your host having a browser.) Place a copy of the backup version on your Web site and test it thoroughly before you leave home. Copy the backup version onto a floppy disk as well and bring it to your talk. If both the presentation version and the floppy fail, you'll still be able to download your online copy. Another backup strategy is to print your slides onto overhead transparencies.

The extra time it takes to make backups is relatively short compared with the time to plan and create a presentation. Even if you never use your backups, you'll feel more confident and relaxed knowing they're ready.

Look and dress professionally. Fairly or not, audiences expect speakers to dress conventionally—that is, according to the norms of their profession. A banker does not dress like a disc jockey (nor vice versa). You don't have to spend a lot of money on clothes, but you should be neat. You want to project the image of someone who knows the expectations of the group and can be trusted with its attention.

Be audible and clear. A speaker's first job is to be heard. If your voice isn't strong, use a microphone (which will likely be available in large rooms). Test it out discretely before speaking (and avoid the worn-out question, "Can you hear me?"). Keep your head up—literally—to ensure your voice isn't muffled. Look at the back of the room and project your voice so that people there can hear without straining. And modulate your voice—that is, let it rise and fall as it would in conversation. A monotone, not surprisingly, is monotonous.

Connect with your audience. Keeping your head down not only muffles your voice but creates the impression that you don't want to be where you are. Make eye contact with different people. Don't focus on one person or even one part of the room but shift your gaze every few seconds. Project yourself as a personable figure who includes everyone.

Assume a natural posture. The way you hold yourself also signals who you are. For example, standing ramrod stiff suggests intellectual rigidity or even hostility. Slouching projects a lack of interest, as if your audience weren't really worth your efforts. Clinging to a lectern indicates fear. Obviously, none of these postures will engage your listeners. Instead, stand erect but relaxed. If possible, get out from behind the lectern and move around; a static, disembodied speaker puts people to sleep.

Amplify what's on the screen—don't read it. Your audience can read; they don't need you for that. Instead, use what's on the screen as a starting point and lead the audience from topic to topic. Augment the content of your slides with examples, definitions, anecdotes, and explanations. Provide extra value to what they see on the screen.

Don't memorize or recite. It's deadly dull hearing people read a prepared text instead of talking conversationally. By all means, think of key expressions ahead of time but don't script your entire talk or try to memorize it. Instead, know your material and (to repeat) speak conversationally about it, as if you were explaining it to a friend or colleague. Although your talk can't be extemporaneous, make it sound that way.

Don't race, don't dawdle. Talk at a steady speaking pace, about the same as when you're on the phone with a client or an associate. Rehearse with a tape recorder and adjust your speed.

Watch out for verbal tics. Nerves can give even experienced speakers various kinds of verbal tics such as giggles or expressions that carry no information. The most common are "er" and "um"; others include "you know" as well as "OK?" Another is the habit of turning statements into questions by letting your voice rise at the end of a sentence. That suggests you are unsure of your ideas or want your audience to grant you permission to continue.

Verbal tics are human but distracting. They have no simple cure, although you can reduce them by simply being aware of their existence and then practicing to overcome them. They are generally the product of nerves; carefully preparing your talk will increase your confidence and make tics less likely to occur.

A C T I O N S

Although the steps that follow are presented in a linear order, you'll have to circle back to repeat some of them as you refine your sense of the audience and material. Indeed, some steps—like gathering information and defining who will listen—have to be done together. You can't know what information to present unless you also know what your audience needs.

Step 1: Gather Your Material

Your material may come from a variety of sources, including documents that you or your colleagues have created (reports, parts of other presentations, promotional materials, etc.). It can include text, graphics, charts, or multimedia. If the material is not at hand, you'll have to gather it, using the same research techniques you would for a written presentation.

Step 2: Analyze the Audience

As you're assembling materials, be specific about your audience:

- Who are they? (Name two or three individuals you expect to be there.)
- What do they need to know about the subject?
- What do they already know?
- What is their level of expertise? What terms can you expect them to know?
- Why do they want to hear about the subject? To make a decision of some kind? To extend their knowledge for its own sake?
- How formal is the occasion?

Step 3: Articulate a Promise

Answer this question: *What is the single most important idea I want my audience to understand?*

If the audience were given a maximum of twenty-five words to express the main point of your talk, what would you want them to say? Avoid generalities (like "Widgets are good"). Focus on a problem that needs solving or a question that needs answering (like "We need to concentrate on getting more local buyers for our widgets"). Recast that twenty-five word statement as your promise, that is, what you and your audience will refer to throughout your talk.

Step 4: Articulate Three Main Points

List three key items from your assembled material that will best help you keep the promise you've just articulated. That is, locate three concrete examples that provide the strongest evidence or support for your main idea. Be specific ("Only 3% of our widget sales are local" or "Our widget prices are 12% cheaper for foreign manufacturers").

Step 5: Prepare a Storyboard

Do rough drafts for the slides that will be the milestones of your talk. Include the text and graphics that will appear on each. Your slides should follow this sequence:

Slide 1: Introduction or overview (the problem to be solved or the question to be asked)
Slide 2: Supporting point A
Slide 3: Supporting point B
Slide 4: Supporting point C
Slide 5: Conclusion or recommendations

Don't worry for now about their final appearance; you'll refine that later. Wait until you've completed initial testing before thinking of additional slides.

Step 6: Design the Look of the Presentation

Choose the layout, colours, and fonts that will appear on all slides or use a template. Ask a colleague for some quick feedback.

Step 7: Test and Revise by Yourself

Let some time pass (a day if possible, but at least a few hours), then go through your presentation. Speak aloud, taking care to talk at the same pace that you'll use in public. Change slides at the appropriate times. Evaluate the following:

Timing: Did you finish within the allotted time? Was there too much information or too little?
Completeness: Did your three main points work together to support your promise? Was there enough concrete evidence?

Logic: Was the presentation persuasive? Does any slide have a weakness?

Structure and Transition: Is it clear how one point leads to the next and how all points keep your promise?

Revise accordingly and repeat this test.

Step 8: Test and Revise with a Colleague

Ask a colleague to act as a touchstone listener. Try to find someone with roughly the same knowledge of the subject as your intended audience. If that's not possible, ask a colleague to try to respond like a typical member of your audience. Have your tester speak to these issues:

- What was the problem or question? Where was it best stated? Where did it need further explanation or examples?
- What was the solution or answer offered? What part was best supported by evidence? What parts of the solution were merely asserted rather than demonstrated?
- What was the most convincing solution or answer? What part of the solution needed more explanation?
- Which slides contain too many words (especially whole sentences rather than phrases)?
- Did you talk directly and conversationally to your audience? Or did you read the screen for them?
- What graphic worked best and why? What graphic needed clarifying and why?
- Were you audible and intelligible? Did you go too fast or too slow? Did you have any verbal tics (such as "um," "er," "you know," or "right?")?
- Were builds or other effects helpful? Or did they distract?
- Did you finish within the time allotted?

Make the necessary revisions and repeat this test.

Step 9: Copy-Edit

Check for:

- Slides in correct order and advancing properly from one to the next
- Legibility (layout, colours, fonts, etc.)
- Effects working properly
- Misspellings, grammatical errors, missing words, or other typos

Step 10: Rehearse

Rehearse aloud. Don't memorize your talk but instead use the slides as prompts.

Step 11: Prepare Leave-Behinds

Prepare a one-page leave-behind for the audience (if you need two pages, print them back to back on the same piece of paper). Include the following:

- Your overview, conclusion, and recommendations
- Three key concrete supporting points
- How people can get in touch with you

Step 12: Prepare Backup Versions

Create a Web-based version of your presentation. Put one copy on a Web site that you can access from where you'll give your talk. Put another on a diskette that you will bring to the talk.

Step 13: Prepare for the Question-and-Answer Session

Anticipate further information your audience might need. Focus on material that you had to omit but still consider important (for example, further evidence, implications of the points you included, or references). Prepare responses to contentious points. Review your material and be ready to speak to it should the audience request that you do.

CHAPTER SUMMARY

Speaking in public gives you a chance to connect directly with your audience, gauging their reactions to you and your ideas. Successful speakers prepare meticulously—analyzing audiences, composing content, structuring ideas, and rehearsing. Computers help that preparation, as well as producing the professional-looking slides that audiences increasingly expect.

Good speakers add value to what their audience sees on the screen. They augment rather than simply read their slides. They also project a professional demeanor with their pace, voice, and manner. The effect they create is that of one colleague explaining a subject to another.

To become a good public speaker, you have to research your material in terms of your audience's needs and the time available to speak. You then must formulate your central idea and the details that will make it convincing. You have to prepare your slides, test your presentation, rehearse, and then deliver your talk engagingly. In addition, you must create leave-behinds and backup versions, as well as frame responses to questions your audience may ask.

CHECKLIST

☐ Audience identified (name one or two members)

☐ Material gathered from pre-existing documents and new sources

☐ Promise articulated

☐ Three key points identified to keep promise

☐ Three pieces of concrete evidence assembled for each key point

☐ Slide template created or chosen

☐ Presentation tested by writer for timing, completeness, logic, and structure

☐ Revisions done based on self-test

☐ Presentation tested with colleague for promise, solution or recommendations, concrete examples, wordiness of slides, amplifying instead of reading slides, graphics, audibility, verbal tics, and timing

☐ Revisions done based on test with colleague

☐ Slides copy-edited (order, legibility, effects, spelling, typos)

☐ Presentation rehearsed aloud

☐ Leave-behinds prepared

☐ Backup versions prepared and tested

☐ Question-and-answer responses prepared

Your additional comments:

EXERCISES

Using a report you have written in another course, prepare a five- to six-minute oral version, allowing an additional one to two minutes for questions and answers. Your audience will be your current classmates, who may or may not have taken the course for which you wrote the report.

Exercise 1

Identify what the members of your audience know about your subject. List any special terms or ideas that you'll need to explain and any you can assume they'll know.

Exercise 2

In a sentence or two, make your promise, that is, state the single most important idea you want your audience to know.

Exercise 3

List three important points that will keep your promise. Add three pieces of concrete evidence for each one.

Exercise 4

Prepare a storyboard by doing rough sketches of the slides you'll use. Decide what you'll cut and what you'll keep to make your three important points while staying within the time limit.

Exercise 5

Design the basic format for your slides, that is, its layout, colours, background, fonts, and graphics (if any).

Exercise 6

List the queries that your audience could ask during the question-and-answer period. Think of what is controversial in your report or where you had to cut to keep within the time limit. Prepare brief responses to each question.

Exercise 7

Rehearse your presentation aloud, timing yourself to ensure that you stay within the time limit. Pay attention to your delivery—that is, how you stand and what you sound like. Try to become aware of any verbal tics and eliminate them.

Exercise 8

Working with one other person, test your presentations for each other. Ask your tester how clear your promise was and how well you kept it, made your key points, and gave concrete examples. Also ask for comments on your design and presentation skills. Include a question-and-answer segment in the testing.

I

A How-to Guide For Fixing the Most Common Writing Mistakes

**What This
Appendix
Covers**

About These Procedures

Where To Put Commas

Ideas About Commas
Commas and Coordinating Conjunctions
Introductory Elements
Non-essential Elements
Manuscript Conventions for Dates and Places

Where Not to Put Commas

Before a Speaking Pause
Comma Splices
Main Clause Followed by a Dependent Clause
Between the Subject and the Verb
Between the Verb and the Object

Main Clauses Run Together

Sentence Fragments

Agreement With Double Subjects

Modifier Placement

A Glossary of Basic Terms

ABOUT THESE PROCEDURES

The procedures that follow will take you step-by-step through checking or correcting your sentences. They are not intended as a method to apply to every sentence you write from now on. Rather, they are a way of learning, reviewing, or correcting.

At first, using these procedures will be slow going, but after some practice, you will find yourself silently applying them as you write. They cannot guarantee that you will produce perfect sentences; they will, however, increase your chances of doing so.

For each procedure, you'll find the following:

- The name of the procedure (with alternate names as applicable)
- A model of the correct form
- A brief overview of the core idea
- Examples
- The terminology you'll need to know before applying the procedure
- A one-sentence overview of the entire procedure
- A series of steps to walk you through the procedure

A glossary of terms for all the procedures is at the end of this appendix.

Use these procedures when:

- You copy edit sentences before submitting a final draft
- Someone tells you that your sentences have errors
- You want to learn or review how to fix common errors

How to Use These Procedures
1. Select a sentence that you wish to check.
2. Read the preliminary materials and consult the glossary for any terms about which you're unsure.
3. Go through the steps, answering the questions about your sentence. Generally, you'll have two choices: *Yes* or *No*. In some cases, *Don't know* will be your third choice.
4. If you answer *Yes* or *No*, you will be told either to go on to another step or exit. If you answer *Don't know*, you will be shown a quick test to apply to your sentence to help you answer the question.

WHERE TO PUT COMMAS

Ideas About Commas

Commas are misused when people neglect two basic principles:

- Commas are logical markers that separate one sentence element from another. Therefore, use them only when you want to separate parts of a sentence.
- Commas aren't speaking pauses, although sometimes—not always—the two do coincide. Therefore, insert commas only when you need to separate sentence elements. Don't punctuate with your ear—that is, don't insert a comma simply because that's where you would pause when speaking.

Commas and Coordinating Conjunctions

The Model

> **First main clause + comma + coordinating conjunction + second main clause**

The Core Idea

When a coordinating conjunction joins two main clauses, a comma must precede it. Using only a comma or only a coordinating conjunction isn't enough; you must use both.

However, when a coordinating conjunction joins two grammatically equal things other than main clauses, there should be no comma. If one is there, remove it.

Note: Inserting a comma before a coordinating conjunction that joins the last element of a series is optional. Although most grammar texts still recommend it, many professional writers leave it out (especially for newspapers and magazines). Be consistent, whichever method you choose.

Examples

Comma required

> Our fees are higher than theirs, *but* we do the job properly.
> The day was bright and warm, *and* we left Halifax on time.
> He'll arrive on Tuesday, *or* she won't get the contract.

Comma not required

> The work is easy but tedious. [*Easy* and *tedious* are equally important adjectives, not main clauses.]

He used both Windows and Macintosh. [*Windows* and *Macintosh* are equally important nouns, not main clauses.]

They had to decide when to sell their house in Montreal and when to buy one in Toronto. [*When to sell their house in Montreal* and *when to buy one in Toronto* are equally important dependent clauses, not main clauses.]

The Procedure in Brief

Put a comma before a coordinating conjunction that joins two main clauses. Remove any comma before a coordinating conjunction that joins anything else.

Know These Terms Before Starting

- Main clause
- Coordinating conjunction
- Grammatically equal
- Series

Actions

Repeat these steps for every coordinating conjunction in your sentence.

Step 1

Does the sentence have a coordinating conjunction?

> **Yes:** Go to Step 2.
> **No:** Exit.
> **Don't Know:** Do any of the following words appear in the sentence: *and, but, or, nor, for, so, yet*?
> > **Yes:** Go to Step 2.
> > **No:** Exit.

Step 2

Does the coordinating conjunction join two main clauses?

> **Yes:** Insert a comma (if one isn't there) and exit.
> **No:** Go to Step 3.
> **Don't Know:** Can the two groups of words on either side of the coordinating conjunction stand by themselves and make complete sense?
> > **Yes:** Insert a comma (if one isn't there) and exit.
> > **No:** Go to Step 3.

Step 3

Does the coordinating conjunction join two equal elements?

> **Yes:** Remove the comma if one is there and exit.
> **No:** Go to Step 4.
> **Don't Know:** Is the word or group of words before the coordinating conjunction equally important as the word or group of words after the coordinating conjunction?
> > **Yes:** If there is a comma before the coordinating conjunction, remove it, then exit.
> > **No:** Go to Step 4.

Step 4

Does the coordinating conjunction join the last item in a series?

> **Yes:** If you wish, you may insert a comma if one is not already there. Be consistent with all other series in your document.
> **No:** There are no other possibilities. Check your understanding of the term and try the procedure again.

Introductory Elements

The Model

Introductory element + comma + subject of sentence

The Core Idea

An introductory element is a word or group of words (other than adjectives) that comes before the subject of a main clause. The comma helps identify the introductory element and prevent misreading or ambiguity.

An introductory element can be a phrase, a dependent clause, a conjunctive adverb, or a single word (such as someone's name when you address them directly, *yes* and *no*, or an adverb that modifes the whole sentence).

You can shift an introductory element to the end of a clause without changing its basic meaning. For example:

> When I *see her*, my heart leaps.
> My heart leaps *when I see her*.

Examples

Phrases

> *From what I've heard*, the bus strike will continue. [*Bus strike* is the subject.]
> *After school*, we went to the movies. [*We* is the subject.]
> *To see the damage*, he climbed up the hill. [*He* is the subject.]

Note: For short prepositional phrases, you can drop the comma:

In Toronto the Jays play at SkyDome.

Dependent clauses

If you build it, Kinsella will come. [*Kinsella* is the subject.]
When she saw the room, Emily knew it had to be painted. [*Emily* is the subject.]
Since you've asked, I will tell you. [*I* is the subject.]

Conjunctive adverbs

Therefore, we have gathered here today. [*We* is the subject.]
However, you have not received permission. [*You* is the subject.]
Consequently, Charlie had to leave. [*Charlie* is the subject.]

Single words (yes/no, *direct address, interjections, adverbs*)

Yes, this is only solution. [*This* is the subject.]
Rebecca, your mom is calling. [*Mom* is the subject.]
Rebecca, please fix the fan. [The subject *you* is implied in imperative sentences.]
Hey, I saw her just yesterday. [*I* is the subject.]
Above, the sun shone brilliantly. [*Sun* is the subject; try reading the sentence without the comma.]

No comma needed

The big barn is around the corner. [*The* and *big* are adjectives that describe the subject (*barn*) and so are not introductory elements.]

The Procedure in Brief

Place a comma after the introductory element that comes before the subject in a main clause.

Know These Terms Before Starting

* Introductory element
* Subject
* Adjective
* Adverb
* Main clause
* Dependent clause
* Phrase
* Direct address
* Interjection

Actions

Step 1

Locate the subject of the clause.

Step 2

Does a word or a group of words (other than adjectives) come before the subject?

> **Yes:** Go to Step 3.
> **No:** Exit.
> **Don't Know:** Can you move that word or group of words to the end of the clause without changing the basic meaning?
> **Yes:** Go to Step 3.
> **No:** Exit.

Step 3

Place a comma after the word or words that come before the subject and its adjectives.

Non-essential Elements (also called non-restrictive elements)

The Model

First part of sentence + comma + non-essential element + comma + rest of sentence

The Core Idea

A non-essential element is a word or a group of words that can be removed from a sentence without changing its basic meaning. A non-essential element can be a conjunctive adverb, a parenthetical expression, direct address, or an adjective clause. A pair of commas must enclose a non-essential element.

Compare these two sentences:

> My brother, *who went to Harvard*, is a doctor.

> The man *who is wearing the red sweater* is the killer.

In the first sentence, the basic idea is that my brother is a doctor; *who went to Harvard* is an adjective clause that adds interesting but not crucial information. It is non-essential and so can be removed without destroying the basic meaning. It therefore requires a pair of commas around it.

In the second example, however, *who is wearing the red sweater* is an essential adjective clause because it points to one man and one man only; it cannot be removed without changing the basic meaning. Essential elements should not be separated from the rest of the clause with commas.

When a non-essential element comes at the end of a clause, you place a comma before it but don't change the clause's closing punctuation (for example, a semicolon, period or question mark).

Examples

Conjunctive adverb, parenthetical expressions, direct address

It is true, *therefore,* that our banking system is sound. [*Therefore* is a non-essential conjunctive adverb.]

There's little chance, *in my opinion*, that war—incoming!—will occur. [*In my opinion* is a non-essential parenthetical expression.]

Your car, *Mr. Smith*, will be ready by sometime next year. [*Mr. Smith* is non-essential direct address.]

Adjective clauses

Whales, *which often range over thousands of miles*, should not be kept in captivity.

Our computer, *which was installed only last week*, won't boot.

The child, *who seemed happy a second earlier*, was now crying loudly.

Non-essential elements at the end of a clause

That would be nice, *wouldn't it?*

The car flipped into a ditch on Elgin Road, *where it was found a week later.*

Her dream of winning the Montreal marathon was not to be, *alas!*

Commas not needed

The book on the table is mine. [*On the table* is an essential prepositional phrase.]

The girl wearing the red dress is Nancy. [*Wearing the red dress* is an essential participial phrase.]

You're fired because you were late again. [*Because you were late again* is an essential dependent clause.]

Know These Terms Before Starting

- Conjunctive adverb
- Parenthetical expression
- Direct address
- Adjective clause

The Procedure in Brief

Place a pair of commas *before* and *after* the non-essential element. Place no commas around an essential element.

Actions

Step 1

Is there a non-essential element?

> **Yes:** Go to Step 2.
> **No:** Exit.
> **Don't Know:** Is there a word or group of words somewhere in the middle of the
> sentence that can be removed without destroying the basic meaning?
> **Yes:** Go to Step 2.
> **No:** Exit.

Step 2

Does the non-essential element come at the end of a clause?

> **Yes:** Go to Step 3.
> **No:** Go to Step 4.

Step 3

Is the there a comma *before* the non-essential element?

> **No:** Add one and exit.
> **Yes:** Exit.

Step 4

Is the there a comma before and after the non-essential element?

> **Yes:** Exit.
> **No:** Add them and exit.

Manuscript Conventions for Dates and Places

The Model

> **First part of date + comma + second part of date**
> **First part of geographical place + comma + second part of
> geographical place**

The Core Idea

The second part of dates and geographical locations need commas after them to separate them from other parts of a sentence.

Examples

Commas required

> My plans to arrive on June 23, 1996, were disrupted by an unexpected snowstorm. Deptford, Ontario, is the setting for the novel *Fifth Business*.

Commas not required

> I want to go home after lunch. [*Home* is not a geographical location such as you would find on a map.]

> I want to go home tomorrow after lunch. [*Tomorrow* is not a date such as you would find on a calendar.]

Know These Terms Before Starting

- Date
- Geographical location

The Procedure in Brief

Place a comma before and after the second part of a date or a geographical location.

Actions

Step 1

Is there a date like January 1, 2000 or a geographical location like Winnipeg, Manitoba?

> **Yes:** Go to Step 2.
> **No:** Exit.

Step 2

Put a comma between the main parts of the date or place name, then go to Step 3.

Step 3

Place a second comma after the second part unless it comes at the end of the clause that requires other punctuation.

WHERE NOT TO PUT COMMAS

Knowing where commas don't go is just as important as knowing where they do. Unnecessary commas send false signals to readers that sentence elements should be separated. That makes extra work for the reader. The next set of procedures, therefore, shows you where to remove existing commas—or avoid inserting them in the first place.

Note once more that it's wrong to put a comma before a coordinating conjunction that joins two equal things. See the procedure for commas and coordinating conjunctions above.

Before a Speaking Pause

Model

An essential part of the sentence + another essential part of the sentence

The Core Idea

The most common reason people insert unnecessary commas is that they assume they need commas where they pause if speaking the sentence. Don't insert a comma where you happen to pause when speaking unless that pause coincides with a legitimate reason to insert a comma.

Examples

Incorrect—commas should be removed

> What our elaborate reorganization and extensive renewal, of the company's personnel and infrastructure means for the Planning Department, is hundreds of hours of exacting and contentious work.

> That your car was damaged in the shop and that you had to spend over three thousand dollars to restore it to its original condition, isn't my fault.

> That you are both our most hardworking employee and a fine person, means that you can expect a raise very soon.

> How well the automobile runs after Chuck tunes it up and changes the oil, remains to be seen.

> [All of these commas only mark speaking pauses.]

Better

> What our elaborate reorganization and extensive renewal of the company's personnel and infrastructure means for the Planning Department is hundreds of hours of exacting and contentious work.

> That your car was damaged in the shop and that you had to spend over three thousand dollars to restore it to its original condition isn't my fault.

That you are both our most hardworking employee and a fine person means that you can expect a raise very soon.

How well the automobile runs after Chuck tunes it up and changes the oil remains to be seen.

Know These Terms Before Starting

- Essential element
- Non-essential element

The Procedure in Brief

Remove any comma that coincides with a speaking pause unless you can specify a legitimate reason to insert the comma.

Actions

Step 1

Is there a comma where you might pause while speaking the sentence aloud?

> **Yes:** Go to Step 2.
> **No:** Exit.

Step 2

Is there a valid reason for that comma? (See "Where to Put Commas.")

> **Yes:** Exit.
> **No:** Remove the comma.

Comma Splice (also known as a comma fault or run-on sentence)

Model

> **First main clause + comma and coordinating conjunction + second main clause**
> **First main clause + semicolon + second main clause**

The Core Idea

Main clauses have to be joined by both a comma and a coordinating conjunction *or* by a semicolon. Using only a comma between two main clauses creates a comma splice.

Examples

Incorrect

Security officers are unable to monitor these areas as often as we'd like, therefore, we should consider other safety measures.

The shipment was delayed by several months, the customers became very angry.

Better

Security officers are unable to monitor these areas as often as we'd like; therefore, we should consider other safety measures. [A semicolon joins the two main clauses.]

The shipment was delayed by several months, so the customers became very angry. [A comma and a coordinating conjunction join the two main clauses.]

Know These Terms Before Starting

- Main clauses
- Coordinating conjunction

The Procedure in Brief

If only a comma separates two main clauses, add the appropriate coordinating conjunction after the comma or replace the comma with a semicolon.

Note: As a matter of style, you can also replace the comma with a period or make one of the main clauses depend on the other.

Actions

Step 1

Can what is on either side of the comma can stand by itself and make complete sense?

> **Yes:** Go to Step 2.
> **No:** Check for other reasons to account for this comma and then exit.

Step 2

Does a comma and nothing else separate the two main clauses?

> **Yes:** Go to Step 3.
> **No:** Exit.

Step 3

Do *one* of the following:

*   Add the appropriate coordinating conjunction after the comma.
*   Replace the comma with a semicolon.
*   Replace the comma with a period and make two separate sentences.
*   Make one clause depend on the other.

Main Clause Followed by an Essential Dependent Clause

Model

Main clause + dependent clause

The Core Idea

There should be no comma after a main clause when it is followed by an essential dependent clause.

Examples

Incorrect—commas should be removed

> You must follow our procedures exactly, when preparing the slides. [*When preparing the slides* is essential because it indicates the specific time to follow procedures exactly.]

> Both soccer teams were disqualified, because their fans began fighting. [*Because their fans began fighting* is essential because it indicates under what specific circumstances the teams were disqualified.]

> Jonathan hasn't been able to eat seafood, after he got sick at Aunt Mabel's. [*After he got sick at Aunt Mabel's* is essential because it indicates the specific event that made him sick.]

Comma required

> Lesley was born in Regina, where she hopes to return soon. [The comma is correct because the writer intends where *she hopes to return soon* to be a nonessential addition to the main idea that Lesley was born in Regina.]

Know These Terms Before Starting

*   Main clause
*   Dependent clause

- Non-essential element
- Essential element

The Procedure in Brief

Remove a comma after a main clause if it is followed by an essential dependent clause.

Actions

Step 1

Is there a dependent clause?

> **Yes:** Go to Step 2.
> **No:** Exit.
> **Don't Know:** Is there a group of words that begins with a subordinate conjunction, has a subject and a verb, but can't stand by itself?
> **Yes:** Go to Step 2.
> **No:** Exit.

Step 2

Does the dependent clause follow the main clause?

> **Yes:** Go to Step 3.
> **No:** Exit.

Step 3

Is the dependent clause essential?

> **Yes:** Go to Step 4.
> **No:** Exit.
> **Don't Know:** Can the dependent clause be removed without changing the basic meaning of the sentence?
> **Yes:** Go to Step 4.
> **No:** Exit.

Step 4

Remove the comma after the main clause (if one is there) and exit.

Comma between the Subject and the Verb

Model

Subject of clause +verb

The Core Idea

There should be no comma between the subject of a clause and its verb. The number of words in the subject makes no difference. Note that a complex subject (such as *the big, old, dilapidated red barn*) may contain a legitimate comma.

Examples

Incorrect

> The long green snake with sharp fangs and a flickering, dangerous tongue, crept closer. [*Crept* is the verb, and everything before it is the subject.]

> A fully integrated, local area network that provides e-mail and full Internet access, doesn't have to cost a great deal. [*Doesn't cost* is the verb, and everything before it is the subject.]

> What the world needs now in these times of trouble and turmoil, is love and understanding. [*Is* is the verb, and everything before it is the subject.]

Better

> The long green snake with sharp fangs and a flickering, dangerous tongue crept closer.

> A fully integrated, local area network that provides e-mail and full Internet access doesn't have to cost a great deal.

> What the world needs now in these times of trouble and turmoil is love and understanding.

Know These Terms Before Starting

* Subject
* Verb
* Clause

The Procedure in Brief

Remove the comma between a subject and the verb.

Actions

Step 1

Is there a subject or a group of words that functions as the subject?

> **Yes:** Go to Step 2.
> **No:** You are not looking at a complete sentence. Exit and rewrite the sentence.

Step 2

Is there a verb or a group of words that function as the verb?

> **Yes:** Go to Step 3.
> **No:** You are not looking at a complete sentence. Exit and rewrite the sentence.

Step 3

Is there a comma between the subject and the verb?

> **Yes:** Go to Step 4.
> **No:** Exit.

Step 4

Remove the comma.

Comma between the Verb and the Object

Model

Verb + object

The Core Idea

There should be no comma between the verb of a clause and its object.

Examples

Incorrect—commas should be removed

> He hit, the ball. [*Hit* is the verb and *ball* is the object.]
>
> The report clearly showed, the flaws of the tax system. [*Showed* is the verb and *flaws* is the object.]

Correct—commas do not separate the verb from the object

> We bought licorice, a chocolate bar, and three packs of gum. [*Bought* is the verb and *licorice, a chocolate bar, and three packs of gum* is the object.]
>
> The children chose, wrapped, and delivered the presents themselves. [*Chose, wrapped, and delivered* is the verb and *presents* is the object.]

Know These Terms Before Starting

- Verb
- Object
- Clause

The Procedure in Brief

Remove the comma between a verb and its object.

Actions

Step 1

Is there a verb or a group of words that functions as the verb?

>**Yes:** Go to Step 2.
>**No:** You are not looking at a complete sentence. Exit and rewrite the sentence.

Step 2

Is there a word or a group of words that functions as the object?

>**Yes:** Go to Step 3.
>**No:** Exit.
>**Don't know:** Locate the word or group of words that receives the action of the verb and try again.

How to Locate the Object
1.   Find the verb.
2.   Put it in the past tense.
3.   Put *What got* in front of the verb and a question mark after the verb.
4.   The word (or group of words) that answers that question is the object.

>**Example**
>Tom hit John.
>*What got hit?*
>*John* is the object.

Step 3

Is there a comma between the verb and the object?

>**Yes:** Go to Step 4.
>**No:** Exit.

Step 4

Remove the comma and exit.

MAIN CLAUSES RUN TOGETHER (SOMETIMES CALLED A RUN-ON SENTENCE)

Model

First main clause + appropriate punctuation + second main clause

The Core Idea

Two main clauses must be separated by the appropriate punctuation, usually a semicolon.

Examples

Each second main clause is in italics.

Incorrect

>The skies threatened *the rains came*.

>Consultants must always consider the needs of their clients *anything else follows from that*.

>I like coffee however, *she likes tea*.

Better

>The skies threatened; *the rains came*.

>Consultants must always consider the needs of their clients; *anything else follows from that*.

>I like coffee; *however, she likes tea*.

Know This Term Before Starting

Main clause

The Procedure in Brief

Place a semicolon between two main clauses not otherwise joined.

   Note: As a matter of style, you can instead insert a comma and the appropriate coordinating conjunction **or** create two sentences.

Actions

Step 1

Are there two main clauses with no punctuation between them?

> **Yes:** Go to Step 2.
> **No:** Exit.
> **Don't Know:** Are there two groups of words that can stand by themselves and make sense?
> > **Yes:** Go to Step 2.
> > **No:** Exit.

Step 2

Insert a semicolon between the two main clauses and exit.

> **Note:** You can instead insert a comma and the appropriate coordinating conjunction *or* make the main clauses into separate sentences.

SENTENCE FRAGMENTS

Model

> **A group of words that can stand by themselves and make complete sense.**

The Core Idea

A main clause must make complete sense and stand by itself; otherwise, it is a fragment. Incorrect semicolons frequently create fragments.

Examples

Incorrect (fragments in italics)

> It is never too late to start over; *because there's always a second chance.*

> Our restaurant will experiment with as many dishes as possible; *and buy all ingredients from local suppliers.*

Better

> It is never too late to start over because there's always a second chance.

> Our restaurant will experiment with as many dishes as possible and buy all ingredients from local suppliers.

Know This Term Before Starting

Main clause

The Procedure in Brief

Remove a semicolon where it creates a fragment, that is, something that can't stand by itself and make sense.

Actions

Step 1

Does the sentence contain a semicolon?

> **Yes:** Go to Step 2.
> **No:** Exit.

Step 2

Can what is on either side of the semicolon stand by itself and make complete sense?

> **Yes:** Exit.
> **No:** Go to Step 3.

Step 3

Remove the semicolon and exit.

AGREEMENT WITH DOUBLE SUBJECTS

Model

> Subject (singular or plural) + *and* + subject (singular or plural) + plural verb
> Subject (singular or plural) + *or* + singular subject + singular verb
> Subject (singular or plural) + *or* + plural subject + plural verb

The Core Idea

Subjects and verbs must agree in number. That is, a singular subject must have a singular verb and a plural subject must have a plural verb. For example:

> Ike is here, but the kids are not.

Confusion arises when a sentence has a double subject, that is, one that consists of two parts joined by *and* or *or*. The form of the verb depends on the conjunction that joins the two parts of the subject:

- Two singular or two plural nouns joined by *and* always take a plural verb.
- Two singular nouns joined by *or* always take a singular verb.
- A singular noun and a plural noun joined by *or* take a verb that agrees with the noun closest to the verb.

Examples

Correct

> Ike and Mike are here.
>
> Either Ike or Mike is here.
>
> Either Ike or the boys are here. [The boys is plural and closest to the verb.]
>
> Either the boys or Ike is here. [Ike is singular and closest to the verb.]

Incorrect

> John and the boys is tall. [The verb should be plural because the two parts of the subject are joined by *and*.]
>
> John or the boys is late. [The verb should be plural because the two parts of the subject are joined by *or* and the plural part is closest to the verb.]

Know These Terms Before Starting:

- Coordinating conjunction
- Double subject

The Procedure in Brief

When there is a double subject, check the coordinating conjunction to make the verb agree in number.

Actions

Step 1

Are the two parts of a double subject joined by *and*?

> **Yes:** Make the verb plural and exit.
> **No:** Go to Step 2.

Step 2

Are the two parts of a double subject joined by *or*?

> **Yes:** Go to Step 3.
> **No:** These are the only relevant conjunctions. Check the sentence and try again.

Step 3

Are the two parts of a double subject singular?

> **Yes:** Make the verb singular and exit.
> **No:** Go to Step 4.

Step 4

Are the two parts of a double subject plural?

> **Yes:** Make the verb plural and exit.
>
> **No:** Make the verb agree in number with the part of the double subject that is closest to it and exit.

MODIFIER PLACEMENT

Model

> **Modifier + what is modified**
> **What is modified + modifier**

The Core Idea

A modifier should be placed as close as possible to what it modifies. Otherwise, readers have to make the connection themselves. A badly placed modifier can result in a meaning quite different from what you intended.

Examples

Problematic

> Driving to Calgary, the sky suddenly darkened. [This says that the sky was doing the driving.]
>
> Don't buy a book for a friend who hates flying about planes. [This says the friend hates flying about planes.]
>
> John only has three dollars. [This suggests either that John is the only person who has three dollars or that John's only interaction with the three dollars is his possession of them.]

Better

> Driving to Calgary, I saw the sky suddenly darken.
>
> Don't buy a book about planes for a friend who hates flying.
>
> John has only three dollars.

Know This Term Before Starting:

Modifier

The Procedure in Brief

Place a modifier as close as possible to what it modifies.

Actions

Step 1

Locate a modifier.

Step 2

- If the modifier describes a verb (or group of words that function as a verb), place the modifier immediately before or immediately after the verb.
- If the modifier describes a noun (or group of words that function as a noun), place it immediately before or immediately after the noun.
- If the modifier describes a word that is not actually present but merely implied, rewrite the sentence.

A GLOSSARY OF BASIC TERMS

Adjective: A word that describes a noun. (The articles *a*, *an*, and *the* are adjectives.)

> **Example**
> *The big red* house fell down. [*The, big*, and *red* all describe the noun house.]

Adverb: A word that describes a verb, an adjective, or another adverb.

> **Examples**
> He ran quickly. [*Quickly* describes *ran*.]
> He ran very quickly. [*Very* describes the adverb *quickly*.]
> It was a quite beautiful sunset. [*Quite* describes the adjective *beautiful*.]

Adjective clause: A dependent clause that does the work of an adjective.

> **Example**
> The house, *which was red*, fell down.

Note: Many authorities insist that adjective clauses beginning with *which* must be non-essential and that adjective clauses beginning with *that* must be essential. Follow this rule unless you know that your audience doesn't use it.

Conjunctive adverb: A word that joins main clauses and shows their logical relationship. There are many conjunctive adverbs, including *therefore, besides, indeed, moreover*, and *nevertheless*.

Examples

I think, *therefore*, I am.

Tom called Fatasha; *however*, she refused to speak.

Consequently, Mr. Holmes, we sent for you.

Note that most adverbs are not conjunctive, as the following example illustrates:

She raced through the store *quickly*. [*Quickly* is an adverb but simply describes the verb.]

Coordinating conjunction: A word that joins two other words (or groups of words) that are equally important. The most common coordinating conjunctions are *and, but*, and *or*. Less frequently used ones are *nor, for, yet*, and *so*. Think of FANBOYS—*for, and, nor, but, or, yet, so*—to help you remember the list.

Examples

I like Ike *and* Mike. [*And* joins two nouns.]

I like either when Ike talks *or* when Mike walks. [*Or* joins two dependent clauses.]

I will hop *but* not skip. [*But* joins two verbs.]

Note that prepositions are not coordinating conjunctions, although they can have a similar linking function, as in this example:

I am eating ice cream *with* whipped cream. [*With* is a preposition showing that *ice cream* is more important than *whipped cream*.]

Dependent clause: A clause that can't stand by itself and make complete sense. (A clause is group of words with a subject and a verb.) A dependent clause always needs to be attached to main clause.

Example

Because I liked Ike [This can't stand by itself despite having a subject and a verb; the reader wants to know what happened because of liking Ike.]

Note the difference from a main clause, such as:

I didn't like Mike. [This main clause can stand by itself.]

Direct address: Using a person's name when speaking directly to him or her.

Example:

Polly, put the kettle on. [I am speaking directly to Polly.]

Note that in direct address the person's name is not the object of a verb, unlike this example:

I like Polly. [I am speaking about Polly.]

Grammatically equal elements (also called coordinate elements): Two words or two groups of words which are equally important to the meaning of the sentence. They are always joined by a coordinating conjunction.

Examples

I liked *Ike* and *Mike*. [The two nouns are equally important.]
I will *meet* and *greet* Ike. [The two verbs are equally important.]

Note that words joined by a preposition are not grammatically equal, as the following example illustrates:

I like Ike with Mike [*Ike* and *Mike* are not joined by a coordinating conjunction but by a preposition; that makes Ike more important.]

Interjection: A non-essential word or phrase that indicates an exclamation.

Example

Hey, that's my Barbie!
Oh, what a beautiful morning!

Introductory element: A word or a group of words that comes before the main clause and introduces it.

Example

Once upon a time, I liked Ike.

There is no introductory element in this version:

I liked Ike once upon a time. [*Once upon a time* doesn't precede the subject.]

Main Clause: A group of words with a subject and a verb that can stand by itself and make complete sense.

Examples

I liked Ike. [This is a sentence with one main clause.]

I liked Ike, but I did not like Mike. [This is a sentence with two main clauses.]

I liked Ike when he lived next door. [This is a sentence with one main clause; *when he lived next door* is a dependent clause because it has a subject and a verb but cannot stand alone.]

Modifier: A word that describes or limits another word.

Examples

The barn is *red*. [The adjective describes a noun.]

He ran *swiftly*. [The adverb describes a verb.]

Jones had a *very* good year. [The adverb describes an adjective.]

Jones had a *very*, very good year. [The adverb describes another adverb.]

Non-essential element (also called non-restrictive element): A word or a group of words that can be removed from the sentence without changing its basic meaning.

Examples
I, *however*, liked Ike. [The main idea is that *I liked Ike*.]
Uncle George, *who liked Ike*, invited him to join us. [*Who liked Ike* is not essential because *Uncle George* already identifies a specific person.]

Note that the same element can be either essential or non-essential depending on what other information is in the sentence:

The man *who liked Ike* is the one in the red shirt. [*Who liked Ike* is essential here because it identifies one specific man and only that man.]

Noun: A word or a phrase that names a person, place, thing, or condition.

Example
The big red house fell down. [*House* is a noun.]

Object: The thing that receives the action of a verb (although not all verbs have objects). You can determine the object (if one exists) by taking the main verb, putting it in the past tense, and placing *What got* before it. For example:

Dick *sees* Jane.
Verb: *sees*
Past tense of verb: *seen*
What got seen? *Jane.*
Therefore, *Jane* is the object.

Example
Jonathan threw out the first *ball.* [*Ball* received the action of Jonathan throwing.]

Note the difference between an object and a subject:

Jonathan threw out the first ball. [Jonathan performed the action; he didn't receive it.]

Parenthetical Expression: A non-essential word or a group of words that interrupts the main message of the clause, adding useful but not crucial meaning.

Example
The sky, *in my opinion*, was falling. [*In my opinion* can be removed]

Note that in this version the same words are not parenthetical:

My opinion was that the sky was falling. [*My opinion* is the subject of the verb and cannot be removed.]

Phrase: A group of words that cannot stand by itself and make complete sense. There are many kinds of phrases, and they generally take their name from their first word or from their function. Here are examples of the most common types:

Prepositional phrase
From all over Manitoba, the trucks began to roll. [The phrase begins with the preposition *from*.]

Infinitive phrase
We decided *to sign the contract*. [The phrase begins with the infinitive form of the verb *sign*.]

Participial phrase
Constructed of bricks, the house withstood the wolf. [The phrase begins with the participle *constructed*.]

Series: A group of three or more items, each having equal value.

Examples
He went to the store and bought *nuts, bolts, and screws*. [Three nouns are in series.]

My dental irrigator was *bought, sold*, and *paid* for. [Three passive verbs are in series.].

I ate, *I played*, and *I slept*. [Three main clauses are in series.]

Subject: The word that performs the action in a main clause or the word about which the sentence primarily speaks.

Example
Jonathan threw out the first ball. [Jonathan performed the main action.]

The first ball was thrown by Jonathan. [*Ball* is the subject of the passive verb *was thrown*.]

II A How-to Guide For Citing the Work of Others

What This Appendix Covers

Ideas

Why You Cite
What You Cite
What You Don't Cite
How You Cite
    Placing Citations in Your Document
    Author-Date System
    Number System

Actions

Preparing the Body Section
Preparing the Reference Section Using an Author-Date Style
Preparing the Reference Section Using a Number Style

IDEAS

Citation formats vary, and it not possible to detail all of them here. What follows, therefore, is a deliberately generic guide; consult the appropriate style manual for additional information on a specific style. The *Ideas Into Action* Web site at **<www.pearsoned.com/keller/>** provides links to resources about styles used by prominent professional organizations.

Why You Cite

You cite work by other authors for three reasons:
- To help readers find the cited material either to learn more about the subject or to verify your claims
- To make clear what parts of your document are based on the intellectual property of others and so avoid charges of plagiarism
- To persuade readers that your use of professional literature is rigorous, knowledgeable, and credible

What You Cite

In general, give credit where credit is due. If you incorporate the intellectual property of identifiable persons or groups, you must acknowledge them. Although an idea may be in the public domain, someone nonetheless owns the particular way that idea is expressed. The clearest examples of something you must give credit for are quotations of the exact words another person wrote or said:

> "The Nimbus 2000 can reach speeds of forty kilometers per hour without stability problems; however, above that, riders experience severe vibrations" (Potter and Weasley, 1999).

> "Collies have a substantial chance of having moderate-to-severe vision problems in later life . . . pups' eyes, therefore, should be checked by a veterinarian ophthalmologist before they are twelve weeks" (Canadian Collie Fanciers, 1997).

> "Our study estimates that fifty percent of productive salmon habitats in the 1970s had been severely degraded by 1995" (Henderson, 1999).

The first example is from a book, the second from a brochure, and the third from a transcription of a personal interview. In each case, the language of the original was reproduced exactly.

However, you don't have to quote others verbatim to incur the responsibility of acknowledging them. Simply changing the language doesn't change your obligation to show where your ideas stop and another person's begin. If you paraphrase someone's words or base an assertion on them, you have to show your intellectual debt, as in these examples:

> Potter and Weasley (1999) have demonstrated that riders have much trouble with the stability of the Nimbus 2000 at speeds above forty kilometers.

> Purchasers of short-hair collie pups need to know that this breed has a significant chance of developing vision problems in later life (Canadian Collie Fanciers, 1997).

> Independent observers such as Henderson (1999) estimate that half of the collapse of the salmon fishery can be attributed to habitat having been seriously damaged.

These principles apply to all intellectual property, including graphics, company logos, recordings, or anything else that you did not create. The Actions section of this appendix shows a method for citing tables and other graphics.

What You Don't Cite

You don't, however, have to cite ideas that are common knowledge and cannot be attributed to a single identifiable source. Here are three such examples:

- Montreal is the largest city in Québec.
- Smoking dramatically increases the risk of lung cancer.
- Canadian federal elections are generally held every four years.

Most educated people would know these ideas to be true or could easily verify them. You need not, therefore, cite a source. However, if a statement were contentious (or at least not widely accepted), you would need to refer to an authority.

For example, forty years ago, scientists debated whether smoking was dangerous. If you were writing about smoking at that time, therefore, you would have needed to cite a reputable source for whatever position you put forward. Today, the general risks of smoking are so well established that no source is necessary. However, you still need to indicate an authority if you assert a precise claim like "Smokers are sixty percent more likely to get lung cancer than non-smokers."

The lesson is that you must know your audience and what they consider common knowledge.

How You Cite

A citation requires an entry in two places:

1. At the point where you use someone else's intellectual property
2. In the list of references

The first entry alerts your reader that the material is borrowed; the second tells your reader exactly where to find the original.

Several professional associations issue style guides that include formats for citing borrowed work. The American Psychological Association (APA) sets documentation style for the social sciences; the Council of Biology Editors (CBE) does the same for the natural sciences and engineering. The Modern Language Association (MLA) is the authority for work published in the humanities. Other professional groups generally adopt or modify one of these styles.

The style you choose depends entirely on what your audience demands. A specific style is not correct or incorrect but rather appropriate or inappropriate. Always check, therefore, that the style you use is the one that your readers consider the standard in their profession. If you can't ask them directly, follow the style used in one of the reputable journals in their field.

Regardless of style, accuracy is paramount. It's easier to be accurate if you collect the necessary information as you go. At the minimum, you'll need to keep records of the following:

- Author(s)
- Title
- Year of publication
- Publisher and place of publication
- Page number(s)
- Volume number for periodicals or series
- URL for sources on the World Wide Web

Other kinds of sources (such as personal communications, brochures, interviews, and television or radio programs) require additional information. Your goal is to make the original easy to find. Err on the side of collecting too much

WORKING SMARTER

Using Your Word Processor for Citations

Your word processor can make citing works more efficient. Begin by creating a file to hold your document's references. If a source is electronic, simply cut and paste the information into your reference file; that reduces the chance of typing errors.

If your source is not electronic and your computer isn't available, enter the information either into a notebook or onto 3 x 5 file cards. If you use a notebook, keep a separate one for each project; if you use file cards, be careful not to lose any. Transfer the information to your word processor file as soon as possible and back it up for safety.

bibliographic information; it's much easier to delete what you don't need than to find the source a second time.

Placing Citations in Your Document

Having gathered the necessary information, you need to put it into your document. The traditional method of placing notes at the bottom of the page or at the end of the document has largely disappeared; this method can force readers to pause, locate the footnote or endnote, then return to where they were, possibly losing the thread of the discussion.

You still may encounter discursive footnotes or endnotes, that is, notes that add information or expand a point rather than direct readers to a source. Although discursive notes are still acceptable in academic writing, professional writers rarely use them. After all, if something is important enough to include, it should be in the body of a document or (in the case of highly technical material) in an appendix. If an idea isn't important, it should be cut. The exception is the sidebar, a short self-contained section (usually two or three paragraphs) holding information that's interesting but not essential. However, sidebars should be used sparingly.

Instead of the traditional footnotes, most professional organizations now require one of two styles: author-date or citation number. The former is more common in the social sciences and humanities, and the latter is more common in science and engineering.

Author-Date System

As its name implies, with the author-date style, the author's name and the year of publication appear in the body of your document, like this:

> Murray's results (1999) show a significant improvement over traditional methods, such as those described by Zane (1996) or Garfeld (1996).

You then place the full bibliographic information about these sources in your reference list. The reference list is arranged alphabetically by author; works by the same author are then listed in chronological order. For example:

> Garfeld, Rhoda R. (1996). Weaning mollusks with lamb chops and barley. *Journal of Odd Practices. 3*, 9–10. <http://www.oddpract.com/1996/Garfeld/>.

> Murray, H. H., & Hollingsworth, M. M. (1999). *So the world is your oyster?* (pp. 43–121) Red Deer, AB: Chatty and Windy.

> Zane, Albert A. (1996). Tracking mollusk breeding for hobbyists. In S. Etchevery (Ed.), *Mollusk breeders handbook.* Toronto: Faloney Press.

Number System

With the number system, you insert a number in square brackets into the body of your document. (Some publications use parentheses instead of square brackets or set the number as a superscript.) The number indicates the citation's position within the sequence of other citations in your document. For example:

> Murray's results [12] show a significant improvement over traditional methods, such as those described by Zane [4] or Garfeld [13].

Assuming that Murray is cited here for the first time, the [12] tells the reader that there have already been eleven citations of other works. Murray's work is the twelfth cited and Garfeld's is the thirteenth. Zane, however, has already been cited—his work was the fourth citation in the paper, as the [4] indicates.

All three names will appear in your reference list in the order that these citations appear in your document—*not* in alphabetical order:

> 4 Zane, A. A. Tracking mollusk breeding for hobbyists. In: Etchevery, S. ed. Mollusk breeders handbook. Toronto: Faloney Press; 1996.
>
> . . .
>
> 12 Murray H. H.; Hollingsworth, M. M. So the world is your oyster? Red Deer AB: Chatty and Windy, 1999:43–121.
>
> 13 Garfeld R. Weaning mollusks with lamb chops and barley. Journal of Odd Practices 3: 9–10; 1996. Available from: <http://www.oddpract.com/1996/Garfeld/>.

Note that these examples are generic. Formatting details vary from one style to another. See the *Ideas Into Action* Web site at **<www.pearsoned.com/keller/>** for links to resources on various bibliographic styles.

ACTIONS

Preparing the Body Section

Step 1

Scan your text for places where you need a citation. Ask yourself: *Are there instances where I have borrowed someone else's intellectual property in one of the following ways:*

- *a direct quote*
- *a paraphrase*
- *an assertion*
- *a statement about which there is disagreement*

> **No:** Go to Step 3.
> **Yes:** Go to Step 2.

Step 2

A. If you are using an author-date style, either insert the year of publication immediately after the first mention of the author's name or insert the author's last name and the year of publication in parentheses at the end of the borrowed material.

Examples

The number of Web sites "dedicated to emerging Pacific economies increased tenfold between 1997 and 1999" (Wynne, 1999).

Wynne (1999) notes that between 1997 and 1999, the number of Web sites focusing on emerging Pacific economies increased by a factor of ten.

B. If you are using a number style, insert a number in square brackets at the end of the borrowed material or immediately after the first mention of the author's name. This number indicates the position of this source within the sequence of citations in your document. If you have previously referred to the same source, use the number from your first citation of it.

Examples

The number of Web sites "dedicated to emerging Pacific economies increased tenfold between 1997 and 1999" [4].

Wynne[4] notes that between 1997 and 1999, the number of Web sites focusing on emerging Pacific economies increased by a factor of ten.

Note: Do not begin a sentence with a citation number in square brackets (as in *[4] notes that between . . .*)

WORKING SMARTER

Entering Citation Numbers

If you are using a number style, insert the author's name and year of publication after each citation number (for example, "[4] Zane 1996"). You will then know at a glance which citation number refers to which source when you generate your works cited section. Once you've prepared the works cited section, remove the name and year from the body of the document, leaving the citation number in square brackets.

Step 3

Ask yourself: *Is there an instance where I have used a table or any other graphic that is someone else's intellectual property?*

> **No:** Go to Step 4.
> **Yes:** Insert a source credit as described below.

If the borrowed material is a table, place the title above it. Below the table, insert *Source:*, followed by the necessary bibliographic information, as illustrated in Figure A2.1.

Features Available on Selected Models 1999

Make and Model	CD/FM/AM	Anti-Lock Brakes	Air Bags
Ford Taurus	Standard	Standard	Standard
Honda Accord	Standard	Standard	Standard
Toyota Tercel	Optional	Optional	Optional
Yugo	N/A	N/A	N/A

Figure A2.1
Citing a table

Source: Importing a used car. (1999). Freedonian Used-Vehicle News, 4*(2), 24.*

If the borrowed material is a graphic other than a table, place its title below the graphic. Then on a new line, insert *Source:*, followed by the necessary bibliographic information, as shown in Figure A2.2.

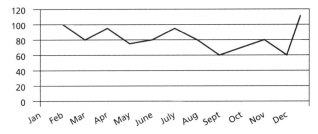

Figure A2.2
Citing a graphic that is not a table

Source: What's next? (1997, August). Freedonian Financial Newsletter, 2*(8), 112.*

Step 4

The material appears to be common knowledge and need not be cited. Repeat scanning your document until you have found all instances where you have borrowed someone else's intellectual property.

Preparing the Reference Section Using an Author-Date Style

Different styles require different formatting (for example, the order of information and what is italicized). Refer to the appropriate style for details.

Step 1

After you have inserted all the necessary citations into the body of your document, create a new section at the end to hold the bibliographic information. Depending on the style sheet, this section might be called "References" or "Works Cited."

WORKING SMARTER

Formatting and Sorting Reference Lists

If your list contains more than a few entries, create a table and paste the bibliographic information into separate rows, beginning each one with the author's name. You can then use your word processor's Sort command to automatically alphabetize the list. (Be sure to make the table's borders invisible in the final version of your document.)

Step 2

A. Go to the top of your document file. With your word processor, search for the first left parenthesis.

B. When you locate a left parenthesis that's part of a citation, copy the author's name and year of publication into the word processor's clipboard.

C. Insert an *xxx* (or other string that is not part of a word) at that point in the document's body.

D. Go to the references section of your document.

E. Paste in the author's name and year of publication.

F. Go back to the top of your document file and search for the *xxx*; remove it and continue searching for left parentheses.

G. Repeat this process until you find no other left parentheses.

Step 3

Go to your references section; remove any duplicate entries, checking that they are indeed duplications and not different works by the same author.

Step 4

Alphabetize the list.

Step 5

Expand the entries in your references list to include all necessary bibliographic information.

> **Example** (using APA style)
>
> Garfeld, Rhoda, R. (1996). Weaning mollusks with lamb chops and barley. *Journal of Odd Practices*, 3, 9-10. <http://www.oddpract.com/1996/Garfeld/>.
>
> Murray, H. H., & Hollingsworth, M. M. (1999). *So the world is your oyster?* Red Deer AB: Chatty and Windy.
>
> Zane, Albert A. (1996). Tracking mollusk breeding for hobbyists. In S. Etchevery (Ed.), *Mollusk breeders handbook.* Toronto: Faloney Press.

Preparing the References Section Using a Number Style

Different styles require different formatting (for example, the order of information and what is italicized). Refer to the appropriate style for details.

Step 1

After you have inserted all the necessary citations into the body of your document, create a new section at the end to hold the bibliographic information. Depending on the style, this section might be called "References" or "Works Cited."

Step 2

A. Open both your document file and the file that holds the bibliographic information you have gathered as you researched your subject.

B. Go to the top of your document file. With your word processor, search for the first left square bracket.

C. When you locate a left square bracket that's part of a citation, go to your bibliography file; then copy the author's name and year of publication. (If you have previously inserted the author's name and year of publication for easy reference, remove them now.)

D. Insert an *xxx* (or other string that is not part of a word) at that point in the body of your document.

E. Go to the references section of your document.

F. Enter the author's name and year of publication.

G. Go back to top of the document file and search for the *xxx*; remove it and continue searching for left square brackets.

H. Repeat the process until you find no other left square brackets.

Step 3

Go to your reference list and expand each entry to include all necessary bibliographic information. The order of entries must follow the sequence in which they appear in the body of your document.

> **Example** (using CBE style)
>
> 4 Zane, A. A. Tracking mollusk breeding for hobbyists. In: Etchevery S., ed. Mollusk breeders handbook. Toronto: Faloney Press; 1996.
>
> . . .
>
> 12 Murray H. H.; Hollingsworth, M. M. So the world is your oyster? Red Deer AB: Chatty and Windy; 1999:43-121.
>
> 13 Garfeld R. R. Weaning mollusks with lamb chops and barley. Journal of Odd Practices. 3:9-10; 1996. Available from: <http://www.oddpract.com/1996/Garfeld/>

INDEX

A

abstractions, 69–71
accurate information, 5
active verbs, 47
active voice, 42
Adams, Cecil, 212
addition, 27
adjective, 322–324, 341
adjective clause, 325, 341
adverb, 322–324, 341
algebra, 70–71
analogous evidence, 9–10
analogy, 238–239
analytical reports, 188–189
anecdotal evidence, 10
appendix, 174, 199
assertion, 28
attached files, 115
audience. *See* readers
Ausubel, David, 92
author-date system, 350, 354–355
automatic lists, 91

B

backgrounds, 277
bad news, 110–112, 120–122
balance, 5, 10–11, 14
bar graphs, 62–64
beta test, 12–13, 14–15
block format, 113–114
body
    citations, 351–354
    citations in, 351–354
    memos, 117
    routine letters, 118
boilerplate files, 114
brevity, 104
Bruner, Jerome, 300
budget plan, 174
bulleted lists, 28
bullets, 95

C

Carson, Rachel, 239
causal description, 221
charts
    flow, 64–65, 75, 136–137, 217–218
    organization, 65, 76
    pie, 64, 75
chronological description, 221
citation
    author-date system, 350, 354–355
    in the body, 351–354
    common knowledge, 348
    how to cite, 348–350
    number system, 351, 355–356
    numbers, 352
    placement of, 350
    purpose of, 247
    Web material, 168
    when, 347–348
    word processor and, 349
clarification, 28
clarity, 5–6, 14
clip art, 56
closing
    bad-news letters, 121
    memos, 117
    routine letters, 119
colon, 28
colour, 95, 276–277
colour wheel, 276–277
column graphs, 62–64, 75

commas
    and coordinating conjunctions, 320–322
    dates, 326–327
    essential dependent clause, 331–332
    fault, 329–331
    ideas about, 320
    introductory elements, 322–324
    main clause, 331–332
    manuscript conventions, 326–327
    non-essential elements, 324–326
    places, 326–327
    before speaking pause, 328–329
    splice, 329–331
    between subject and verb, 332–334
    between verb and object, 334–335
common comparisons, 243–244
common writing mistakes
    commas, where not to put, 327–335
    commas, where to put, 320–327
    main clauses run together, 336–337
    modifier placement, 340–341
    sentence fragments, 337–338
    subject agreement, 338–340
comparisons, 237–241
    bad, 241
    claiming too much, 241
    common, 243–244
    drawing attention to itself, 241
    good, 241
    misreading the audience, 241
    multi-dimensional, 238–239
    multiple, 247
    one-dimensional, 238
    by professionals, 239–240
    revisions, 247–248
    testing, 247–248
    too-clever, 247
    uncommon, 243–244
    weak, 246
complex information, 66–68
computer conventions, 95, 97
conjunctive adverb, 325, 341–342
contrast, 28
conversation, 45
coordinate elements. *See* grammatically equal
coordinating conjunctions, 320–322, 330, 342
copy-edit
    bad-news letters, 122
    memos, 118
    presentations, 312
    proposals, 179
    routine letters, 119
Coren, Stanley, 212
correspondence, 112–114
    bad news, 110–112, 120–122
    block format, 113–114
    brevity, 104, 106
    covering letters, 112
    credibility, 106
    direct writing, 106
    e-mail, 114–115
    format, 112–114
    honesty, 104
    imagine your audience, 104–105
    language of, 105–106
    memos, 107–109, 116–118
    plain writing, 106
    purpose of, 107
    respect, 104
    routine letters, 118–119

    routine messages, 109–110
    saying no, 110–112
    types of, 107–116
    voice mail, 115–116
covering letters, 112
    proposals, 176–177
    reports, 199
credibility, 4, 5–6
    accurate information, 5
    balance, 5, 10–11
    clarity, 5–6
    correspondence, 106
    evidence, 8–11
Crick, Francis, 240
critical path, 169, 174

D

dash, 28
data-gathering, 193–194
dates, 326–327
decomposing, 219–220
demonstration, 27
dependent clause, 322–324, 342
descriptions
    audiences, 218–222
    causal, 221
    chronological, 221
    decomposing, 219–220
    functional, 221
    and graphics, 221–222
    hierarchical, 221
    mixed, 218
    physical, 210–213, 223–226
    presenting, 220–221
    process, 210, 213–218, 226–228
    size, 221
    spatial, 221
    world, 210
descriptive report, 188–189
details, 12, 14
diagrams, 57–59, 75
direct address, 322–324, 325, 342
document design
    colour, 95
    emphasis, 97
    fonts, 93–94
    grids, 85–87, 96
    heading, 96
    headings, 92–93
    house styles, 84–85, 96
    instructions, 142–144
    less is more, 84
    list-making, 96–97
    planning, 85
    proposals, 178
    purpose, 84
    reports, 200
    styled text, 94
    template, 96
    typewriter conventions, 95
    usability testing, 97–98
    visualization, 96
    white space, 87–91, 97, 142
Donne, John, 241
drag-and-drop editing, 21
drawing programs, 59

E

e-mail, 114–115
editing
    drag-and-drop, 21
    physical descriptions, 225
    process descriptions, 228

split screen, 23
editors as audience, 288–290
Educational Psychology: A Cognitive View, 92
Einstein, Albert, 240
Elbow, Peter, 244
electronic outliner, 30, 134
em dashes, 95
embedded text links, 263
emphasis, 97
empirical evidence, 9
essential dependent clause, 331–332
evidence, 8–11
    analogous, 9–10
    anecdotal, 10
    balanced, 10–11
    empirical, 9
    presentation in threes, 10
    selection, 14
executable files, 115
executive summary, 175
experts, 136–137, 149
external proposal, 161–162

F
feasibility report, 187
field test your document, 33–34
flaming, 115
flow charts, 64–65, 75, 136–137, 217–218
fonts, 93–94, 273–275
    families, 273
    styled text, 274–275
format, 11, 14
    bad-news letters, 121–122
    block, 113–114
    citation, Web site, 168
    correspondence, 112–114
    media releases, 294
    memos, 108
    persuasion, 11
    reference lists, 354
    reports, 192
frames, 266–267, 270
freewriting, 244
Fuller, Buckminster, 259
functional description, 221

G
general readers
    knowledge of, 237
    needs of, 236
    wants of, 236–237
geographical location, 326–327
glossary of basic terms, 341–345
grammar checkers, 15
grammatical parallelism in lists, 91–92
grammatically equal, 320–322, 343
graphics
    abstractions, 69–71
    algebra, 70–71
    bar graphs, 62–64
    callout writing, 76
    choosing, 74–75
    column graphs, 62–64, 75
    complex information, 66–68
    credit for, 72
    delighting graphics, 54
    and description, 221–222
    diagrams, 57–59, 75
    flow charts, 64–65, 75
    image maps, 264–265
    instructing readers, 54
    instructions, 141, 143–144
    integration into text, 76
    line graphs, 61–62, 75
    links, 263–264
    logic, 69
    organization charts, 65, 76
    other kinds of, 66

overdone, 72–73
perception, 69–70
persuasion with, 66
photos, 55–57, 75
pie charts, 64, 75
preparation, 75–76
readers' understanding of, 71–72, 76–77
rollover, 264
simple information, 66–68
tables, 59–61, 75
testing, 77
when to use, 73–74
graphs
    bar, 62–64
    column, 62–64, 75
    line, 61–62, 75
grids, 85–87, 96

H
headings, 27, 32, 33
    previewing information, 92–93
    revise, 96
    styles, 93
headlines, media releases, 293
Henry IV, Part I, 238–239
hierarchical description, 221
hierarchy, 28
honesty, 104
horizontal alignment, 273
house styles, 84–85, 96
HTML, 260

I
Ideas Into Action Web site, 11, 54, 276, 347, 351
image maps, 264–265
index, 202
infinitive phrase, 345
instructions
    audience analysis, 138–139
    cautions, 145–146
    content of, 130–133
    difficult terms, 147
    document design, 142–144
    explicit, 130
    field-tested, 131
    final draft, 150
    first draft, 145–147
    flow charts, 136–137
    graphics, 141, 143–144
    knowing how, 132–133
    list materials, 146
    plain language, 139–140
    sample, 131–132
    sequential, 130
    stand-alone, 130–131
    steps in sequence, 146
    task analysis, 133–137
    telling how, 130–131
    testing, 144–145
    usability testing, 137
    visual markers, 142–143
    warnings, 145–146, 147
    white space, 142
    why, 132–133
interjection, 322–324, 343
internal proposal, 161–162
Internet
    research, 166–168
    writing for. *See* Web sites
introductory element, 322–324, 343
investigative reports, 187
italics, 95

J
justified text, 88

K
Kennedy, Des, 215

L
The Language Instinct, 215
Lanham, Richard A., 41
Lawson, Robert W., 240
layers, 270
layout grids, 268–270
letters. *See* correspondence
Life Itself: Its Origins and Nature, 240
line graphs, 61–62, 75
links, 277, 279–280
list-making, 32, 33, 96–97
lists
    automatic, 91
    bulleted, 28
    freewriting, 244
    grammatical parallelism, 91–92
    numbered, 28
    reference, 354
    white space, 90–91, 271–272
Lives of a Cell, 239
Living Things We Love To Hate, 215
logic, 28, 69
long sentences, 43

M
macros, 195
main clause, 320–322, 322–324, 330, 331–332, 336–337, 343
manuscript conventions, 326–327
Marcus, Stephen, 244
margins, 88
mechanical objects, 211–212
media releases, 294
    audience, 292
    clearing, 295
    delivery of, 295
    editors as audience, 288–290
    electronic versions, 294
    elements of, 290–292
    format, 294
    headlines, 293
    opening paragraph, 292
    recipients, 295
    revisions, 293, 294
    subhead, 293
    supporting information, 293
    testing, 293, 294
    timing of, 290
memos, 107–109, 117
    audience, 116
    body, 117
    closing, 117
    copy-edit, 118
    format, 108, 117
    length, 108–109
    opening paragraph, 116–117
    purpose of, 116
    revisions, 117
    testing, 117
metaphors, 238
Mike and Ike, story of, 242
mistakes. *See* common writing mistakes
modifier, 343
modifier placement, 340–341
multi-dimensional comparison, 238–239
multiple comparisons, 247

N
natural objects, 212
natural processes, 215–216
navigational devices, 261–267
    consistency, 292
    embedded text links, 263
    frames, 266–267
    graphic links, 263–264
    image maps, 264–265

multiple paths, 262
pull-down menus, 265–266
and the reader, 261–262
rollover graphics, 264
site maps, 266
testing, 262
text links, 262–263
non-essential elements, 324–326, 344
non-restrictive element. *See* non-essential
  elements
noun, 344
number system, 351, 355–356
numbered list, 28

O
object, 344
on-site documentation, 194
On Writing Well, 44
one-dimensional comparison, 238
one-off report, 188
opening paragraph
  bad-news letters, 120
  media releases, 292
  memos, 116
  routine letters, 118
organization charts, 65, 76
organizing information, 20–21
  field-testing, 198
  general procedure, 31–34
  problem-solving, 24–26
  signaling your structure, 26–29

P
paint programs, 59
paragraph length, 89–90, 97, 273
parentheses, 28
parenthetical expression, 325, 344
participial phrase, 345
passive voice, 42–43
perception, 69–70
periodic report, 187
persuasion
  accurate information, 5
  balance, 5, 10–11
  beta test, 12–13
  clarity, 5–6
  credibility, 5–6
  details, 12
  evidence, 8–11
  format, 11
  with graphics, 66
  and proposals, 163–170
  public speaking, 300
photos, 55–57, 75
phrase, 322–324, 344–345
physical descriptions, 210–213, 223–226
  audience, 223
  decomposing, 219, 223–224
  edit, 225
  graphics, 224
  identify parts, 225
  major features of object, 223
  mechanical objects, 211–212
  natural objects, 212
  other phenomena, 212–213
  presentation planning, 224
  reader orientation, 224–225
  readers' bearings, 225
  revisions, 226
  testing, 225–226
physical presentation, 12
pie charts, 64, 75
places, 326–327
Plain English
  and content, 39–40
  long sentences, 43
  plain words, 44–45
  purpose of, 38
  simplicity, 43–44

strategies for writing, 40–46
  subject, 42–43, 46
  tortuous sentences, 38–39
  usability, 45–46
  verbs, 40–42, 46
plain language, 139–140
  conversational, 140
  short sentences, 139–140
  steps, 140
  unfamiliar terms, 140
plain words, 44–45, 47
planned processes, 214–215
policy report, 188
power of three
  evidence presentation, 10
  exploiting, 29–30
  headings, 32
  public speaking, 302
prepositional phrase, 345
prepositions, 47
presentation software, 303–305
presentations. *See* public speaking
presenting, 220–221
problem-solving, 24–26
  existence of problem, 24
  objective standards, 24–25
  possible solutions, 25–26
process descriptions, 210, 213–214,
  226–228
  audience, 226
  with decisions, 216–218
  decomposing, 219–220, 226–227
  edit, 228
  graphics, 227
  identify steps, 227
  major steps, 226
  natural, 214, 215–219
  planned, 214–215
  reader orientation, 227
  readers' bearings, 228
  revisions, 228
  testing, 228
progress report, 187
promises to your audience, 22–23, 31,
  241–243, 302, 310
proposals
  appendix, 174
  budget plan, 174
  copy-edit, 179
  cost, 169
  covering letters, 176–177
  credentials, 169
  critical path, 169, 174
  delivery of, 179
  document design, 178
  effectiveness, 170
  executive summary, 175
  existence of problem, 164–165
  external, 161–162
  formal components of, 170–171
  internal, 161–162
  introduce yourself and the problem,
    171
  management plan, 173–174
  and persuasion, 163–170
  problem description, 172
  problem-solving, 168–169, 173
  purpose of, 160–161
  readers of, 164
  resources, 160
  revisions, 178–179
  sample request for, 162–163
  solicited, 162
  solution, 169
  table of contents, 177
  title page, 177–178
  unsolicited, 162
  what should be, 172–173
Providence, 10

psychology, 69–70
public speaking
  audibility, 308
  audience, 300–301, 310
  backup, 308, 313
  basic principles of design, 305–308
  builds, 306–307
  clarity, 308
  copy-edit, 312
  delivery of presentation, 308–309
  design elements, 305
  design of, 311
  key phrases vs. whole sentences, 306
  leave-behinds, 307, 313
  main points, 311
  material for, 310
  persuasion, 300
  posture, 309
  power of three, 302
  presentation software, 303–305
  professional appearance, 308
  promise to audience, 302, 310
  question-and-answer sessions,
    307–308, 313
  rehearsal, 313
  revisions, 311–312
  slide presentation, 302–303
  storyboard, 311
  testing, 311–312
  timing of talk, 301
  verbal tics, 309
pull-down menus, 265–266
punctuation, signaling with, 28–29

Q
quotation marks, 95

R
read aloud, 45
readers
  analysis, 138–139
  analyze, 13
  descriptions, 218–222
  first question, 6
  general. *See* general readers
  and graphics, 71–72, 76–77
  imagine your, 31, 33, 104–105
  maintaining interest, 7–8
  misreading, 241
  navigational devices, 261–262
  organizing for, 20–21
  promises to. *See* promises to your
    audience
  proposal, 164
  reports, 189–190
  target audience, 8
  technical writing, 246
  thinking like, 21–22
  from thinking to doing, 26
  touchstone, 31, 33, 45, 46
  Web, 256–257, 259–260
real users, 12–13
relative pronouns, 47
*Relativity: The Special and the General
  Theory*, 240
reports, 192
  analytical, 188–189
  appendix, 199
  audience for, 189–190
  covering letters, 199
  data-gathering, 193–194
  descriptive, 188–189
  document design, 200
  feasibility, 187
  field-testing, 197
  final draft, 201
  format, 192
  importance of, 186
  index, 202

interviews, 193–194
investigative, 187
on-site documentation, 194
one-off, 188
periodic, 187
policy, 188
preliminary draft, 195–196
problem description, 190–191
progress, 187
sample, 186
site, 187
source records, 194
submission of, 202
summary, 198–199
table of contents, 193, 202
three-part structure, 191–192
title page, 200–201
topic of, 190
types of, 186–188
what should be vs. what is, 191
research, Internet, 166–168
resources, 160
respect, 104
Revising Business Prose, 41
revisions, 15
bad-news letters, 121
comparisons, 247–248
media releases, 293, 294
memos, 117
physical descriptions, 226
process descriptions, 228
proposals, 178–179
public speaking, 311–312
routine letters, 119
rhetoric, 4
rollover graphics, 264
routine letters, 118–119, 119
routine messages, 109–110
run-on sentence, 329–331, 336–337

S
sans serif, 93–94
saving extra material, 26
saying no, 110–112
semicolon, 28
sentence fragments, 337–338
sequence, 27
series, 320–322, 345
serif, 93–94
Shakespeare, William, 238–239
signaling
headings, 27
punctuation, 28–29
technical writing, 242–243
words and phrases, 27–28
Silent Spring, 239
simile, 238
simple diagrams, 58–59
simple information, 66–68
site maps, 266
site report, 187
size, 221
slide presentation, 302–303
social act of writing, 4–5
solutions, 25–26
sorting, 32, 354
spacing, 95
spatial, 28
spatial description, 221
specialized fonts, 94
spell checkers, 12
Spinker, Steven, 214–215
split screen, 23
spreadsheets, 60
stock photos, 56
storyboard, 311
storytelling, 241–242
The Straight Dope, 212
structure. See organizing information
Style: Ten Lessons in Clarity and Grace, 41

styled text, 94, 274–275
subject, 42–43, 46, 322–324, 345
subject agreement, 338–340
subordinate conjunctions, 47
summary, 175–176, 198–199
symbols, 95, 237–241

T
table of contents
proposals, 177
reports, 193, 202
tables, 59–61, 75
target audience, 8
task analysis, 133–137
expert knowledge, 136–137
importance of, 133–135
performing, 135–136
technical writing
analogy, 238–239
audience, 246
common comparisons, 243–244
common ground, 246–247
comparisons, 237–241
Einstein's Relativity, 240
and general readers, 236
metaphors, 238
multi-dimensional comparison,
238–239
multiple comparisons, 247
one-dimensional comparison, 238
possibilities, 244–245
promises to your audience, 241–243
signaling, 242–243
simile, 238
storytelling, 241–242
symbols, 237–241
too-clever comparisons, 247
uncommon comparisons, 243–244
weak comparisons, 246
template, 260, 261, 279
testing
bad-news letters, 121
comparisons, 247–248
debrief, 148
distance from user, 148
document design, 97–98
expert advice, 149
field, 147–149
graphics, 77
instructions, 131, 144–145, 147–149
media releases, 293, 294
memos, 117
navigational devices, 262
physical descriptions, 225–226
process descriptions, 228
public speaking, 311–312
records, 148–149
reports, 197
routine letters, 119
structure, 198
subjects, 147
usability, 45–46, 48
Web sites, 278
text links, 262–263
Thomas, Lewis, 239
title page
proposals, 177–178
reports, 200–201
too-clever comparisons, 247
tortuous sentences, 38–39
Turner, Neely, 239
typewriter conventions, 95

U
uncommon comparisons, 243–244
unfamiliar terms, 140
usability, 45–46, 48
document design, 97–98
instructions, 137, 147–149
Web sites, 281–282

V
verbs, 40–42, 46, 47
version control, 141
vertical alignment, 272
visual markers, 142–143
voice mail, 115–116

W
weak comparisons, 246
the Web. See Web sites; World Wide Web
Web-safe colours, 277
Web sites
alpha test, 280
appearance, 268–277
audience, 259–260, 278
backgrounds, 277
beta test, 280–281
colour, 276–277
content, 279, 282
embedded text links, 263
fickleness of readers, 256–257
fonts, 273–275
frames, 270
graphic links, 263–264
horizontal rules, 275–276
HTML, 260
idea connections, 267
image maps, 264–265
layers, 270
layout, 261, 268–277, 280
layout grids, 268–270
links, 279–280
navigational devices, 261–267
network of ideas, 257–258
pages of, 259
planning, 258–259, 278
prototype, 278
prototyping strategies, 260
pull-down menus, 265–266
reader navigation, 281
relative control, 268
rollover graphics, 264
screen design, 281–282
site maps, 266
template, 260, 261, 279
testing, 278
text links, 262–263
text on, 256
usability testing, 281–282
white space, 270–273
Web writing. See Web sites
white space, 87–91, 142
horizontal alignment, 273
lists, 271–272
and lists, 90–91
margins, 88
paragraph length, 89–90, 97, 273
relationships among ideas, 88–89
vertical alignment, 272
Web sites, 270–273
William the Conqueror, 44
Williams, Joseph M., 41
word processors, 60–61
words and phrases, signaling with, 27–28
World Wide Web
citation format, 168
copying information, 167
copyright, 167–168
credentials of Web authors, 166–167
finding material, 166
importance of, 256
writing for the Web. See Web sites
writing mistakes. See common writing
mistakes
Writing To Learn, 240

Z
Zinsser, William, 44, 240